THE HOWARD STREET TUTORING MANUAL

THE HOWARD STREET TUTORING MANUAL

Teaching At-Risk Readers in the Primary Grades

Darrell Morris

THE GUILFORD PRESS
New York   London

© 1999 The Guilford Press
A Division of Guilford Publications, Inc.
72 Spring Street, New York, NY 10012
http://www.guilford.com

Printed in the United States of America

This book is printed on acid-free paper.

Last digit is print number: 9   8   7   6   5   4   3   2

Library of Congress Cataloging-in-Publication Data

Morris, Darrell.
      The Howard Street tutoring manual : teaching at-risk readers in
   the primary schools / Darrell Morris. — 2nd ed.
           p.   cm.
      Rev. ed of: Case studies in teaching beginning readers. c1992.
      Includes bibliographical references and index.
      ISBN 1-57230-444-8 (pbk.)
      1. Reading (Primary)—Illinois—Chicago—Case studies.
   2. Individualized reading instruction—Illinois—Chicago—Case
   studies.   3. Tutors and tutoring—Illinois—Chicago—Case studies.
   I. Morris, Darrell.   Case studies in teaching beginning readers.
   II. Title.
   LB1525.M718   1999
   372.41'7'0977311—dc21   98-32002
                                                                CIP

Contents

Preface

When I began writing the first edition of this book in the mid-1980s, tutoring programs for at-risk beginning readers were uncommon in the nation's public schools. Certainly reading failure in the primary grades was an acknowledged problem. Nonetheless, one-to-one tutoring by certified teachers was thought to be too costly, and volunteer tutors were not even considered as potential providers of direct reading instruction. Overwhelmingly, school-based remedial reading efforts focused on small-group pull-out instruction, usually beginning no earlier than third grade.

Things have changed over the past decade. The advent and subsequent spread of Reading Recovery across the nation has popularized and legitimated the use of carefully trained teachers to tutor at-risk first-grade readers. In addition, President Clinton's America Reads Challenge initiative of 1997 has shone a huge spotlight on the role of *volunteer* reading tutors in grades 1, 2, and 3. In effect, one-to-one tutoring is now recognized as an effective school-based strategy for preventing reading failure in the primary grades (Invernizzi, Rosemary, Juel, & Richards, 1997; Wasik, 1998; Wasik & Slavin, 1993).

I am encouraged by reading education's recent emphasis on early intervention, that is, identifying at-risk readers in first grade and providing them with intensive, one-to-one instruction. However, my experience in the schools has led me to believe that one-to-one tutoring is not a panacea, but rather a *potentially* powerful tool that must be used in creative ways. In fact, to reduce reading failure significantly in the primary grades, I believe at least three things must happen.

First, we must provide effective reading instruction to low readers in the classroom. I have worked with hundreds of teachers over the years, and my observation has been that the majority feel that their undergraduate training did not fully prepare them for the challenge of teaching their lowest readers. We should stop pretending otherwise. In first through third grade, effective instruction refers to guided contextual reading and systematic word study that is skillfully paced to the learning rates of individual children. Providing such instruction in a class of 24 children is very difficult; teachers need and deserve help in the form of high-quality in-service training.

Interestingly, a supervised tutoring experience for classroom teachers may be the best way to begin. By tutoring one of his/her own low-reading students (and reflecting on the tutoring process with a trainer), the classroom teacher can see the learning-to-read process up close and gain understanding of it (Morris, in press). This kind of seeing and understanding, which occurs more easily in a one-to-one context than in a classroom, can lead thoughtful teachers to question and even revise their classroom instruction (e.g., adding a third reading group in the morning language arts block; patching together a graded set of reading materials that will offer needed word control to low readers; or systematizing and "slowing down" phonics instruction so that struggling readers learn how to decode words). Tutoring, then, may be a first step in helping teachers to rethink what can be accomplished with low readers in the classroom.

Second, we must find ways to provide at-risk first-grade readers with intensive tutorial help outside the classroom. The success of such programs as Reading Recovery and Success for All in the United States has shown that almost every child can learn to read if given effective one-to-one instruction beginning early in first grade. It is true that these programs, which use carefully trained certified teachers to tutor on a daily basis, are expensive—in fact, cost-prohibitive in some school districts with large numbers of at-risk readers. Nonetheless, we cannot abandon a concept that works (i.e., tutoring) because of the expense of particular programs. Instead, we must begin to develop a variety of first-grade tutorial efforts, all the while looking for ways to make them more cost-effective. In this vein, several programs have recently produced promising results using part-time teachers or paraprofessionals working under the close supervision of a reading specialist (Sanders & Buhle, 1997; Santa & Hoien, 1999).

Third, we must make effective use of volunteer reading tutors in the primary grades. It is unlikely that most schools will ever be able to provide a paid, professional tutor for every struggling reader in grades 1 through 3. Even if a school district were able to do so in grade 1, there would still be children in grades 2 and 3 desperately in need of tutorial help. One way around this problem is to use volunteer tutors (parents, college students, retirees, etc.) to teach low readers in grades 2 and 3. Volunteer tutoring programs do present problems of recruitment, lesson planning, supervision, and allotment of school time and space; in truth, such programs will *not* work without the leadership of a committed reading specialist. Nonetheless, carefully supervised volunteer programs offer several advantages: they serve large numbers of children, they are cost-effective, and they provide a vehicle for involving the community in one of the school's most important tasks—teaching children to read.

This revised edition of *The Howard Street Tutoring Manual* can be used for each of the purposes mentioned—that is, to train classroom teachers, reading specialists, preservice teachers, and even volunteer tutors to work effectively with low-reading primary-grade students. The manual will have its maximum influence when the teachers or tutors who read it are simultaneously engaged in a practicum (university- or field-based) in which they tutor one or more low-reading children under the supervision of an expert reading clinician. Of course, no reading manual can tell a practitioner *exactly* what to do or say with every child he/she will encounter. Those that attempt to do so will either fail, through oversimplification, to address the unique needs of each student, or become hopelessly bogged down in endless detail. This admittedly imperfect manual attempts to find a middle ground between simplicity and specifics, while explaining some of the *whys* involved in understanding literacy development.

This second edition of the manual contains substantial revisions. For example, the "Emergent Reader" chapter (Chapter 3) has been rewritten to reflect my recent experience with the Early Steps reading intervention model. In addition, the chapter on assessment has been expanded, word study (or phonics) is covered in more detail in the instructional chapters, and graded lists of reading books are included for the first time. These changes notwithstanding, the in-depth case study format and the underlying developmental theory remain consistent with the first edition.

Reading failure in the primary grades has been a national concern for more than 30 years. Thus far, we have addressed the problem by instituting new reading programs, new grouping procedures, and new accountability designs. We have not, however, invested seriously in teacher training. In my opinion, such an investment is long overdue. If, over the next decade, we can train teachers to meet the needs of low readers *in the classroom*, and professional and volunteer tutors to accelerate the children's learning *outside the classroom*, then I am confident that we can significantly increase the number of children who read at or near grade level by the end of third grade. If this tutoring manual plays even a small part in helping educators accomplish this goal, it will have served its purpose.

ACKNOWLEDGMENTS

Over the past decade I have had an opportunity to work with a remarkable group of reading teachers in the western counties of North Carolina. Their ideas, energy, and commitment have certainly influenced my own thinking about early reading intervention. All of these teachers deserve acknowledgment but space permits me to name only a few. Stamey Carter contributed significantly to the development of Early Steps, a first-grade tutorial model on which Chapter 3 of this manual is based. Stamey also helped develop the graded book lists that are found at the end of each case study chapter. Sue Batters, Luwonna Ellis, Ardease Greene, Judy Henderson, and Frances McNeil are reading teachers who each year supervise volunteer tutoring programs in their respective schools. Their unheralded but highly successful work has convinced me that the ideas in this tutoring manual have practical, real-world merit.

I also want to take this opportunity to thank some of my academic siblings who, like me, were trained at the University of Virginia's McGuffey Reading Center: Mary Abouzeid, Donald Bear, Janet Bloodgood, Karen Broaddus, Jeff Cantrell, Ann Fordham, Tom and Laurie Gill, Marcia Invernizzi, Francine Johnston, Bob Schlagal, Charlie Temple, Shane Templeton, Jo Worthy, and Jerry Zutell. These colleagues' willingness to carry forward a rich, yet underappreciated, clinical tradition has for 20 years nurtured and stimulated my own work in the field of reading. Finally, I want to express my thanks to two people who made the publication of this book possible. Chris Jennison of The Guilford Press believed in this unorthodox, formula-defying work from the start. He was also a delight to work with. Verda Ingle, my wife, provided unwavering moral support, a helpful critical reading, and, as usual, a careful editing of the final text that improved its readability.

Preface to the First Edition

This is anything but a traditional reading textbook. It is narrow in scope (addressing the needs of primary-grade readers), yet fairly comprehensive in theoretical orientation. Its content includes much that is old and familiar, but some that is new and heretofore seldom mentioned in the literature. The book is informally written, yet intentionally precise in its description of teaching procedures. Finally, it is a personal book, in that I believe in and wish to share the ideas found within its pages.

The motivation for writing *Case Studies in Teaching Beginning Readers* grew out of my 10-year involvement in a real after-school tutoring program on the North Side of Chicago. Shortly after our tutoring effort began, it became apparent that some type of teaching manual was needed to guide the efforts of the volunteer tutors and thereby enhance quality control in our program. I eventually decided on a "case study" manual, with the three cases to span the nonreader through the third-grade reader, the kinds of students we were working with at Howard Street. It was my hope that the case studies, considered separately, would demonstrate how various teaching strategies and materials relate to a child *at a given stage* in early reading development. At the same time, the three cases, taken together, would show how a beginning reader changes over time, and how teaching strategies must evolve or change to meet the developmental needs of the learner.

As I began to write, back in 1982, I quickly realized that a formulaic, "cookbook" type of manual was not going to work; I had too deep a respect for the complexities of beginning reading and writing, and could not write about teaching procedures without sharing "why this works this way" with the prospective tutor. Careful writing about the teaching of reading takes time and, with various other responsibilities and interruptions, this book took 8 years to complete. The advantage of such a long labor, however, is that the book's pedagogical content has been tested and modified in a real-world laboratory (the tutoring program) over an extended period of time. These teaching strategies do work.

This book will be useful to reading professionals who are attempting to establish, in their school or community, a one-to-one tutoring program for struggling primary-grade readers. The book describes how to start such a program, how to supervise the work of the volunteer tutors, and how to evaluate the effectiveness of the tutoring effort. However, the real core of the book—and the part over which I labored the longest—is the section on instruction (Chapters 3–5). These chapters, I believe, will render the book of value to anyone who is interested in teaching youngsters to read: supervisors of a tutoring program, the volunteer tutors themselves, school-based reading specialists, learning disability teachers, and even classroom teachers.

The teaching strategies described in this manual are grounded theoretically in the language-experience approach to teaching reading, probably best explicated by Russell Stauffer (1970) and taught to me by the late Edmund H. Henderson at the University of Virginia. Henderson was a teacher in the finest sense of the word, and I owe him a huge intellectual debt. He would not have agreed with every statement in this book, but I think he would have applauded its overall goal—the attempt to talk seriously about the teaching of beginning reading.

At this time I wish to thank two groups of people who, much more than they realize, sustained me in the long and sometimes frustrating process of writing this book and bringing it to publication. First, there is the selfless group of teachers who over the years supervised the volunteer tutors at Howard Street: in chronological order, Megan Tschannen-Moran, Elaine Weidemann, Warren Clohisy, Bev Shaw, Ellen Knell, Judy Ebright, and Betty Boyd. Second, there is the group of reading clinicians at the National College of Education Reading Center who willingly donated their valuable time, again and again, to help with assessment and teaching tasks at Howard Street: Carol Ivy, Betty Johnson, Laurel Kaplan, Barbara Kaufman, Laurie Nelson, Barbara Platt, Jan Sabin, and Charlotte Wolfe. I am extremely fortunate to have worked closely with each of these dedicated teachers and doubly fortunate to be able to claim each of them as a friend.

Finally, I want to thank my wife, Verda Ingle, for her unflagging support of this project. Not only did she skillfully fulfill the roles of critical reader, illustrator, typist, and copy editor, but also she, more than anyone else, believed in the worth of this effort, from start to finish. For that, I thank her from the bottom of my heart.

January 30, 1992

CHAPTER 1

The Tutoring Model

My main purpose for writing this book was to produce a useful teaching manual for tutors who work with beginning readers. That manual can be found in Chapters 2 through 5. The pedagogical ideas in the manual, however, did not result from scholarly work conducted in the privacy of my university office. Rather, they evolved over 10 years' time in the context of my directing an after-school storefront tutoring clinic in a poor Chicago neighborhood. Because many of the teaching ideas grew out of this specific, real-life context, I feel it is important to share with the reader some background about the origin and development of the Howard Street Tutoring Program.

My first college teaching job, in 1979, was at National College of Education (now National-Louis University), a small suburban teacher-training institution just 3 miles north of the city of Chicago. Shortly after my arrival at National, a colleague, Elaine Weidemann, asked whether I might be interested in an after-school tutoring program that she and a friend were trying to establish on the far-north side of Chicago. Anxious to become involved in the city and its public schools, I responded yes. I met a few days later with Elaine and her friend, Megan Tschannen-Moran, and thus began my 10-year involvement in an inner-city tutoring program for low-reading primary-grade children.

Tschannen-Moran, a young Northwestern University-trained educator, lived in the poor, Black–Hispanic neighborhood known as Jonquil Terrace. Comprising three square blocks of apartment buildings and shops in the far-northeast corner of Chicago, Jonquil was not unlike scores of other low-income neighborhoods in the city. High unemployment, low levels of education, inadequate housing, drugs, and violent crime were common problems faced by the adults and children living within its borders. Megan and her husband, Bob, a minister, were part of a small but tenacious community group, Good News North of Howard, that was trying in various ways to stabilize and improve the quality of life in the neighborhood.

One of the Good News group's projects (and its members were not short on ideas or determination) was to start a private, alternative school in two dilapidated storefronts that the group had rented on Paulina Street, less than one block north of the busy Howard Street El stop. Megan was in charge of this project. So that the local public school, only two blocks away, would not resent the encroachment of a perceived competitor, and because Megan was sincerely concerned about the children who attended that public school, she was determined to offer some type of after-school tutoring for those children as well. Her idea was to end the Good News alternative school's day at 2:30 P.M., the same time that the public school dismissed its students. Then, as the Good News students departed, a group of low-reading public school students could walk over to the alternative school (the storefronts) and receive tutoring in reading from adult volunteers. Megan envisioned the tutoring program operating two afternoons per week (e.g., Monday and Wednesday from 3:00 to 4:00 P.M.).

I was very much interested in Megan's concept of an after-school volunteer tutoring program for the public school children. From my clinical training in reading education at the University of Virginia, I had become convinced that one-to-one tutoring, even only two or three times a week, could make a significant difference in poor children's literacy development. I also liked the idea of a grass-roots, community-based initiative, one that would be free of bureaucratic interference. Finally, I was curious about the potential effectiveness of adult volunteer tutors. I knew that I, a reading specialist, could teach children to read in a one-to-one situation, but could we train volunteers with little or no background in reading to become effective tutors? This was the challenge.

Over the first few years of the tutoring program, we learned some important lessons, mostly through trial and error (see Morris, Tschannen-Moran, & Weidemann, 1981; Morris, 1993a):

1. *If volunteer reading tutors are to be successful, they require close, ongoing supervision by a reading specialist.* We learned this lesson the hard way when, in Year 1, two of our eight college-educated volunteers became overwhelmed with the tutoring task and quit. Moreover, it became clear that although the other volunteers continued to show up for tutoring each time, they were often frustrated. They were uncomfortable with lesson planning and unsure about how much effort to demand of the children. We quickly had to move in and provide needed professional support.

2. *Volunteer tutoring programs should be kept small to ensure quality control.* In our second year, we succumbed to the universal temptation to "expand the program." With the best of intentions, we went from 8 tutor–child pairs in Year 1 to 14 tutor–child pairs in Year 2. Unfortunately, we discovered that one hard-working supervisor could keep up with, at most, 10 tutor–child pairs. Thus, our well-intentioned expansion served to compromise the quality of the entire program.

3. *The interpersonal bond that develops between volunteer and child is a major factor in a tutoring program's success.* We recognized, early on, that the bonding between tutor and child was what kept the volunteers coming back, week after week, month after month (a crucially important element in a volunteer tutoring

program). Over the course of a year, the volunteers experienced good and bad days, tutoring-wise; however, their commitment to and affection for their students was unwavering.

4. *A volunteer tutoring program can significantly improve the reading ability of low-reading primary-grade students.* From the start of the tutoring program, we documented the children's reading growth through careful record keeping and beginning-of-year/end-of-year testing. In the eighth and ninth years of the program, we conducted a more rigorous evaluation, comparing the achievement of the tutored children with a closely matched comparison group. Results showed that the tutored group consistently outperformed the comparison group on several measures of reading and spelling ability (Morris, Shaw, & Perney, 1990).

I moved away from the Chicago area in 1989, but the Howard Street Tutoring Program continued to operate under the able leadership of Beverly Shaw and Betty Boyd. The program is now in its 20th year of consecutive operation, serving 20+ children each year from the same inner-city public school.

Having established new academic roots at Appalachian State University in western North Carolina, in 1989 I began helping rural school systems set up early intervention programs for at-risk first-grade readers. The intervention model, which I have sometimes called First Steps or Early Steps, has an in-school tutoring component that serves two purposes: (1) to teach at-risk or low-readiness children to read in first grade and (2) to train reading teachers and classroom teachers, through an intensive tutoring experience, to better understand and meet the needs of low-reading first graders.

Early Steps has met with some success (see Morris, 1995; Santa & Hoien, 1999), but we have found that many low-reading first graders, even after a full year of daily one-to-one tutoring by a certified teacher, still require careful support as they move into second grade. For this reason, several North Carolina school districts have also instituted follow-up second-grade tutorial programs based on the original Howard Street model.

The Howard Street tutoring model is attractive to the schools, at this point, for several reasons: (1) Early Steps has convinced both teachers and administrators of the power of one-to-one tutoring, (2) the schools realize that some children leaving Early Steps have not quite made it "over the hump," that they need an extra push in second grade, (3) the school-based reading teacher, having gone through the Early Steps tutorial training, is well-prepared to train adult volunteers to tutor low-reading second graders, and (4) volunteer tutors do not tax the budgets of rural school systems with limited financial resources.

It has been interesting to watch the Howard Street tutoring concept, originally designed as a stopgap, out-of-school program for inner-city children, evolve in a totally different setting. In rural North Carolina low-reading second and third graders *are tutored during the school day by volunteers who are supervised by the school-based Title 1 reading teacher.* Thus, from small and humble beginnings in a Chicago storefront, the Howard Street model has become an integral part of several school districts' systemic efforts to prevent reading failure in the primary grades. (See also the Book Buddies program: Invernizzi et al., 1997.)

This chapter will describe in some detail how to implement the Howard Street tutoring model. First, however, let us examine more generally the need for reading tutors in the primary grades.

THE NEED FOR READING TUTORS

In our society, 6-year-olds enter first grade expecting to learn to read. Their parents expect them to learn to read, and so do their teachers. Regrettably, these expectations are not always met. Many first and second graders (perhaps 25%) fall significantly behind their peers in reading and remain behind throughout the elementary grades (Juel, 1988; Slavin, 1994; Stanovich, 1986). Because much school learning across the grades depends on reading competence, early and sustained failure in reading can have devastating consequences—in the lives of low readers and their families and in the socioeconomic life of the community. For example, the high school dropout, juvenile delinquency, and adult illiteracy rates that receive continuing attention in the media can often be traced to reading failure in the first few years of school.

The reasons for reading failure in the primary grades have been debated for more than 100 years (Huey, 1908); at various points, the *teacher* (poorly trained), the *child* (lack of "readiness"), and the *spelling system* (hopelessly irregular) have borne the brunt of the blame. Overall, however, the debate has centered on what is the best *method* for teaching beginners to read (e.g., phonics, whole word, sentence-based, etc.). It is remarkable how this war of teaching methods has raged across the decades—from Flesch (1955) to Veatch (1959), Chall (1967), and Smith (1971)—up to the current battle between "code-emphasis" (Adams, 1990) and "whole-language" proponents (Watson, 1989). The characters have changed, but the epic struggle for the hearts and minds of teachers (and publishers) has remained the same.

Although issues of teaching method should continue to be addressed, there are other ways of thinking about the problem of reading failure in the primary grades. I suggest that the *opportunity* to learn to read is of critical importance. In a typical first- or second-grade classroom, with only 90 minutes of reading instruction and a 1:24 teacher:student ratio, there is surprisingly little time available for individual children to read aloud under the classroom teacher's direct supervision. This lack of supervised reading time, a long-standing, systemic problem in elementary schools, is particularly harmful to those low-achieving beginning readers who desperately need practice in a situation where feedback is available. Like most of us facing a difficult task, the struggling beginning reader requires help when trouble arises (e.g., in confronting an unknown word) and reassurance when things are going well.

Like many other opportunities in our society, the opportunity to learn to read is not equally available across socioeconomic (SES) groups. When comparing middle-SES and lower-SES schools, one finds that middle-class schools often have smaller class sizes and more highly trained support staff (reading specialists). There are also fewer low-reading children in a middle-SES (as opposed to a low-SES) primary-grade classroom, as a result of the children's differential access to crucial preschool education or "reading readiness" experiences. This makes it possible for the middle-class school to provide more intensive help to those few children who do get off to a slow start in reading. In addition, the middle-SES child who *is* having difficulty with reading in first or second grade is more likely to be tutored at home by a parent than is a low-SES child. (Several factors operate here, including the availability of quiet time and appropriate physical space in the home, parents' educational background, and their knowledge of how elementary schools work.) Finally, if neither the school nor the school–home combination is getting the job done, the middle-class parent is in a much better position, economically, to seek outside professional assistance for his/her low-reading child—for example, the services of a private tutor or of a local university-sponsored reading clinic. In summary, there is redundancy built into middle-class children's educational experience that gives them more chances at learning to read.

I have argued previously that life circumstances—for example, growing up in a poor neighborhood in a large city or in a poor, isolated rural area—can systematically limit a child's chances to learn to read. This is a discouraging but not surprising finding in a free, capitalistic society where many kinds of opportunities are unequally distributed. However, there is another side, a hopeful side to this opportunity-to-read analysis. In both middle- and lower-SES schools, authorities estimate the incidence of organically related reading disability (dyslexia) to be less than 4% (Vellutino et al., 1996). This leaves a large population of low-reading first and second graders in all schools who have the *potential* to learn, but not adequate opportunity. The chief task facing humane educational planners—and a big task it is when one takes into account scarcity of resources and institutional inertia (Sarason, 1972)—is to modify the existing educational system so that sufficient opportunity is provided and potential realized (see Clay, 1993; Slavin, Madden, Karweit, Dolan, & Wasik, 1994). A secondary task, but one that can be addressed immediately, is to supplement existing educational offerings with innovative, low-expense programs that provide children with the needed opportunity to learn to read. The situation is not complicated. There are hundreds of thousands of 6-, 7-, and 8-year-olds moving through the public schools each year who are not developing adequate literacy skills. On the other hand, there are even more literate adults in this country who have the time and knowledge to help these children learn to read. Volunteer tutoring programs, if well conceptualized and supervised, can make an important difference.

Why Tutoring Makes a Difference

Anyone who has ever taken *group* lessons in tennis, golf, or ice skating at a local recreation center can appreciate the power of individual instruction. No matter how talented the instructor, in group lessons the best he/she can do is model the athletic behavior and then let the participants try it on their own. Given the group context, there is limited time for the instructor to provide learners with immediate feedback geared to their individual needs.

The opposite is true in individual lessons. For example, a skillful golf pro, when working with only one student, can zero in on that student's grip of the club, his/her stance, and the particular characteristics of his/her golf swing. Moreover, instead of speaking in generalities about proper grip, stance, and swing (information that can be found in any golf manual), the pro can take into consideration the idiosyncratic nature of the single student's golf game, providing feedback and advice that may apply to the student's game (e.g., "Slow down and shorten your backswing"), but not to that of another beginning golfer. Is it any wonder that when people of means seek such athletic instruction, they opt for individual, not group, lessons?

In many ways, and for many children, learning to read is a much more complex act than learning to hit a golf ball. There is considerable failure when children are taught to read in groups, and, not surprisingly, instruction tailored to the needs of the individual child has proven to be more effective. In fact, today more than ever before, researchers and practitioners are beginning to appreciate the power of one-to-one tutoring in preventing reading failure in the primary grades (Clay, 1993; Pinnell, 1989; Invernizzi et al., 1997).

In explaining the potential of a one-to-one instructional setting, Wasik and Slavin (1990) have argued that there are four components of effective instruction, which they call the QAIT model.

1. **Q**uality of instruction: Skillfulness with which information or processes are presented so that they are easily learned by students. Quality of instruction involves what is taught and how it is presented.
2. **A**ppropriate *level of instruction*: Ability to present lessons at the student's optimum learning level, that is, lessons that are neither too difficult nor too easy for the student.
3. **I**ncentive: Timeliness in providing reinforcement and corrective feedback to the student in the act of learning.
4. **T**ime: Provision of enough instructional and practice time so that the material or skill can be learned.

Wasik and Slavin maintain that one-to-one tutoring can potentially affect all four components of the QAIT model, above. First, providing a tutor with careful training and good materials should ensure a reasonable *quality of instruction*. Second, a tutor can completely adapt the *level and pace of instruction* to the needs of the child being tutored. If the child requires additional instruction at a given level, this can be provided; if the child is "catching on," the tutor can quickly move forward. Wasik and Slavin correctly note that such individualized pacing is not possible in "even one-to-two or one-to-three instruction, where adaptation to individual needs becomes progressively more difficult" (p. 6).

Third, a tutor can devote full attention to his/her student, providing *feedback or incentive* at exactly the moment it is called for in the learning process. Such timely feedback, whether it be praise or correction, enhances learning and increases student motivation. And fourth, if tutoring is provided as a supplement to classroom instruction, it adds to *instructional time*. Moreover, this additional tutorial time should be of a high quality because of the aforementioned factors.

Wasik and Slavin's analysis is helpful in that it explains why tutoring can work, and work well. However, as these authors note, the tutoring setting provides only the *potential* for student learning. The start-up and subsequent closing of hundreds of volunteer tutoring efforts during the decade of the 1960s showed that there is no magic, no automatic success, to be had from placing well-meaning adult volunteers with low-achieving schoolchildren. It has been our experience that *each* of the components in the QAIT model must be carefully considered if tutoring is to make a difference with low-reading primary-grade children. The key is adequate training/supervision of the tutors, and this issue will be of central importance as we move now to a description of the Howard Street Tutoring Program.

A VOLUNTEER TUTORING PROGRAM

The Howard Street tutoring model can be implemented either during the school day or after school hours. In the program description that follows, volunteer tutors, under the supervision of a reading specialist, work with low-reading second graders on Monday and Wednesday afternoons from 1:00 to 1:45 P.M.

Identifying Low Readers and Recruiting Tutors

In September the reading specialist asks the three second-grade teachers in her school to identify the lowest 5 readers in their respective classrooms. The reading teacher pretests these 15 children, using a set of *graded word recognition lists*, a set of *graded reading passages*, and a *spelling inventory* (see Chapter 2). The 10 students scoring lowest on the pretest measures are selected to participate in the tutoring program.

Because the program includes only low-reading second graders, the reading ability range of the students is appreciably narrowed (initially, early- to mid-first-grade reading levels). This greatly simplifies the training and supervision of the volunteer tutors. It is one thing to provide volunteers with techniques they can use with children who read at a first-grade level; it is quite another to provide them with the variety of techniques and knowledge required to work successfully with children whose reading ranges from a first-grade to a fifth-grade level.

One may ask why the volunteer tutoring is focused on second graders instead of first graders. Actually, the pedagogical ideas in this manual (see Chapters 3 to 5) can be used to tutor low readers from first through fourth grade. My personal conviction is that intensive one-to-one reading help for at-risk children should be provided as early as possible. Nonetheless, experience has led me to believe that trained teachers and paraprofessionals are more effective with first graders than are volunteers (but see Invernizzi et al., 1997; Johnston, Invernizzi, & Juel, 1998). Ideally, a professionally staffed reading intervention in first grade (e.g., Reading Recovery, Early Steps) would be followed by volunteer tutoring in second and third grades. This ideal has become a reality in several school districts in western North Carolina, and the achievement results are encouraging.

In the *recruitment of tutors*, volunteers come from all walks of life: undergraduate education and liberal arts majors in local universities, graduate students in education or psychology looking for practicum experiences, parents whose children are in school, parents whose children are away at college, employees of businesses that grant release time for volunteer work in the schools, retirees looking for meaningful volunteer work, and so on. Because of population density, cities and suburbs would seem to offer a more plentiful source of potential tutors. However, tutor recruitment is really a question of commitment and energy. I have seen one reading teacher in an isolated rural community build up a solid volunteer tutoring corps by personally contacting her school's parent–teacher association (PTA), along with local church and civic groups.

In the start-up years, printed flyers and a few contacts at local universities, churches, and civic organizations can be used to attract potential tutors. After a few years of operation, a word-of-mouth recruitment network usually proves to be fairly reliable in securing the needed number of tutors. Most volunteers, particularly the college students, tutor for only 1 year. However, a small group of community volunteers (parents, retirees) often return year after year, finding the tutoring to be a collegial and rewarding experience.

The Tutoring Model

The volunteer tutors and their second-grade students show up for tutoring at 1:00 P.M. on Mondays and Wednesdays. (On Tuesdays and Thursdays, the reading teacher works with the same students in small groups.) Tutoring is done in the reading resource room and in a nearby music room.

The reading instruction provided the students is based on several assumptions:

1. *Children learn to read by reading, just as they learn to ride a bicycle by jumping on and trying to ride.* Therefore, the most valuable tutoring activity is to support

beginning readers in their attempts to read interesting, well-written stories. (The number of minutes spent reading is an important consideration.)

2. *Over time, low readers must be paced efficiently through reading material that is graded in difficulty.* The tutor must know when to slow down, when to spend more time at a given difficulty level to ensure a needed level of student mastery. The tutor must also know when to move forward, when to increase the difficulty level so that appropriate challenge can lead to new student learning.

3. *Word study or phonics plays an important role in a program designed to help beginners learn to read and spell.* At minimum, children should be led to automatize the basic one-syllable spelling patterns in English (CVC, CVCe, CVVC) so that they can draw efficiently on this knowledge in their contextual reading and writing efforts. Efficient instructional pacing is also important in word study, with higher-level features (e.g., consonant blends and short vowels) being introduced as lower-level ones (beginning consonants) are mastered.

Given the preceding assumptions, a typical 45-minute tutoring lesson takes the following form:

1. *Contextual reading at the child's instructional level (18 minutes).* The tutor supports the child in reading and comprehending well-written stories. A true beginning reader will *echo read* simple pattern books; a mid-first-grade-level reader will *partner read,* or alternately read with the tutor, pages of a basal story or trade book; and a late-first-grade (or higher) reader will *read independently*, requiring only incidental support from the tutor.

2. *Word study (10 minutes).* Word categorization activities and games (see Bear, Invernizzi, Templeton, & Johnston, 1996; Morris, 1982) are used to help children internalize basic spelling patterns. Depending on a child's developmental level of word knowledge, he/she may categorize or "sort" beginning-consonant elements, short-vowel word families (rhyming words), or vowel patterns. Figure 1.1 provides an example of a word family sort and a vowel pattern sort.

A child must master a given sort before moving on to the next one. Mastery means that the student can both read and spell the target word patterns with a

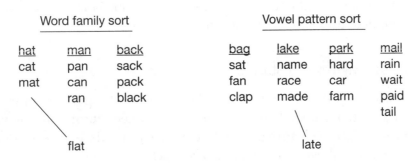

FIGURE 1.1. Word sort activities.

degree of automaticity and confidence. (Detailed instructions for conducting word study lessons are found in Chapters 3, 4, and 5.)

3. *Easy reading (10 minutes).* This reading is done in trade books (e.g., Harper & Row's I Can Read books). The child may reread a favorite book or partner read with the tutor a new but easy book. The purpose is to build sight vocabulary, increase fluency, and strengthen the child's confidence as a reader.

4. *Reading to the child (7 minutes).* At the end of each lesson, the tutor reads a quality selection to the child. This may be a fairy tale, a fable, a short picture book, or a chapter from a longer book.

Note that this is the basic lesson plan for a low-reading second or third grader. For a beginning first grader or virtual nonreader, a different lesson plan, featuring a structured writing component, is used (see "Atticus," Chapter 3).

Two hours of focused reading practice per week may not seem like a lot, but it does make a difference. Given such practice in a supportive environment, low readers begin to progress and, as they do, the pacing of their instruction becomes an important concern (Barr, 1974). In reading acquisition, there is an optimal level of task difficulty that will produce the biggest gains in learning—a level at which the reader is sufficiently challenged but not overwhelmed. In the Howard Street model, we carefully monitor each child's current "instructional level," moving the student forward quickly when performance warrants such a move (e.g., to a higher contextual reading level or to a new or more complex set of word patterns). The supervisor of tutors plays a critical role in these instructional pacing decisions.

The Role of the Supervisor

A unique characteristic of this tutoring program is the close monitoring of the reading lessons by a reading specialist "supervisor." The supervisor's most important responsibilities are described briefly in the paragraphs that follow.

Identifying the Low Readers and Recruiting Tutors

During the first 2 weeks of school the supervisor pretests low-reading second graders in her school (see Chapter 2). At the same time, she is actively involved in recruiting volunteer tutors for the program.

Getting the Tutoring Lessons Started

One of the most difficult parts of the supervisor's job is getting the program started in September. Remember that most of the volunteer tutors are neophytes when it comes to teaching reading. Therefore, they require close supervision during the first month if they are to master basic teaching techniques and establish "good tutoring habits" (e.g., emphasizing contextual reading, minimizing transition time between tutoring tasks, providing timely encouragement to a child for a job well done, etc.).

Over the years we have learned that on-the-job training for the volunteer tutors is much more efficient than preservice lectures on "how to tutor." Therefore, the supervisor begins the program each year by working with only two tutor–child pairs. On Day 1, the supervisor teaches a child (see the *lesson plan* in the preceding section) while the volunteer tutors watch. There is a debriefing after the lesson, with the supervisor carefully explaining the basic instructional routines the volunteers have just observed. On Day 2, the volunteers do the tutoring and the supervisor observes; again, a careful debriefing afterward allows the new tutors to ask questions and to receive constructive feedback on their performance. Once the first couple of tutors have gained their "sea legs," usually after three or four lessons, the supervisor starts another two or three tutor–child pairs. In this way, the program stair-steps up to 10 children being served by the end of October, with each *beginning tutor* having received special attention from the supervisor in the early lessons.

Ongoing Supervision

From the inception of the tutoring program, we have recognized the need to provide some type of ongoing support to the volunteer tutors. We do not expect an undergraduate music major or a retired accountant to be an instinctively good teacher of beginning reading. Rather, we anticipate that such volunteers will get "stuck" from time to time in their new tutoring role, requiring the assistance of an experienced reading teacher. By providing consultation and supervision throughout the year, we are able to build up the competence and confidence of the volunteer tutors and help them (and the children they work with) avoid the damaging feelings of inadequacy and discouragement.

The most important in-service support is provided to the tutors on an individual basis. In the early years of the program the supervisor observed the tutoring lessons and then met with individual tutors before, after, or even during the sessions to make suggestions or provide feedback. If a tutor was having difficulty, the supervisor was right there to model a specific teaching procedure with that tutor's child. Planning or sequencing of instruction across tutoring lessons was the responsibility of the volunteer in consultation with the supervisor. This proved to be a fairly workable system, but we discovered over the years that busy volunteers did not always have time, before or after the tutoring sessions, to consult with their supervisors regarding lesson planning, nor did some have the requisite knowledge to plan by themselves at home (e.g., which story to read next or which word patterns to sort next).

Eventually we adopted a lesson-planning approach in which the supervisor, a trained reading specialist, assumes more responsibility. It works as follows. A lesson plan notebook (8½" × 11" spiral) is kept for each child. After a Monday tutoring session, the supervisor takes the 10 notebooks home and plans the next tutoring lesson for *each* child in her group. (*Note*: The supervisor draws on her first-hand observations of the Monday tutoring lessons in making lesson plan suggestions for Wednesday.) When the volunteer tutor comes in on Wednesday afternoon, he/she picks up the lesson plan book for his/her student, notes the specific tutoring activities for the day, locates the needed materials, and proceeds to get to work. The volunteer is already familiar with the teaching routines (support reading, word sorting, reading to the child); what the notebook offers—free of charge, so to speak—is an appropriate plan for that specific lesson (e.g., *which* stories to read, *which* word patterns to sort). Following the lesson, the tutor quickly jots down in the notebook relevant comments on the child's performance that day, and these comments are then considered by the supervisor in planning the child's next lesson. In this way, the lesson plan notebook becomes an important secondary dialogue between supervisor and tutor regarding the child's reading/writing development across the year. (See sample lesson plan in Figure 1.2.)

The supervisor's careful lesson planning ensures quality control in the program. Through the lesson plans, the supervisor is able to differentiate skill instruction (beginning consonants for one child, short-vowel word families for another) and adjust the pace at which individual children progress through the graded reading materials (primer, late-first, early-second, and so on). Such instructional "fine-tuning" increases student achievement, but does come at a cost. That is, the supervisor of 10 tutor–child pairs must spend approximately 2 hours of planning per tutoring day during the fall and up to 1.5 hours per tutoring day during the spring.

Preplanned lessons for the individual children are crucial, yet equally important is the supervisor's physical presence *during* the tutoring period. As she walks among and observes the 10 tutor–child pairs, she sends an implicit message to child and volunteer alike: "This tutoring is serious business." During a lesson the supervisor can model a new teaching technique for a tutor or provide assistance

LESSON PLAN

1. **Guided reading:**
   "A Pet in a Bowl"
   Laidlaw, 2-1

2. **Word sort:**
   e vowel patterns
   (e, ee, ea)

3. **Easy reading:**
   Partner-read the first half of
   the tradebook *Silly Sam*

4. **Read to** John:
   Paul Bunyan (deLeeuw)

TUTOR'S COMMENTS

1. John did all the reading, so we stopped after 8 pages. He missed just a few words, and his comprehension was good. This level is just about right.

2. Some confusion on *ee* and *ea* at first, but he ended up doing a nice job. Should work on these patterns a few more times.

3. We alternated pages and finished the book. John liked it.

4. No time today.

FIGURE 1.2. Sample lesson plan (with tutor's comments).

when an old technique does not seem to be working. Moreover, the supervisor's firsthand observations of the tutoring enable her to make informed and necessary adjustments in upcoming lessons (e.g., to move a child up one reading level or one skill level).

Assessing the Program's Effectiveness

In May the supervisor posttests the tutored students on the same reading/spelling tasks that were administered at the beginning of the school year:

1. *Word recognition*: Ability to read individual words on lists graded in difficulty (early-first-grade through third-grade lists)
2. *Passage reading*: Ability to read a set of passages graded in difficulty (early-first-grade through third-grade passages)
3. *Spelling*: Ability to spell a 20-word list of first- and second-grade words

Table 1.1 shows the pretest–posttest scores of 10 second graders who were tutored in a rural North Carolina school during the 1995–1996 school year.

Note in the table that on the September pretest, only 2 of the 10 second-grade students could read a primer or mid-first-grade-level passage. After a year of tutoring, however, seven of the children could read a second-grade passage, and five were on grade level (2-2 or better).

In a large school (or school system) where there are more low-reading second graders than can be tutored in a given year, a reading teacher can conduct a more rigorous evaluation of the Howard Street tutoring model. To do so, the teacher, in

TABLE 1.1. Pretest–Posttest Reading Performance of 10 Tutored Students

	September pretest		May posttest	
Student	Word recognition[a]	Passage reading[b]	Word recognition	Passage reading
Charlie	Below PP	Below PP	PP	Primer
T.J.	Below PP	PP	Primer	1-2
April	Below PP	PP	Primer	1-2
Marcus	PP	PP	1-2	2-1
Josh	PP	PP	Second	2-1
Christy	PP	PP	Second	2-2
Michael	PP	PP	Second	2-2
Stacey	PP	PP	Second	2-2
Bridgett	PP	Primer	Second	2-2
Victor	Primer	Primer	Third	Third

[a]To attain a given word recognition level (e.g., preprimer [PP]), student had to score 50% or better on *flash* presentation of a 20-word list.

[b]To attain a given passage-reading level (e.g, 1-2 or late-first-grade), student had to read with 90% accuracy at a minimally acceptable rate.

September, pretests a large number of low-reading second graders. Next, he/she rank orders the children based on their pretest *word recognition scores*. Starting at the bottom of the rank-ordered list, the reading teacher pairs successive children, assigning one to the *tutored group* and one to the nontutored or *comparison group*. The tutored group, of course, will receive a full year of one-to-one reading instruction from volunteers. In May the reading teacher administers the same test battery to both groups, tutored and nontutored. Achievement differences between the two groups will speak to the effectiveness of the volunteer tutoring effort.

Such a training study was carried out in the late 1980s at the original Howard Street tutoring site in Chicago. Thirty low-reading second and third graders, who received 1 year of tutoring instruction, were compared with 30 closely matched, nontutored students. The results were clear. The tutored students significantly outperformed the comparison group on each achievement measure: word recognition, passage reading, and spelling (see Morris et al., 1990). Figure 1.3 illustrates how the two groups performed on the *passage reading* task.

Although Figure 1.3 clearly shows that, overall, the tutored group outperformed the comparison group on *passage reading*, the figure also shows that tutor-

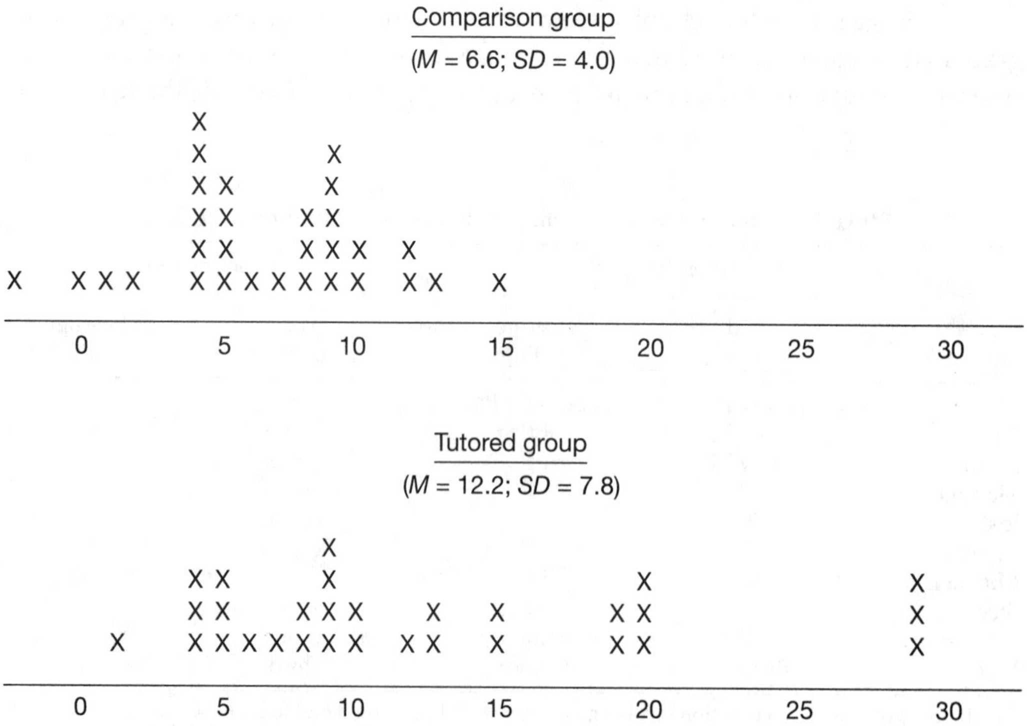

FIGURE 1.3. Months of passage reading gain for students in the tutored group and the comparison group.

ing did not produce a full year's reading gain (10+ months) for every tutored child. Still, 15 of the tutored children (50%) made such a gain, as compared with only 6 of the comparison-group children (20%). More important, only 7 (or 23%) of the tutored group made what may be termed "limited progress" during the year: 5 or fewer months of reading gain. This is significant when one realizes that 14 (or 47%) of the nontutored children made 5 or fewer months of reading gain. On the other end of the continuum, 10 of the tutored children (34%) made quite large gains in passage reading, whereas only 1 nontutored child showed such growth.

Program Implications

Interpreting Program Effectiveness

Results in both Chicago and North Carolina show that the Howard Street tutoring model can help at-risk primary-grade children learn to read. In the Chicago training study, one-third of the tutored children achieved accelerated growth in reading, moving this group, ability-wise, back into the educational "mainstream" of their public school classrooms. Another 30% of the tutored children gained a full year in reading. Although this second group did not show accelerated or "catch-up" growth, they did begin to learn to read and spell at a normal rate (1 year of achievement for 1 year in school). Finally, a third group of tutored children (less than 30%) progressed in reading but at a slower rate than their peers.

It is encouraging to find that a volunteer-staffed tutoring program, operating on a small budget (the part-time salary of the supervisor), can make this kind of difference in disadvantaged children's educational experience. And it is important to keep in mind that we were working with the lowest readers (bottom quartile) in a poor inner-city school. On the other hand, it should be clear that the reading gains the tutored children made were hard won. To achieve just a half-year difference in reading achievement between the tutored and comparison groups, it took 50 hours per child of well-planned, closely supervised one-to-one tutoring. These observations are not to question the worth of the tutoring effort or the significance of the children's accomplishment, but to point out that such a volunteer tutoring effort produces measurable gains, not miracles.

One may ask why some low-reading second graders benefit more than others from 50+ hours of one-to-one tutoring. Skill differences among the tutors and tutor–child dyad characteristics (good personality matches versus not-so-good matches) may account for some of the achievement variation in the tutored group. However, a better explanation results from viewing the lowest readers in a second-grade classroom as being on a continuum—a continuum of "readiness" or potential for learning to read.

For example, although 10 low-reading second graders may all start out in September as "beginning readers" (preprimer or below), our experience shows that there will be differences in their subsequent responsiveness to instruction. In fact, there are surely different reasons that these children did not learn to read *in first grade*. Some may not have been developmentally ready to respond to the basal reading instruction offered in first grade (lacking prerequisite alphabet knowledge and/or phoneme awareness); others may have been ready, but received poor instruction owing to teacher inexperience or too-large class size; and still others (a small percentage, no doubt) may have serious and basic problems in processing written language.

The first two aforementioned groups—those children who were not "ready" for traditional reading instruction in first grade, and those who were ready but were not taught—are highest on the "readiness" continuum at the beginning of second grade ("best bets," if you will). These children should benefit most from consistent tutoring in reading during the second-grade year. On the other hand, those few children who experience some basic difficulties with written language processing (e.g., internalizing the alphabet, "hearing" sounds within words, establishing an initial sight vocabulary) will undoubtedly make slower progress in reading and writing over a year's time, *regardless* of the quality of the tutoring effort.

It should be pointed out that, based on a September reading assessment (see preceding section), it is almost impossible to predict which children will be very successful and which will experience only moderate success in the year-long tutoring program. Only by working with a child over a few months' time (15 to 20 sessions) can we begin to gauge accurately that child's aptitude for learning to read and write. Even then, some children will surprise, starting off torturously slowly in the fall but progressing quickly after they "catch on" to the reading process after the Christmas break. Although a tutoring program of the kind described in this manual is not a panacea for severe learning problems, note in Figure 1.3 that the seven tutored children who made less than 6 months' progress on the passage-reading measure *did improve* (1 to 5 months gain). Furthermore, a sensitive tutor can make the slow learner or disabled reader (choose your terminology) "feel" this improvement, however modest it may be, thereby strengthening the child's needy academic self-image.

Thus far, little mention has been made of the tutoring program's relationship with the neighborhood public school. In Chicago this relationship was a friendly but limited one. The principal and teachers supported our storefront tutoring effort and made it easy for us to operate in the school; for example, they provided us with space for pre- and posttesting and helped us get information forms to and from the children's homes. However, as in many Chicago public schools in the late 1980s, children in this school were taught to read only in grade-level materials. That is, second graders read in second-grade basals, third graders read in third-grade basals, and so on, *regardless* of the students' actual reading levels. Because the Howard Street program was committed to tutoring low readers at their *instructional level* (which for our children was 1 to 2 years below their classroom basal placement), there was little room for meaningful professional dialogue between the classroom teachers and the tutoring program supervisor.

In rural North Carolina schools in the 1990s the situation has been different. The volunteer tutoring is conducted on school grounds during the school day and supervised by the school-based reading teacher. Because the supervision of volunteer tutors is part of the reading teacher's job description, the children's tutorial instruction is tightly integrated with their school-based remedial reading instruction. Moreover, the reading teacher, by communicating regularly with a tutored child's classroom teacher, can sometimes influence the reading instruction offered in the classroom, as illustrated in the following example:

RT: I've moved Marcus up to a 2-1 book in tutoring. Do you think he could be moved up to your middle reading group in the classroom?

CT: I *have* noticed a difference in his reading. I'll have Marcus "visit" the middle reading group next week and see how he does.

In closing this section, let me briefly address the relationship between tutoring and classroom reading instruction. Low readers in the primary grades *must* read stories and study word patterns on a daily basis with their classroom teacher. Moreover, for progress to be made, the stories read and word patterns studied have to be at the children's "instructional" or developmental level. Tutoring should never be seen as an alternative to or replacement for such classroom instruction. In fact, most low readers, if they are to catch up, will require effective classroom reading instruction *and* effective tutorial assistance. It is the combination that can accelerate the children's reading progress, allowing them to make up the distance between themselves and their average-achieving peers.

Replication Requirements

What does it actually take to launch a small volunteer-staffed tutoring program of the kind described in this chapter? First, a physical setting must be located. A community-based after-school program might use a couple of rooms in a local community center, YMCA, or church. Or, quite possibly, the neighborhood public school may make available a few classrooms for after-school tutoring. During-school tutoring programs can make use of the reading resource room, other specialist rooms (music, art, counseling), or the school cafeteria, particularly in the early morning or late afternoon. Next, reading material must be acquired. Seven hundred dollars ($700) will purchase more than enough books to get the tutoring program started. All that is needed are 75 to 100 paperback trade books (early-first to second-grade reading levels) and three or four sets of used basal readers (late-preprimer to third-grade levels only). Lists of suggested trade books and used basals can be found in the appendices at the ends of Chapters 3, 4, and 5.

With the tutoring site and sufficient reading materials secured, the next tasks are to identify the children to be tutored (no problem here) and to recruit a small group of committed adults who can volunteer 2 hours per week to tutor children in reading. Recruitment of volunteer tutors may be a problem at first, but this will become an easier task in succeeding years. Again, churches, community groups, local universities, retirees, and parents of students in the school are logical starting points.

In putting together a small volunteer tutoring program of the kind described in this chapter, the most crucial piece of the puzzle is the *supervisor* of tutors. The supervisor is truly the hub around which the tutoring program revolves. In the beginning the supervisor's greatest challenge is to convince both the neophyte tutors and the struggling beginning readers that they are going to be successful. Through model teaching, discussion, lesson planning, and consistent encouragement, the supervisor gradually educates the volunteer tutors, who, in turn, teach their respective students to read. To accomplish these tasks, the effective supervisor must possess several characteristics: (1) theoretical knowledge of the beginning reading process, (2) experience in teaching beginners to read, (3) confidence (based on items 1 and 2) that almost all children can learn to read and write, and (4) an ability to work constructively with adults in a mentor–apprentice relationship.

Although the supervisor's role is demanding, it is also intellectually stimulating and personally fulfilling. Working through adult volunteers to meet the learning needs of individual children is a new experience for most educators; moreover, guiding the differentiated, one-to-one instruction of 10 beginning readers over the course of a school year can only deepen a person's knowledge of the learning-to-read process. Despite its challenge, remember that the supervisor's job is part-time—only 2 hours per week of on-site supervision, along with lesson planning (up to 4 hours per week) that can be done at one's convenience.

A well-trained reading specialist is the obvious person to fill the supervisor's position, although a first- or second-grade teacher with expertise in teaching beginning reading can also do the job. Reading teachers, given the flexibility of their schedules, can supervise during or after school, whereas classroom teachers are usually limited to supervising after school. It should go without saying that teachers should receive a stipend for after-school service of this kind.

A promising way to begin a volunteer tutoring program is for *two teachers to work together the first year* in supervising a small group of volunteers (perhaps eight). Sharing the supervision of a small number of tutor–child pairs 2 days a week offers several advantages:

1. The problem of recruiting a large number of volunteer tutors the first year is mitigated.
2. Close monitoring of the individual tutor–child pairs is possible when there is such a small, 1:4, supervisor:tutor ratio. The careful supervision of the tutoring lessons will not only help the volunteer tutors but will also benefit the neophyte supervisor who is learning a new craft.
3. The amount of time needed for outside lesson planning is small when each supervisor is responsible for only four tutor–child pairs.
4. When two teachers share supervising for the first year, there is an impor-

tant opportunity for dialogue. By observing tutoring lessons together and discussing the needs of individual children and tutors, the supervisors can support each other in planning future lessons. This will greatly enhance the co-supervisors' understanding of the operation of the tutoring program. Two heads are better than one, both in terms of producing results and understanding process.

After 1 year of sharing responsibilities, each supervisor should feel more confident in doing the job alone. Furthermore, because of an experience factor, each will be able to supervise more tutor–child pairs in Year 2.

One cautionary note is in order. There is an inherent tendency for volunteer service programs to expand too quickly, particularly when there is a great need for the service. We made this mistake in the Howard Street Tutoring Program, expanding to 14 tutor–child pairs in the second year of operation (see Morris, 1993a). After a few months we realized that it was impossible for one supervisor, no matter how knowledgeable or energetic, to direct such a large program. Sufficient support was unavailable to the volunteers, and this adversely affected their feelings of competence and the quality of their tutoring. We did learn from our mistake; in Year 3 we went back to 10 tutors per supervisor.

Again, it is important to start small and build up gradually over a few years' time. An experienced supervisor can eventually monitor the work of 10 volunteer tutors; such an effort may not "save" every low reader in a school, but it is a significantly large candle to light an otherwise dark room.

Other Tutoring Models

The Howard Street tutoring model is only one approach to meeting the needs of low-reading primary-grade children. At present there are several *in-school* early reading intervention programs that have been successfully field-tested across the country. Noteworthy among these are Reading Recovery (Pinnell, 1989) and Success for All (Slavin et al., 1994). Although Reading Recovery and Success for All use different teaching methods and materials, the programs have similar features:

1. Both programs work with *first graders,* attempting to identify at-risk learners early in the first-grade year before they have fallen significantly behind their peers in reading ability.
2. Both programs feature one-to-one, in-school tutoring in reading 5 days per week.
3. Both programs use carefully trained professional teachers to do the tutoring.
4. Both programs are expensive.

The Howard Street tutoring model described in this chapter is not an adequate replacement for powerful, professionally staffed intervention programs. In terms of their potential to reduce reading failure in the primary grades, Reading Recovery and Success for All dwarf any volunteer-staffed tutoring effort. Identifying at-risk readers early in first grade and using carefully trained teachers to tutor the children 5 days a week can make an enormous educational difference. It is my earnest wish that intervention programs of this type will continue to flourish and enjoy public support over the next decade.

Nonetheless, volunteer tutoring programs do have two important roles to play in our schools. First, carefully supervised volunteer tutoring, instituted in second and third grade, can reinforce or even accelerate the achievement effects of a professionally staffed first-grade intervention program. Second, in those schools (and there are many) that do not have the resources to afford a professionally staffed first-grade intervention program, volunteer tutoring in the primary grades can be a "lifeline" to literacy, enabling many children to learn to read who otherwise would not.

This chapter has outlined one way to establish a small volunteer tutoring program for low-reading primary-grade children. The chapters that follow provide detailed case-study descriptions of how to assess and teach beginning readers functioning at different ability levels. It is my hope that these descriptions will be of help both to supervisors of tutoring programs and to the volunteer tutors themselves.

CHAPTER 2

The Initial Reading Assessment

A first step in any tutoring effort is to find out what the child can do as a reader. An informal yet careful reading assessment will allow the tutor, from the start, to plan appropriate lessons keyed to the instructional level and skill needs of the learner. The initial assessment will also provide useful benchmarks against which the child's future gains in reading can be compared. Because we are focusing only on beginning readers in this tutoring manual (early-first-grade through second-grade *reading levels*), the variability in reading skill from one child to the next will be limited, to a degree. Even so, assessment will show that any group of so-called beginning readers will be a heterogeneous lot, with the children differing across several important dimensions. Among these are the following:

1. *Motivation for learning to read:* The child's desire to learn to read, manifested in an interest in books, an ability to sustain attention, and a willingness to take risks in new learning tasks.
2. *Familiarity with the sound or cadence of written language:* The child's tacit awareness of differences between spoken language and written language (book language). Many children learn the more formal cadence or rhythm of written language by being read to in the preschool years. Those children who have not been read to in the home or school will, of course, be deficient in this area.
3. *Concept of story:* The child's awareness of plot or predictable sequences of events in stories.
4. *Meaning vocabulary:* The store of spoken word meanings the child brings to the task of learning to read.
5. *Alphabet knowledge:* The child's ability to name and write the letters of the alphabet (upper- and lowercase).
6. *Word awareness:* The child's awareness that written words are units separated by spaces in a line of print. (This awareness is evidenced by the child's ability to point to individual words as he/she reads.)
7. *Sight vocabulary:* The number of printed words the child recognizes immediately, that is, without having to "sound out" the letters.

8. *Phoneme (or sound) awareness:* The child's awareness that spoken words are composed of sequences of phonemes or sounds (/man/ = /m/ + /ă/ + /n/). Phoneme awareness is crucial in learning to read an alphabetic written language like English, because the beginner must eventually learn, in some manner, to map individual letters (*b, t, m,* etc.) or letter clusters (*ch, -ck*) to their phonemic equivalents in the spoken language.

9. *Spelling ability:* The child's ability to construct or "invent" spellings based on his/her knowledge of speech sound relationships and alphabet letter names. (For example, a first-grade boy may spell *dress* "DRAS" because he accurately perceives a speech sound similarity between the short e sound in *dress* and the sound of the letter name, A.)

10. *Decoding ability:* The child's ability to "sound out" or decode regularly spelled words via the application of letter–sound knowledge.

11. *Contextual reading ability:* The child's ability to read short written stories or books accurately and fluently.

12. *Comprehension:* The child's ability to extract meaning from what he/she reads.

A list of understandings or abilities that may play a role in learning to read could go on and on. I will stop here because the preceding list, however incomplete it may seem to some, does capture the theoretical perspective that will guide this manual's discussion of assessment and teaching strategies to use with beginning readers.

If assessment of reading ability is a first step in the tutoring process, what tasks should the initial assessment battery include? The fact that we will be working with remedial beginning readers (children who have received classroom instruction but have fallen behind their peers in achievement) narrows our assessment focus a bit. That is, generally, the major problem confronting the struggling beginning reader is how to become an efficient processor of the print on the page—how to read written words and sentences in an accurate and fluent manner. Therefore, our initial assessment will concentrate on the child's ability to read (and spell) isolated words, and his/her ability to read orally first- and second-grade passages. Comprehension of text can also be a significant problem for beginning readers. However, it stands to reason that comprehension at the early stages of reading is, in large part, dependent on the beginner's ability to read the words on the page. (It is true that as the child's word recognition proficiency increases, comprehension becomes the primary goal of reading instruction. This position is reflected clearly in Chapter 5.)

This section includes a set of assessment tasks to use with beginning readers. A brief rationale for each task is provided, along with specific directions for administration and scoring. The assessment tasks are as follows:

1. Word recognition (graded lists)
2. Oral reading of graded passages

3. Spelling
4. Word awareness (optional)
5. Alphabet knowledge (optional)

WORD RECOGNITION (GRADED LISTS)

Rationale

Word recognition is central in learning to read. By examining a beginning reader's ability to recognize first- and second-grade words arranged on lists of graded difficulty, the tutor can obtain an indication of the child's sight vocabulary and decoding skills. In fact, the child's performance on such a word recognition assessment will provide a good first estimate of his/her reading instructional level.

Administration

Using a "timed–untimed" procedure to present each word, the tutor has the child read successive lists of first- and second-grade words:

Preprimer list (20 words)*
Primer list (20 words)
First-grade list (20 words)
Second-grade list (20 words)

Third-grade list (20 words)
Fourth-grade list (20 words)

Administration of the word recognition task begins with the first word in the preprimer list. Using two blank 3″ × 5″ index cards to cover the page, the tutor "flashes" the first word to the child for approximately ¼ second. Johnson, Kress, and Pikulski (1987) have provided a clear description of this timed or flash presentation:

> To rapidly present a word to the child, the two cards are held together immediately above the first word on the list. The lower card is moved down to expose the word; the upper card is then moved down to close the opening between them. This complete series of motions is carried out quickly, giving the child only a brief presentation of the word. It is important, however, that the word be exposed completely and clearly. (p. 57)

If the child responds correctly to the flash presentation of the first word, the tutor proceeds to flash the next word, continuing down the list in this manner until a

---

*See Appendix 2.1 at the end of this chapter for ready-to-administer copies of the word lists mentioned here, along with score sheets for the tutor's use.

given word is misread. At that point, the tutor opens the cards to frame the misread word and allows the child ample time to analyze or decode the word if he/she can. This is the untimed presentation. Following the child's untimed response, the tutor resumes flashing the listed words until subsequent errors necessitate the need for other untimed presentations.

The tutor should record the child's responses as the listed words are presented. A pencil and a score sheet corresponding to the child's test list should be at the tutor's side (away from the child) during the administration of the word recognition test. *Only errors need be recorded.* As long as the child is responding accurately on the flash presentations, the tutor need not pick up the pencil. When the child does misread a flashed word, the tutor routinely:

- Opens the cards, initiating the untimed presentation.
- Quickly writes down the child's flash response.
- Waits for and then records the untimed response.
- Readies the child for the flash presentation of the next listed word.

For example, if the child reads "day" for "by" on the flash presentation, the tutor opens the cards, immediately records *day* in the Flash column of the score sheet, and waits for the child's untimed response. If the child correctly identifies "by" when given additional time, the tutor simply records a check (✓) in the Untimed column. If the child makes another incorrect response, "die," the tutor writes *die* in the Untimed column. Finally, if the child fails to respond to the untimed presentation of the target word, "by," the tutor records a 0 in the Untimed column.

At the end of each list, the tutor quickly adds the number of words read incorrectly, along with the number of no-responses (0's). The tutor does this separately for the Flash and Untimed columns. If the total number of errors equals 10 or more *in the Untimed column*, the tutor can stop the test. If the total number of errors in the Untimed column is less than 10, the tutor administers the next list. Figure 2.1 shows the word recognition performance of two children on the primer-level list.

Scoring

The first step in scoring is to determine the child's percentage of *correct* responses on each list, as shown here:

	Preprimer		Primer		1-2	
	Flash	*Untimed*	*Flash*	*Untimed*	*Flash*	*Untimed*
Dante	75	80	30	35	—	—
Herbert	85	95	65	90	25	35

Dante

		Flash	Untimed
1.	back	black	0
2.	eat		
3.	sun		
4.	bird	0	0
5.	pat	play	pan
6.	saw	0	say
7.	feet	0	0
8.	lake	like	0
9.	hid	0	0
10.	cut	cup	cap
11.	about	0	0
12.	one		
13.	rain	0	0
14.	water	0	0
15.	two		
16.	how	0	who
17.	window	0	0
18.	need		
19.	that's		
20.	mother	mom	✓
% correct		30	35

Herbert

		Flash	Untimed
1.	back	black	✓
2.	eat		
3.	sun		
4.	bird		
5.	pat	pet	✓
6.	saw	say	✓
7.	feet		
8.	lake	like	✓
9.	hid		
10.	cut		
11.	about		
12.	one		
13.	rain		
14.	water	where	whert
15.	two		
16.	how		
17.	window	were	wind
18.	need		
19.	that's		
20.	mother	mom	✓
% correct		65	90

FIGURE 2.1. Two children's word recognition performance on the primer-level list. The next list should be administered to Herbert (above 50% on untimed), but word recognition testing can be discontinued for Dante (below 50% on untimed).

A score of 60% or above in the Flash column usually indicates that the child has adequate *sight vocabulary* to read at that level. Thus, given the preceding examples, we might predict that Herbert, but not Dante, will experience success reading in primer-level material. This is because Herbert's primer-level flash score (65%) is significantly higher than Dante's (30%). It is important to remember that the flash score (an indicator of sight vocabulary) is a much better predictor of contextual reading ability than the untimed score (an indicator of decoding skill).

A second way to analyze word recognition performance is to look at the amount of "pickup" or improvement between the flash and untimed scores on given lists. A good amount of improvement from the flash to the untimed score is an indicator that the child, given sufficient time, can decode words at that level of difficulty. Conversely, negligible improvement can signal the child's lack of decoding skill at that level. Notice, in Figure 2.1, that Herbert was able to identify five additional words on the untimed presentations (65% to 90%), but Dante could identify only one additional word (30% to 35%). Thus, Herbert not only possesses a larger primer-level sight vocabulary than his classmate, but he also has greater ability to decode words at this level.

A third way to analyze a child's word recognition performance is to look at the types of errors he/she is making on individual words. For example, Herbert misread four one-syllable words on the flash presentation: *back, pat, saw,* and *lake.* In each case, however, he was off by only one letter (sound) and was quickly able to correct these errors on the untimed presentations. In contrast, on two of the three two-syllable words that Herbert misread on the "flash" (*water* and *window*), he substituted a known sight word that bore little resemblance to the flashed word. Even when given more time with these two-syllable words, he was unable to decode them.

On the primer-level list, Dante obviously had difficulty reading one- and two-syllable words on both the flash and untimed presentations. From his responses, one can tentatively surmise that Dante has not yet internalized simple one-syllable vowel patterns (e.g., "play" for *pat*, "like" for *lake*, "cup" for *cut*). Unfortunately, there are not enough responses to make a reliable analysis. What is distinctive about Dante's protocol is the large number of 0's or no-responses in both the flash and Untimed columns. Is this a child who has little or no decoding ability at the primer reading level, or is Dante just a cautious child, afraid to take a decoding risk when he meets a word not presently in his limited sight vocabulary? More observation in other reading and writing contexts will be needed to answer this question. (*Note*: This preliminary analysis of errors on these introductory word recognition lists will not be the tutor's final check on the child's phonics knowledge or decoding ability. A more detailed analysis of errors on specific word patterns [e.g., CVC—*man, top*; CVCe—*lake, rope*; CVVC—*nail, road*] will be carried out once tutoring begins.)

Before ending this section on word recognition assessment, a word of caution is in order. Learning to "flash" a list of words to a child—and to score responses quickly as one goes along—is not the easiest of tasks to master. There is a subtle coordination involved in the flash technique that can be picked up only through practice and more practice. Probably the best way to learn the technique is to observe it being modeled by an experienced reading teacher, to practice on one's own, and then to get feedback from the reading teacher regarding one's proficiency. Fortunately, once the motor routine of crisply flashing the words is mastered, the skill will not be lost over time. It cannot be overstressed how essential this assessment procedure is to the tutor or teacher who works with beginning readers.

ORAL READING (GRADED PASSAGES)

Rationale

Few would question the diagnostic importance of an oral reading sample. In fact, a careful record of a child's oral reading is the best "window" we can have into the developing reading process. For example, does the child read the words in the text with adequate accuracy (e.g., 90%)? Does his/her reading have rhythm or cadence? On meeting new words, does the child rely more on contextual cues or letter–sound cues? Does he/she self-correct errors that disrupt the meaning of the text? Does the child take risks, or depend on teacher assistance when he/she is in doubt? These and other questions can be answered by analyzing the child's oral reading.

Administration

To assess oral reading, one needs a set of graded passages (easy to hard) and procedures for scoring and interpreting the child's reading of these passages. In our oral reading inventory, there are eight passages or difficulty levels: early-first grade through fourth grade (see Appendix 2.2).

Emergent (29 words)
Preprimer (69 words)
Primer (100 words)
1-2 (100 words)

2-1 (100 words)
2-2 (100 words)

Mid-third (100 words)

Mid-fourth (100 words)

With the exception of the first two levels (emergent and preprimer), each passage contains 100 words and is accompanied by three comprehension questions.

Where to begin the oral reading assessment depends on the child's grade placement. A first grader should start with the *emergent* passage, a second grader with the *preprimer* passage, and a third grader with the *primer* passage. The assessment begins with the tutor providing a brief introduction to the first passage, as in the following example for primer level:

TEACHER: In this story, little mouse and his mother see pictures in the clouds.

Then the tutor asks the child to read the 100-word passage orally and answer three questions. If he/she is successful, the tutor brings out the next passage (1-2), and the same routine is repeated. The child reads, orally, successive passages until he/she clearly reaches a frustration level. Frustration level is technically determined by an error quantity above a maximum limit, for example, more than 10 word-reading errors on a given passage. Other signs of frustration may include a significant decrease in the child's reading rate or fluency, an increase in the number of errors that change the meaning of text, and an increase in the need for tutor assistance in pronouncing words.

Scoring

In discussing how to score the oral reading sample, we will first take up the issue of *coding* or transcribing the child's oral reading and then move to *analyzing* the coded sample.

Because first-grade-level readers are notoriously slow in moving through text, the tutor will be able to code oral reading—that is, record the child's errors—as the child reads. To do so, the tutor will need a photocopy of the pages being read. (Tape-recording the oral reading is also highly recommended as a later check on coding reliability.) The coding system itself (see Figure 2.2) is traditional and straightforward, with five types of oral reading errors to be marked.

In this coding system, repetitions can be marked by underlining the repeated word or phrase (<u>the boy</u> was). However, repetitions will not be counted as scoreable errors.

Figure 2.3 shows the coding of a third-grade girl's reading of a late-first-grade (1-2) passage.

1. **Substitutions:**   Write the substituted or mispronounced word over the word in the text.

   saw
   (the   boy   was)

2. **Omissions:**   Circle the omitted word.

   (the   (big)   boy)

3. **Insertions:**   Use a caret to indicate the inserted word(s).

   big
   (the ˄ red   ball)

4. **Self-corrections:**   Place a check (✓) next to the marked error to indicate that the child has self-corrected. (A self-correction is usually a substitution error that the child spontaneously corrects.)

   saw ✓
   (the   boy   was)

5. **Examiner help:**   Place an "H" above each word that has to be provided by the examiner (the tutor). The tutor should refrain from providing help unless it is clearly necessary to do so—that is, unless the child refuses to attempt the unknown word or is noticeably unsuccessful in decoding it. (Wait 3 to 5 seconds before providing help.)

   H
   (the   boy   was)

FIGURE 2.2. Coding system for oral reading errors.

One hot summer day Frog and Toad

I
sat by the pond. "I wish we had

some sweet, cold ice cream," said Frog.

"What a good idea," said Toad.

"Wait right here, Frog. I will be

wanted ✓
back soon." Toad went to the store. ←

He bought two big ice-cream cones.

liked ✓
Toad licked one of the cones. "Frog likes ←

chocolate best," said Toad, "and so do I."

sŏf H
Toad walked along the path. A large, soft

dripped
drop of chocolate ice cream slipped down

on
⌄his arm. "This ice cream is melting in

the sun," said Toad.

fast
Toad walked faster. Many drops of melting

ice cream / flew through the air.

FIGURE 2.3. Coding of a 1-2 passage (100 words). Reprinted from Lobel (1976, pp. 30–33). Copyright 1976 by Harper Trophy. Reprinted by permission.

Note in Figure 2.3 that most of the child's errors were *substitutions* and that two of these were self-corrected. Her attempt to sound out the word *soft* was unsuccessful, and the tutor supplied the word.

Having established a system for coding oral reading, let us now address the scoring and analysis of a coded sample. The first score to obtain is the *oral reading score*, or the percentage of words read accurately in a passage (100% minus the percentage of reading error). The six passages, *primer* through *fourth grade*, each contain 100 words. To compute an oral reading score for these passages, we simply subtract the number of reading errors (1 error = 1%) from 100%. Looking back at the coded sample in Figure 2.3, we find 7 scoreable errors in this 100-word, *Level 1-2* passage. By subtracting the number of errors (7) from 100%, we obtain an oral reading score of 93%. (*Note:* The *emergent* and *preprimer* passages contain fewer than 100 words—29 and 69 words, respectively. Therefore, subtract 3.4% per error on the *emergent* passage and 1.4% per error on the *preprimer* passage.)

The question confronting us now is, how is an oral reading score of 93% to be interpreted? Unfortunately, setting firm criteria for oral reading accuracy in first-grade material is problematic. Experts in the field will disagree. The following, then, are useful but tentative accuracy criteria for interpreting a child's oral reading performance.

Emergent	85% accuracy
Preprimer	85%
Primer	90%
1-2	90%
2-1 and above	92%

Notice that the accuracy criterion increases from 85% in early-first-grade reading material to 90% in late first grade and, finally, to 92% in second grade. Although these criteria may be considered too liberal (too low) in some reading diagnosis circles, keep in mind that self-corrections are being counted as errors in this scheme. If we had chosen not to count them as errors, the accuracy criterion would probably be one or two points higher at each reading level. The assumption is that if a child meets the accuracy criterion at a given grade level (e.g., a 90% score on the 1-2 passage), he/she can be instructed at this level.

For illustrative purposes, let us examine the following scores attained by our third-grade girl on the oral reading passages:

Primer	96%	4 errors
1-2	93%	7 errors
2-1	90%	10 errors
2-2	84%	16 errors

This particular set of scores is instructive because it highlights the usefulness of our oral reading criteria, at the same time suggesting a need for caution and flexibility in applying the criteria. For example, it is clear that the child was comfortable reading the 1-2 passage, her 93% score easily exceeding the 90% criterion. Furthermore, most observers would agree that this third grader was probably frustrated on the 2-2 passage, reading only 84% of the words accurately. What is not so clear is how to interpret the child's 90% score on the 2-1 passage. Can we be sure that because the reader missed the criterion at this level (92%) by two points (two misread words), this means that she should not be instructed in Level 2-1 reading materials? Of course we cannot be sure. This is the limitation of the oral reading score—of any numerical score, for that matter—in a clinical evaluation. That is, in borderline cases other information about the child's oral reading performance must also be considered: rate of reading, quality of errors, self-correction, amount of teacher support required, and so forth. It is to these additional characteristics of oral reading that we now turn.

The child's *reading rate* on passages at the primer level and above is easy to obtain. (The rate need not be measured on the simple emergent and preprimer passages.) Using a watch with a second hand, the tutor first records how many seconds it takes the child to read the passage. Then, with the help of the following formula, he/she can quickly compute the reading rate in words per minute (wpm).

$$\text{Reading rate (wpm)} = \frac{60 \times \text{No. of words read}}{\text{No. of seconds to read passage}}$$

Because *number of words read* remains constant across the passages (i.e., 100 words), the rate formula becomes:

$$\text{Reading rate (wpm)} = \frac{60 \times 100, \text{ or } 6{,}000}{\text{No. of seconds to read passage}}$$

An example will help. If the child takes 115 seconds to read the 100-word 1-2 passage, his/her rate is 52 wpm.

$$\text{Reading rate (wpm)} = \frac{6{,}000}{115} = 52$$

Interpreting the reading rates of beginning readers calls for caution and common sense. Sixty words per minute (60 wpm) has often been cited as an average rate for first graders reading first-grade material (McCracken, as cited in Guzak, 1985). But what is an "average" or acceptable rate for remedial second or third graders reading first-grade material? The following criteria, based on this author's clinical experience, are suggested:

60 or more wpm: A good, solid reading rate

40–59 wpm: A possibly acceptable rate, depending on the presence of appropriate intonation and phrasing in the child's reading

Below 40 wpm: An unacceptably slow rate of reading

As with the oral reading accuracy criteria, the tutor must exercise judgment when the child's rate bounds two criterion levels; that is, the rate is close to 40 wpm or close to 60 wpm. Exercising judgment amounts to taking into consideration other aspects of the child's oral reading performance, including the number of reading errors made, the number of self-corrections, and the amount of tutor assistance provided.

With the oral reading sample coded, it requires little effort to conduct an *analysis of the substitution errors* made by the reader. Probably the simplest way to proceed is to list each substitution beside the corresponding text word. Again, let us refer to the oral reading protocol in Figure 2.3.

Text word	Child's substitution
we	I
went	wanted (s-c)
licked	liked (s-c)
slipped	dripped
faster	fast

A quick "eyeball" analysis of the substitution errors shows unequivocally that this child is attending to the letter sounds in words (e.g., "liked" for *licked*).

Many tutors may choose to conclude their analysis of the child's substitution errors at the graphic or letter–sound correspondence level. However, by going a little further and analyzing substitutions from both a graphic and a meaning perspective (Does the substitution preserve meaning?), one can sometimes gain valuable insight into a child's reading behavior (Goodman, 1969; Chittenden, 1983). This is particularly true when the substitution errors are considered in relation to the child's self-correction responses (see the following chart).

Text	Substitution	Meaning	Graphic	Self-correction
we	I	+	0	
went	wanted	0	+	+
licked	liked	0	+	+
slipped	dripped	+	+	
faster	fast	+	+	

The reader of this 1-2 passage self-corrected twice, both times on a word that disrupted the meaning of the text. She did not self-correct any of three substitutions that preserved meaning.

Even if the tutor chooses not to analyze self-corrections in the detailed manner described here, he/she should still record the number of self-corrections, along with the *number of tutor helps required.*

Level	Total errors	No. of self-corrections	No. of helps
Primer	4	3	0
1-2	7	2	1
2-1	10	2	2
2-2	16	1	5

Notice in the preceding chart that as the reading process starts to break down (total errors increasing), the number of self-corrections decreases and the number of tutor helps increases.

The following chart summarizes what we have learned about the oral reading sample depicted in Figure 2.3.

Level	No. of words	Total errors	Oral reading score	Rate	Self-corrections	Helps
1-2	100	7	93%	52 wpm	2	1

Question: Based on the numbers in the preceding chart, can we interpret this as an adequate oral reading performance by the child? Why or why not? How to code, score, and interpret an oral reading sample will be addressed again at several points in this manual, specifically at the beginning of each of the case study chapters (Chapters 3, 4, and 5).

SPELLING

Rationale

On first look, one might question the inclusion of a spelling task in a battery designed to assess beginning reading ability. However, there are good reasons for doing so. First, spelling ability and word reading ability are highly correlated in the early primary grades (K–2). Morris and Perney (1984) reported a .82 correlation between first graders' January spelling ability (assessed according to a developmental scheme) and their May, end-of-year, word recognition ability. Second, and more important, we can gain insight into a child's ability to read words by looking at how he/she spells words. This is because *an abstract, developing word knowledge underlies the ability to do both* (Ehri, 1980; Gill, 1992; Henderson, 1990; Perfetti, 1992).

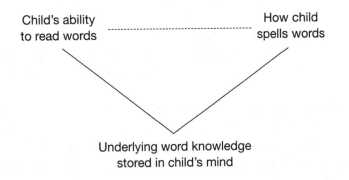

Two aspects of this developing word knowledge that have received much attention in the research literature are *phoneme awareness* (awareness that words are composed of sequences of individual sounds or phonemes: /man/ = /m/ + /a/ + /n/) and *orthographic awareness* (knowledge of the frequently occurring letter sequences or spelling patterns in our written language: CVC—*man, red, hot*; CVCe—*lake, pole*; and CVVC—*boat, feel*). Researchers have shown conclusively that success in learning to read is contingent on the child's development of these understandings (Adams, 1990; Gibson & Levin, 1975; Liberman & Liberman, 1992). Regarding assessment, we are fortunate in that a quick qualitative analysis of a beginning reader's spelling attempts (see "Scoring" on page 36) will reliably reveal the amount of phonemic and spelling pattern awareness possessed by the child at a given point in time. More on this later.

Administration

The spelling task begins with the tutor modeling a sound-it-out spelling of the sample word, "mat."

> We are going to write the word "mat." What letter should I write down first? [The examiner offers praise for the correct response, *M*, and writes the letter on the paper. If the child gives the wrong letter or fails to respond, the examiner still writes down the letter *M*.] *M* is the first letter in "mat." What letter should we write down next? [And so on.]

With the sample word completed, the examiner hands the pencil to the child and says:

> Now I'm going to call out some more words, and I want you to try to write them. Remember, for each word, think about what letter comes first, what comes next, and so on. Okay, the first word is "bike."

If the child is unable to provide the beginning letter in the first four spelling words (*bike, fill, plate,* and *mud*), then the testing can be stopped. On the other hand, if the child is able to produce the beginning consonant letter *in even one of the first four words*, then the entire 20-word list should be administered. (For younger children, the test can be administered in two sessions.)

In administering the spelling test, the tutor should pronounce each word naturally, use it in a phrase or sentence if necessary, and then repeat the word a final time. The 20 spelling words, with accompanying sentences, are listed in Figure 2.4.

As the child attempts to spell the words, the tutor can provide encouragement when it is needed—for example, "Okay, you tried hard on that one," or "Good, you got the beginning and ending letters on that word." The tutor should encourage the reluctant speller to try his/her best, to listen for and write down the sounds that he/she hears.

Scoring

Traditionally, scoring a spelling test has been a right–wrong proposition. The examiner determines the number of correct spellings out of the number of words attempted by the child (e.g., 7 out of 10) and comes up with a spelling score (70% accuracy). However, because beginning reader–writers, by definition, are able to spell very few words correctly, such a right–wrong scoring approach often yields little useful information. For example, compare the two spelling samples in Figure 2.5.

On the 20-word list, Thomas and Brandy both scored 0 if we consider only the number of words spelled correctly. However, even a cursory glance reveals

First-grade words

1.	bike	I ride my <u>bike</u>.
2.	fill	I <u>fill</u> the basket.
3.	plate	Food is on the <u>plate</u>.
4.	mud	We play in the <u>mud</u>.
5.	flat	The table is <u>flat</u>.
6.	bed	I sleep on the <u>bed</u>.
7.	drive	My mom can <u>drive</u> the car.
8.	chop	He likes to <u>chop</u> wood.
9.	wish	Make a <u>wish</u>.
10.	step	Take one <u>step</u>.

Second-grade words

11.	plant	I can <u>plant</u> a flower.
12.	dress	That is a pretty <u>dress</u>.
13.	stuff	Take that <u>stuff</u> outside.
14.	chase	I <u>chase</u> my cat.
15.	wise	The old man is <u>wise</u>.
16.	shopping	We go <u>shopping</u>.
17.	train	You can travel on a <u>train</u>.
18.	cloud	See the <u>cloud</u> in the sky.
19.	thick	That is a <u>thick</u> piece of wood.
20.	float	Can you <u>float</u> in the water?

FIGURE 2.4. First- and second-grade spelling list. These words were selected from the first- and second-grade lists of the Qualitative Inventory of Word Knowledge (Schlagal, 1992), an inventory that has been used extensively in spelling research.

	Thomas	Brandy
bike	BC	BIK
fill	FL	FEL
plate	PT	PAT
mud	MD	MOD
flat	FT	FAT
bed	BD	BAD
drive	JV	JIV
chop	CHP	CHIP
wish	W	WES
step	CP	SDAP
plant	PT	PAT
dress	JS	JAS
stuff	SDF	SOF
chase	CHS	CHAS
wise	YS	WIS
shopping	—	SIPN
train	CHN	CHAN
cloud	CD	COD
thick	—	THEK
float	FT	FOT

FIGURE 2.5. Two children's performance on the spelling assessment.

that Brandy's spellings seem to be a bit more sophisticated. For example, unlike Thomas, Brandy represents vowel sounds in her spellings. Because a *quantitative* analysis (number correct) fails to differentiate these two spellers, does there exist a *qualitative* system for analyzing children's early spelling attempts? The answer is yes, and it is to such a qualitative or developmental scoring system that we now turn.

Much has been learned over the past 25 years regarding the development of spelling ability in young children. Beginning with Read's pioneering studies (1971, 1975), one can cite the important contributions of many, including Beers and Henderson (1977), Chomsky (1971, 1979), Ehri (1992), Gentry (1978), Henderson and Beers (1980), Henderson (1990), Templeton and Bear (1992), and Zutell (1979). Figure 2.6 presents in abbreviated form what these researchers have discovered.

As shown in Figure 2.6, once children can write the letters of the alphabet, their early *Semi-Phonetic (1)* spellings often include only the beginning consonant (B for *bike*; F for *fill*). Later in this stage, *Semi-Phonetic (2),* they represent the consonant boundaries (beginning and end) of one-syllable words (BK for *bike*, FL for *fill*). Note in the figure that, on occasion, they represent the beginning consonant and vowel but omit the ending consonant (e.g., FE for *fill*, PA for *plate*). These are

| Spelling | Semi-Phonetic | | Letter-Name | | Within-Word Pattern |
	(1)	(2)	(3)	(4)	(5)
bike	B	BK	BOK	BIK	BIEK
fill	F	FL, FE	—	FEL	FIL
plate	P	PT, PA	PAT	PLAT	PLAET
mud	M	MD	—	MOD	MUDD
flat	F	FT, FA	—	FAT	FLATE
bed	B	BD	—	BAD	BEDD
drive	J	JV	JIV	JRIV	DRIEV
chop	H	CHP	—	CHIP	CHOPE
wish	Y	WE	WES	WESH	WISHE
step	C	SP	SAP	STAP	STEPP
plant	P	PT	PAT	PLAT	PLANTE
dress	J	JS	JAS	JRAS	DRES
stuff	S	SF	SOF	STOF	STUF
chase	H	CHS	—	CHAS	CHAIS
wise	W	WZ	—	WISS	WIZE
shopping	S	SPN	SIPN	SHIPEN	SHOPING
train	T	TN	TAN	TRAN	TRANE
cloud	K	CD	KOD	CLOD	CLOWD
thick	F	THC	—	THEC	THIK
float	F	FT	FOT	FLOT	FLOTE

FIGURE 2.6. Developmental stages in young children's spelling.

still semi-phonetic attempts, for the child is unable, developmentally, to attend to the sequence of sounds in the word—that is, beginning, middle, and end.

Next comes a *Letter-Name,* or Phonetic, stage in which vowels begin to appear consistently in the children's spellings. In this stage the children "sound their way through" the word to be spelled, making one-to-one sound–letter matches as they write. Long vowels are represented with the corresponding letter-name (PLAT for *plate,* JRIV for *drive*). Short vowels are also represented with letter-names, but, curiously, with those letter-names that bear a phonetic similarity to the specific short-vowel sound. For example, the short *i* and long *e* sounds are articulated in a similar manner (the tongue is in a similar position in the vocal tract). When the neophyte speller attempts to represent the short *i* in *fill,* he/she lacks a letter-name referent (there is no alphabet letter "ih."). Thus the child tacitly chooses the nearest long vowel letter-name, E, and spells *fill,* FEL. The following are other phonetically appropriate short-vowel–letter-name pairings:

- *a* as in *flat* is spelled with an A—FLAT
- *e* as in *step* is spelled with an A—STAP
- *i* as in *thick* is spelled with an E—THEK
- *o* as in *chop* is spelled with an I—CHIP
- *u* as in *stuff* is spelled with an O—STOF

Early in the Letter-Name stage (3), young spellers represent the vowel sound in a consonant-blend word, but often omit the latter part of the blend (PAT for *plate,* SOF for *stuff*). Later in this stage (4), they represent both parts of the consonant blend (PLAT, STOF).

With extended opportunities to read and write, many normally achieving first graders move into a *Within-Word Pattern* spelling stage (5) near the end of the school year. Now the children begin to represent short vowels "correctly" (FIL for *fill,* DRES for *dress*) and mark long vowels (PLAET for *plate,* FLOTE for *float*), even though the vowel markers are often misplaced. Within-Word Pattern spellings, although still incorrect in the conventional sense, are a clear step forward developmentally. They indicate that the children are beginning to abandon their earlier conception of spelling as a fixed, one-to-one (one sound = one letter) code. Instead, these young spellers are searching actively for the legitimate patterns of letters (CVC—*mat*; CVVC—*tail*; CVCe—*lake*) that actually map the sounds of the spoken language to the English spelling system.

Using the model of development depicted in Figure 2.6, let us now analyze the two spelling samples on page 35. One need not take a graduate course in spelling theory to see that Thomas is a Semi-Phonetic stage speller and Brandy a Letter-Name stage speller. Such global, stage-based assessments are interesting and potentially informative. However, the tutor's real task is to identify specific developmental characteristics of the child's spelling and to understand the significance of these characteristics for reading–writing instruction.

For example, Thomas represents only the consonant boundaries of words in his spelling attempts (BC, FL, PT, etc.). From this we can infer that his phoneme awareness is incomplete. If a child lacks conscious awareness of certain sound elements in spoken words (vowels, in Thomas's case), how is he to learn that, in written language, letters map to these sounds—*a* to /ă/, *e* to /ĕ/, *i* to /ĭ/, and so on? As tutoring begins, Thomas may be able to process beginning and ending consonant cues in words that he meets in text; however, he will have difficulty—for a while, anyway—processing or getting into memory the vowel element in these words.

Brandy, on the other hand, represents both consonants and vowel sounds in her spellings (BIK—*bike*; FEL—*fill*; PAT—*plate*; MOD—*mud*). She "hears" or discriminates the vowel sounds accurately, but she needs to learn which alphabet letters go with which short-vowel sounds in written English. That is, short i (as in *fill*) is represented with the letter *i*, not the letter (name) *e*, as the child's ear informs her. From Brandy's spellings we can infer that (1) she possesses a larger sight vocabulary than her classmate, Thomas; (2) she may be able to process both vowel and consonant cues in her attempts to read (get into memory) printed words; and (3) she could benefit immediately from word study activities that focus on the short vowels and consonant blends.

A final comment on these two spelling samples pertains not so much to what Thomas and Brandy put in, but rather to what they left out as they attempted to spell the 20 words. Although both children showed evidence of phoneme awareness in their spellings—Brandy to a greater degree than Thomas—neither child demonstrated orthographic or spelling pattern knowledge (see Within-Word Pattern stage in Figure 2.6). As mentioned earlier, Brandy's "letter-name" spellings of the short vowel words (FEL–*fill*; MOD–*mud*; SDAP–*step*) revealed her lack of knowledge of the basic closed-syllable, short-vowel patterns in English. She also failed to put in an extra vowel letter to mark her long-vowel spellings (BIK–*bike*; JIV–*drive*; CHAS–*chase*). Finally, note Brandy's spelling of *thick* (omission of the final -*ck*) and of *dress* and *stuff* (omission of final consonant doublet). These spellings also indicate a lack of spelling pattern knowledge.

It is important to keep in mind that Thomas and Brandy are beginners, early- to mid-first-grade readers at best. The dearth of orthographic knowledge shown in their spellings results directly from their lack of experience with written language, very possibly from a lack of time spent reading text and attempting to write their own texts. As Thomas and Brandy progress in learning to read, their word knowledge will grow and evolve. Over a few months of tutoring, it is very likely that Thomas will move into the Letter-Name or vowel-awareness stage of spelling, and that Brandy will begin to show distinct signs of pattern awareness in her spelling attempts.

As we have seen in the preceding example, an informal, developmental assessment of a child's spelling can yield valuable information. For some purposes, however (e.g., reporting pretest–posttest results to a school or funding agency), a tutoring program may need a more formal-looking numerical spelling score for each child. Such scores are easily obtained. Figure 2.6 shows how a number or point value can be assigned to each level in our developmental spelling scheme: Semi-Phonetic (1 to 2 points), Letter-Name (3 to 4 points), Within-Word Pattern (5 points), and Correct (6 points). To determine a child's developmental spelling score on the 20-word test, the tutor simply assigns the appropriate number of points to each spelling attempt, then totals the number of points acquired across the 20 spelling words. To illustrate, we will again use the spelling samples produced by Thomas and Brandy (see Figure 2.7).

Thomas's tendency to represent beginning and ending consonants in his spelling attempts resulted in mostly 2-point spellings and a total score of 35. Brandy, who systematically sounded her way through each word, produced 3 and 4-point letter-name spellings for a total score of 70. Remember that each child would have scored 0, appearing to have equal ability, if a correct–incorrect scoring system had been used.

Although on first look it may seem tedious to assign an individual score to each spelling attempt, the tutor will find that, with experience, he/she can usually do so quickly and accurately. There is one note of caution. Not all children will produce spellings as systematic and isomorphic with the scoring system as were Thomas's and Brandy's. Obviously, those spellings that do deviate from the developmental pattern will be interesting and important from the standpoint of assessment. To assist the tutor in judging the developmental appropriateness of a

	Thomas		Brandy	
bike	BC	(2)	BIK	(4)
fill	FL	(2)	FEL	(4)
plate	PT	(2)	PAT	(3)
mud	MD	(2)	MOD	(4)
flat	FT	(2)	FAT	(4)
bed	BD	(2)	BAD	(4)
drive	JV	(2)	JIV	(3)
chop	CHP	(2)	CHIP	(4)
wish	W	(1)	WES	(3)
step	CP	(2)	SDAP	(4)
plant	PT	(2)	PAT	(3)
dress	JS	(2)	JAS	(3)
stuff	SDF	(2)	SOF	(3)
chase	CHS	(2)	CHAS	(4)
wise	YS	(2)	WIS	(4)
shopping	—	(0)	SIPN	(3)
train	CHN	(2)	CHAN	(3)
cloud	KD	(2)	COD	(3)
thick	—	(0)	THEK	(4)
float	FT	(2)	FOT	(3)
		35		70

FIGURE 2.7. Developmental scoring of two spelling samples.

wider range of spelling attempts, Appendix 2.3 provides additional scoring examples for each developmental level. Not all possible ways children will spell the 20 words are included in Appendix 2.3. However, the figure contains enough examples to facilitate commonsense scoring judgments on idiosyncratic spelling attempts.

The basic reading assessment battery has now been described. It includes three tasks: (1) word recognition (graded lists), (2) oral reading passages, and (3) spelling. Administration time will vary from 20 to 30 minutes, depending on how many word recognition lists and oral reading passages are attempted by a given child.

For a few children, those who are off to a very late start in learning to read or those who are experiencing specific difficulty with written-language learning, some additional assessment may be necessary. This is because a true beginner may be unable to perform on the basic assessment tasks—that is, be unable to read a preprimer word list, unable to read aloud a preprimer passage, and unable to represent even beginning consonants in his/her spelling attempts. In such a case, the tutor needs to learn what the child *can* do, what he/she does know about written language. The following sections describe two optional assessment tasks, *word awareness* and *alphabet knowledge*, that address this concern.

WORD AWARENESS (OPTIONAL)

Rationale

Word awareness, as defined here, refers to the beginning reader's ability to match spoken words to written words as he/she reads (see Morris, 1996). For example, having memorized a short poem or storybook page, can a 6-year-old boy read the few lines of print, pointing accurately to the individual words as he goes along? Until the child can do so, he will be unable to learn new sight words from his reading or attend effectively to letter-sound cues within words in text (e.g., beginning consonant cues). Thus, word awareness—the ability to "read the spaces," in Clay's (1991b) terminology—assumes crucial importance in the learning-to-read process.

Administration

First, the tutor must decide whether the word awareness task should be administered. The following rule of thumb applies: If a child is unable to read the preprimer passage *and* if he/she scores below 50% on the preprimer word recognition list (untimed), then administer the word awareness task. Conversely, if the child is able to read the preprimer passage *or* if he/she scores 50% or above on the PP1 word list, do *not* administer the task.

The word awareness task requires the child to (1) finger-point read three different sentences, and (2) identify preselected target words within the sentences. A relevant drawing is paired with each test sentence to provide a context for reading (see Figure 2.8 as well as Appendix 2.4 for all three "Katie" sentences).

The tutor introduces the task by asking the child what he/she thinks is happening in the first drawing. After acknowledging the child's response, the tutor says:

> The sentence down here [pointing to the printed sentence] tells what is happening in the drawing. Watch while I read the sentence, pointing to each word. [The tutor finger-point reads the sentence.] Now, this time *you* read the sentence and point to the words. [If necessary, the tutor moves the child's finger to the first word (Katie) to help him/her get started.]

Upon the child's completion of his/her finger-point reading attempt, the tutor immediately points to a target word within the sentence ("Can you read this word?")—and then to a second target word ("What about this one?"). After recording the child's responses (see "Scoring" on page 42), the tutor moves on to the next test sentence.

All three test sentences (see Appendix 2.4) should be administered because the child's performance may vary a bit from sentence to sentence. However, the entire word awareness task will take only 2 to 3 minutes to administer and score.

Scoring

Figure 2.9 is a score sheet for recording the child's responses on the word awareness task.

Katie is walking in the rain.

FIGURE 2.8. First of three test sentences in the "Katie" book.

	Point	Words	

2   1
(1) Katie is *walking* in the *rain*   _____   1 _____   2 _____

1   2
(2) *She* sees a *big* dog.   _____   1 _____   2 _____

2   1
(3) The *dog* shakes *water* on Katie.   _____   1 _____   2 _____

FIGURE 2.9. Score sheet for word awareness task ("Katie" book).

The score sheet should be filled in as each sentence is completed. Finger-point reading attempts are scored in an all-or-nothing (+ or 0) manner. That is, the child receives credit only if he/she points to and reads correctly each word in the sentence (self-corrections are acceptable). Note also that there is room on the score sheet for the tutor to write in the child's word identification responses. It is not necessary to derive a numerical performance score on the word awareness task. The tutor administers the task seeking the answer to just one question: How well can the child match spoken words to written words in finger-point reading a memorized sentence? Interestingly, beginning readers will differ in the amount of word awareness they possess. Some will finger-point read with ease and identify target words within the sentences without hesitation. Others may occasionally stumble in finger-point reading, particularly on two-syllable words, in which they may point once for each syllable.

Child:	Walk	ing	in
Text:	Walking	in	the

When later asked to identify a single word within the sentence, these children may go back to the beginning of the sentence and finger-point over to the target word, using context as a word identification aid. (*Note*: Such a strategy would have to be viewed as a strength.) Finally, a few beginning readers may show little or no ability to finger-point read a printed sentence or to locate and identify words within the sentence. For these youngsters, an early objective of the tutoring lessons will be to enhance their awareness of word units in text.

ALPHABET KNOWLEDGE (OPTIONAL)

Rationale

The alphabet letters (upper- and lowercase) are the building blocks of our writing system. The child who is able to recognize and name these letters brings important, task-specific perceptual knowledge to the learning-to-read effort (Adams,

1990; Ehri & Wilce, 1985). Furthermore, to produce phonetic or "sound-it-out" spellings in his/her writing, the child must know, among other things, the names of the alphabet letters and how to write the letters.

Administration

The alphabet knowledge task need *not* be administered if the child represents at least 15 of the 20 beginning consonants appropriately on the 20-word spelling test. This task contains two parts: recognition and production. *Recognition*: The child names the alphabet letters, upper- and lowercase, as the tutor points to them in random order. *Production*: The child writes the alphabet letters as the tutor dictates the letter names in random order. See Appendix 2.5 for a randomized alphabet sheet that can be used for both the recognition and production task.

Scoring

Along with recording the number of correct responses on both the recognition and production task, the tutor should note the specific letters that the child misses. The tutor should also note the relative speed of the child's letter identification attempts (assuming accuracy, the quicker the child's response, the better).

On the production task, the child should receive credit for writing either the upper- or lowercase form of a letter.

A SAMPLE ASSESSMENT

To conclude this chapter on the initial reading assessment, let us follow one child through the entire test battery. On the first task, the graded *word recognition lists*, Shawn, a low-reading third grader, achieved the following scores:

	Flash (%)	Untimed (%)
Preprimer	90	95
Primer	85	90
1-2 (late first)	55	70
Second	15	35
Third	—	—

As shown in the preceding chart, Shawn's word recognition ability began to falter on the late-first-grade list and "bottomed out" in second grade. On the second-grade list, given ample time to read or even "sound out" the words, he could recognize only 7 of 20. The tutor also noticed that on the preprimer and primer lists, where Shawn seemed to perform well, his correct word recognition responses on the flash presentations were not always automatic. That is, he would sometimes hesitate a moment after a word had been flashed before responding. Based on this child's word recognition performance, the tutor anticipated that Shawn would be successful reading the early-first-grade passages (preprimer and primer), but that he might experience difficulty reading the 1-2 and 2-1 passages.

The *oral reading passages* were administered next. Shawn's scores on the passages are presented in the following table.

Level	No. of words	Total errors	Oral reading score (%)	Rate (wpm)	Self-corrections	Helps
Primer	100	2	98	57	1	0
1-2	100	6	94	54	3	0
2-1	100	19	81	37	2	5

A discernible pattern in the oral reading scores shows that Shawn was able to read the first-grade passages with an acceptable degree of accuracy, his reading rate being slow but consistent on the primer and 1-2 passages. On the 2-1 passage there was a significant drop in his oral reading accuracy (94% to 81%) and his rate (54 wpm to 37 wpm). Notice also that self-corrections decreased and tutor helps increased on the second-grade passage. Clearly, the second-grade passage was too difficult for this child.

Shawn's performance on the third assessment task, *spelling*, was encouraging (see Figure 2.10).

Spelling word	Shawn's spelling
bike	BIK
fill	FIL
plate	PLAT
mud	MUD (c)
flat	FLAT (c)
bed	BED (c)
drive	DRIV
chop	CHOP (c)
wish	WESH
step	STEP (c)
plant	PLAT
dress	DRES
stuff	STOF
chase	CHAS
wise	WIS
shopping	SHOPING
train	TRAN
cloud	CLOD
thick	THIK
float	FLOT

FIGURE 2.10. Shawn's spelling assessment.

Although he spelled only 5 of the 20 words correctly, his errors were developmentally sound, revealing considerable knowledge of the spelling system. For example, he represented short vowels conventionally, for the most part (FIL, MUD, CHOP, DRES, THIK, etc.). He also showed good knowledge of both consonant blends (FLAT, DRIV, STOF) and consonant digraphs (CHOP, THIK, WESH, etc.). What Shawn still has to learn is that long-vowel spellings usually contain a "silent letter" or marker. He spelled *bike*—BIK; *plate*—PLAT; *train*—TRAN; *float*—FLOT; and so on.

Given Shawn's relatively strong performance on the first-grade word recognition lists, perhaps we should not be surprised by the level of orthographic knowledge he displayed in his spellings. Still, keep in mind that he is a third grader reading, at best, at a late-first-grade level. Many children who fall significantly behind in reading in the primary grades become frustrated or overwhelmed by the spelling system and begin to show deviant patterns in their spelling attempts—for example, omitted letters, juxtaposed letters, randomly inserted letters. The fact that Shawn's spellings are readable and interpretable within a developmental framework means that he has not given up and is still trying to make sense of the English spelling system.

Having administered and scored the three assessment tasks, the tutor charted Shawn's performance on the entire battery. (*Note*: The optional tasks, *word awareness* and *alphabet knowledge*, were not administered.)

	Word recognition (graded lists)		Oral reading	
	Flash (%)	*Untimed (%)*	*Accuracy (%)*	*Rate (wpm)*
Preprimer	90	95	—	—
Primer	85	90	98	(59)
1-2	55	70	94	(54)
2-1	15	35	81	(37)
2-2			—	—

Spelling: No. of words spelled correctly—5 of 20
Developmental stage—Phonetic/Within-Word Pattern

Initial assessment data of the kind shown in the preceding chart has two major functions. Its first and most immediate purpose is to help the tutor plan the initial reading lessons. This involves finding appropriately challenging materials for the child to read (not too easy, not too hard) and determining specific skill areas in need of improvement. In the case before us, the assessment results suggest that Shawn should begin with *Level 1-2* reading material. His word recognition, in and out of context, is adequate at this level. Although we do not have a measure on Shawn's reading *comprehension*, it is assumed that the tutor will, through questioning, hold this third grader accountable for comprehending the Level 1-2 stories he reads. Regarding *word recognition* training, the assessment results (word recognition and spelling tasks) suggest that the tutor should review with Shawn the short-vowel patterns (*man, bed, hit*, etc.) and then begin work on the various long-vowel patterns (*cake, hide, meat, coat*, etc.). Finally, it is true that Shawn's *reading rate* is very slow, even in first-grade reading material. However, the best remedy here is for the tutor to provide the child with lots of supported reading practice in both instructional-level (1-2) and easier independent-level materials.

A second, less immediate, function of the initial assessment information is its eventual use as pretest data in a pre–post evaluation design. That is, the readministration of the very same reading–spelling tasks after 8 months of tutoring will allow the tutor to gauge how much progress the child has made in learning to read.

We have seen that it is possible to glean instructional implications from an initial reading assessment. However, this is only a start. Assessment, in truth, should be an ongoing process, an integral part of the teaching act across time. As we move in the following chapters to case studies on teaching beginning readers, it will become clear that the assessment procedures described in this chapter can be used informally to monitor a child's reading–writing development throughout a year of tutoring.

APPENDIX 2.1. Word Recognition Assessment: Test Lists and Accompanying Score Sheets (Preprimer through Fourth Grade)

Test Lists (What the Child Reads)

Preprimer	Primer	Late-first
1. and	1. back	1. leg
2. cat	2. eat	2. black
3. me	3. sun	3. smile
4. is	4. bird	4. hurt
5. go	5. pat	5. dark
6. play	6. saw	6. white
7. where	7. feet	7. couldn't
8. like	8. lake	8. seen
9. thing	9. hid	9. until
10. old	10. cut	10. because
11. your	11. about	11. men
12. up	12. one	12. winter
13. sad	13. rain	13. shout
14. big	14. water	14. glass
15. for	15. two	15. paint
16. by	16. how	16. children
17. dog	17. window	17. table
18. not	18. need	18. stand
19. who	19. that's	19. head
20. here	20. mother	20. drove

(cont.)

Note: These word recognition lists were developed by randomly sampling the graded lists in *Basic Reading Vocabularies* (Harris & Jacobson, 1982).

APPENDIX 2.1. *(cont.)*

Test Lists (What the Child Reads)

Second	Third	Fourth
1. able	1. accept	1. average
2. break	2. favor	2. hamster
3. pull	3. seal	3. select
4. week	4. buffalo	4. tobacco
5. gate	5. slipper	5. brilliant
6. felt	6. receive	6. liberty
7. north	7. legend	7. prance
8. rush	8. haircut	8. solemn
9. wrote	9. dresser	9. disease
10. perfect	10. icy	10. impress
11. change	11. thread	11. miracle
12. basket	12. plop	12. wrestle
13. shoot	13. bandage	13. coward
14. hospital	14. further	14. explode
15. spill	15. moat	15. opinion
16. dug	16. closet	16. suffer
17. crayon	17. window	17. vast
18. third	18. unroll	18. relationship
19. taken	19. storyteller	19. furnace
20. prize	20. yarn	20. clan

(cont.)

APPENDIX 2.1. (*cont.*)

Score Sheets (for the Examiner)

Level: Preprimer	Flash	Untimed	Level: Primer	Flash	Untimed
1. and			1. back		
2. cat			2. eat		
3. me			3. sun		
4. is			4. bird		
5. go			5. pat		
6. play			6. saw		
7. where			7. feet		
8. like			8. lake		
9. thing			9. hid		
10. old			10. cut		
11. your			11. about		
12. up			12. one		
13. said			13. rain		
14. big			14. water		
15. for			15. two		
16. by			16. how		
17. dog			17. window		
18. not			18. need		
19. who			19. that's		
20. here			20. mother		
Percentage correct			Percentage correct		

(*cont.*)

APPENDIX 2.1. *(cont.)*

Score Sheets (for the Examiner)

Level: First	Flash	Untimed	Level: Second	Flash	Untimed
1. leg	_____	_____	1. able	_____	_____
2. black	_____	_____	2. break	_____	_____
3. smile	_____	_____	3. pull	_____	_____
4. hurt	_____	_____	4. week	_____	_____
5. dark	_____	_____	5. gate	_____	_____
6. white	_____	_____	6. felt	_____	_____
7. couldn't	_____	_____	7. north	_____	_____
8. seen	_____	_____	8. rush	_____	_____
9. until	_____	_____	9. wrote	_____	_____
10. because	_____	_____	10. perfect	_____	_____
11. men	_____	_____	11. change	_____	_____
12. winter	_____	_____	12. basket	_____	_____
13. shout	_____	_____	13. shoot	_____	_____
14. glass	_____	_____	14. hospital	_____	_____
15. paint	_____	_____	15. spill	_____	_____
16. children	_____	_____	16. dug	_____	_____
17. table	_____	_____	17. crayon	_____	_____
18. stand	_____	_____	18. third	_____	_____
19. head	_____	_____	19. taken	_____	_____
20. drove	_____	_____	20. prize	_____	_____

| Percentage correct | _____ | _____ | Percentage correct | _____ | _____ |

(cont.)

APPENDIX 2.1. (*cont.*)

Score Sheets (for the Examiner)

Level: Third	Flash	Untimed	Level: Fourth	Flash	Untimed
1. accept	_____	_____	1. average	_____	_____
2. favor	_____	_____	2. hamster	_____	_____
3. seal	_____	_____	3. select	_____	_____
4. buffalo	_____	_____	4. tobacco	_____	_____
5. slipper	_____	_____	5. brilliant	_____	_____
6. receive	_____	_____	6. liberty	_____	_____
7. legend	_____	_____	7. prance	_____	_____
8. haircut	_____	_____	8. solemn	_____	_____
9. dresser	_____	_____	9. disease	_____	_____
10. icy	_____	_____	10. impress	_____	_____
11. customer	_____	_____	11. miracle	_____	_____
12. thread	_____	_____	12. wrestle	_____	_____
13. plop	_____	_____	13. coward	_____	_____
14. bandage	_____	_____	14. explode	_____	_____
15. further	_____	_____	15. opinion	_____	_____
16. moat	_____	_____	16. suffer	_____	_____
17. closet	_____	_____	17. vast	_____	_____
18. unroll	_____	_____	18. relationship	_____	_____
19. storyteller	_____	_____	19. furnace	_____	_____
20. yarn	_____	_____	20. clan	_____	_____

Percentage
correct _____ _____

Percentage
correct _____ _____

APPENDIX 2.2. Oral Reading Assessment:
Graded Reading Passages and Accompanying Score Sheets
(Beginning-First Grade through Fourth Grade)

Reading Passages (What the Child Reads)

On the first-grade passages (emergent, preprimer, primer, and 1-2), the child *reads directly from the trade books* listed here:

Emergent passage (29 words): Entire text of Joy Cowley's *The Storm* (1983). Storybox series, The Wright Group.

Preprimer passage (69 words): Entire text of June Melser's *Look for Me* (1982). Storybox series, The Wright Group.

Primer passage (100 words): Pages 18–23 from Arnold Lobel's *Mouse Tales* (1972). Harper Trophy.

Late-first-grade (1-2) passage (100 words): Pages 30–33 from Arnold Lobel's *Frog and Toad All Year* (1976). Harper Trophy.

The child also reads the early second-grade (2-1) passage directly from the following trade book:

Early-second-grade (2-1) passage (100 words): Pages 15–16 from Joyce Milton's *Wild, Wild Wolves* (1992). Step into Reading series, Random House.

The child reads the last three passages (late-second-grade, third-grade, and fourth-grade) from the test pages (pages 53, 54, and 55, respectively) that follow:

Late-second-grade (2-2) passage (100 words): Pages 6–8 from Margaret Wetterer's *Kate Shelley and the Midnight Express* (1990). Carolrhoda Books.

Third-grade (3) passage (100 words): Page 58 from Farley Mowat's *Owls in the Family* (1981). Bantam.

Fourth-grade (4) passage (100 words): Page 1 from Eve Bunting's *Blackbird Singing* (1980). Scholastic.

(*cont.*)

APPENDIX 2.2. (*cont.*)

Kate stood at the kitchen window with

her younger sisters and brother. They saw

lightning flash. They heard thunder crack

in the hills. Then the rain came.

As the rain poured down, they watched the

water rising in Honey Creek. Soon it overflowed

its banks and flooded part of the yard.

"I'm going to let the animals out of the barn,"

Kate said. "If the water keeps rising,

they could drown."

"Be careful you don't slip in the water,"

her mother warned.

Kate ran down the hill. She waded through

muddy water to the barn. She led out the

two horses and shooed them to higher ground.

2-2

(*cont.*)

Mother and Dad and I were having dinner. The dining room windows were open because it had been such a hot day. All of a sudden there was a great *swooosh* of wings—and there, on the window sill, sat Wol. Before any of us had time to move, he gave a leap and landed on the floor beside my chair. And he hadn't come empty-handed. Clutched in his talons was an enormous skunk. The skunk was dead, but that didn't help matters much because, before he died, he had managed to soak himself and Wol with his own special brand of perfume.

3

(*cont.*)

I stood behind Mom, watching her paint. She had set up her easel in her favorite place, with the house behind her and the stand of trees in front. Fred Johnson, our fat black cat, lay at her feet, his tail moving just enough to make the tasseled grass sway. The smell was horrible here, so close to the foulness of the droppings under the trees.

Mom's picture was only partly finished, and I knew she was waiting for the birds.

Her head tilted back, then swung expectantly toward the west, and I heard them coming, too, heard them before I saw them.

APPENDIX 2.2. *(cont.)*

Score Sheets (for the Examiner)

Beginning-First-Grade Passage
(Emergent)

From Joy Cowley's *The Storm*.
Copyright 1983 by The Wright Group.
Reprinted by permission.

Introduction

Please read this book, called *The Storm*.

―――――――――――――――――――

Here comes the cloud.

Here comes the wind.

Here comes the lightning.

Here comes the thunder.

Here comes the rain.

Here comes the rainbow.

and here comes . . .

the sun.

―――――――――――――――――――

Words:	29
Errors:	____
Error quotient:	3.4
Accuracy:	____ %
Self-corrections:	____

Emergent

(cont.)

APPENDIX 2.2. (*cont.*)

Score Sheets (for the Examiner)

Early-First-Grade Passage (Preprimer)

From June Melser's *Look for Me.*
Copyright 1982 by The Wright Group.
Reprinted by permission.

Introduction

Let's see what happens in this book, called
Look for Me.

Mom looked for David

in the toy box.

"No, he's not here," she said.

She looked for him

up the chimney.

"No, he's not here," she said.

She looked for him in the clock.

"No, he's not here," she said.

She looked for him in the teapot.

"No, he's not here," she said.

Where is that boy?

[Giggle, giggle]*

Mom looked for David under the rug.

"Here he is," she said.

Words:	69
Errors:	____
Error quotient:	1.4
Accuracy:	____ %
Self-corrections:	____

---

*Do not count mistakes on "Giggle, giggle" as
errors.

Preprimer
(*cont.*)

APPENDIX 2.2. *(cont.)*

Score Sheets (for the Examiner)

Mid-First-Grade Passage (Primer)

From Arnold Lobel's *Mouse Tales*, pp. 18–23. Copyright 1972 by Arnold Lobel. Used by permission of HarperCollins Publishers.

Introduction

Read this to see what pictures the little mouse and his mother see in the clouds.

"Look!" said Mother. "We can see pictures

in the clouds." The little mouse and his

mother saw many pictures in the clouds.

They saw a castle . . . a rabbit . . . a mouse.

"I am going to pick flowers," said Mother.

"I will stay here and watch the clouds,"

said the little mouse. The little mouse saw

a big cloud in the sky. It grew bigger and

bigger. The cloud became a cat. The cat

came nearer and nearer to the little mouse.

"Help!" shouted the little mouse, and he

ran to his mother. "There is a big cat in the

sky!" cried /* the little mouse. "I am

afraid!" Mother looked up at the sky. "Do

not be afraid," she said. "See, the cat has

turned back into a cloud again."

---

*Slash (/) indicates completion of 100 words. Oral reading accuracy score derived from this 100-word sample.

Questions

1. What were the little mouse and his mother doing at the beginning of the story?
   (*Looking at clouds.*)
2. Where did the mother mouse go?
   (*To pick flowers.*)
3. Why did the little mouse shout, "Help!"?
   (*He was scared by a cloud that looked like a cat.*)

Words:	100
Errors:	____
Error quotient:	1.0
Accuracy:	____ %
Self-corrections:	____
Time:	____min. ____sec.
Rate:	6,000/sec. = ____wpm
Comprehension:	____/3

Primer

(cont.)

APPENDIX 2.2. *(cont.)*

Score Sheets (for the Examiner)

Late-First-Grade Passage (1-2)

From Arnold Lobel's *Frog and Toad All Year*, pp. 30–33. Copyright 1976 by Arnold Lobel. Use by permission of HarperCollins Publishers.

Introduction

Let's see what happens in this Frog and Toad story that takes place in the summer.

One hot summer day Frog and Toad sat

by the pond. "I wish we had some sweet,

cold ice cream," said Frog. "What a good

idea," said Toad. "Wait right here, Frog. I

will be back soon." Toad went to the store.

He bought two big ice-cream cones. Toad

licked one of the cones. "Frog likes

chocolate best," said Toad, "and so do I."

Toad walked along the path. A large, soft

drop of chocolate ice cream slipped down

his arm. "This ice cream is melting in the

sun," said Toad. Toad walked faster. Many

drops of melting ice cream / flew through

the air. They fell down on Toad's head. "I

must hurry back to Frog!" he cried.

Questions

1. Where did Toad get the ice cream?
   (*At the store.*)
2. What kind of ice cream did Toad get?
   (*Chocolate.*)
3. What happened to the ice cream as Toad walked along the path?
   (*It began to melt.*)

Words:	100
Errors:	____
Error quotient:	1.0
Accuracy:	____ %
Self-corrections:	____
Time:	____min. ____sec.
Rate:	6,000/sec. = ____wpm
Comprehension:	____/3

1-2

(cont.)

APPENDIX 2.2. *(cont.)*

Score Sheets (for the Examiner)

Early-Second-Grade Passage (2-1)

From Joyce Milton's *Wild, Wild Wolves*, pp. 15–16. Copyright 1992 by Joyce Milton. Used by permission of Random House.

Introduction

Let's read from this book that tells how real wolves live.

_____

A hungry wolf can eat 20 pounds of meat

at a single meal. That's like eating one

hundred hamburgers! To get all this meat,

wolves usually hunt big animals like deer

and moose. But a hungry wolf will chase

and eat a rabbit or a mouse. It may even

go fishing! Wolves live in groups called

packs. The pack members "talk" to each

other with their bodies. When a wolf is

scared, it holds its ears close to its head.

When a wolf is happy, it wags its whole

tail. If it wags just the tip, watch out! It is

getting / ready to attack.

_____

Questions

1. What does the story say that tells you wolves eat a lot?
   (*They eat as much meat as 100 hamburgers; or they eat 20 pounds of meat in one meal.*)
2. What animals do wolves hunt and eat?
   (*Deer, moose, rabbits, mice.*)
3. What do you call a group of wolves?
   (*A pack.*)

Words:	100
Errors:	____
Error quotient:	1.0
Accuracy:	____ %
Self-corrections:	____
Time:	____min. ____sec.
Rate:	6,000/sec. = ____wpm
Comprehension:	____/3

2-1

(cont.)

APPENDIX 2.2. *(cont.)*

Score Sheets (for the Examiner)

Late-Second-Grade Passage (2-2)

From Margaret Wetterer's *Kate Shelley and the Midnight Express*, pp. 6–8. Copyright 1990 by Carolrhoda Books. Reprinted by permission.

Introduction

This passage describes a rainstorm on a farm.

Kate stood at the kitchen window with her

younger sisters and brother. They saw

lightning flash. They heard thunder crack

in the hills. Then the rain came. As the rain

poured down, they watched the water

rising in Honey Creek. Soon it overflowed

its banks and flooded part of the yard. "I'm

going to let the animals out of the barn,"

Kate said. "If the water keeps rising, they

could drown."

"Be careful you don't slip in the water," her

mother warned. Kate ran down the

hill. She waded through muddy water to

the barn. She led out the two / horses

and shooed them to higher ground.

Questions

1. Who was watching the storm with Kate?
   (*Her sisters and brother.*)
2. What happened to the water in the creek?
   (*Overflowed its banks; flooded the surrounding land.*)
3. Why did Kate go down to the barn?
   (*To free the animals so they wouldn't drown.*)

Words:	100
Errors:	____
Error quotient:	1.0
Accuracy:	____ %
Self-corrections:	____
Time:	____min. ____sec.
Rate:	6,000/sec. = ____wpm
Comprehension:	____/3

2-2

(cont.)

APPENDIX 2.2. (*cont.*)

Score Sheets (for the Examiner)

Third-Grade Passage

From Farley Mowat's *Owls in the Family*, p. 58. Copyright 1981 by Farley Mowat. Used by permission of Little, Brown and Company.

Introduction

In this passage, a pet owl named Wol brings home a surprise for the family.

Mother and Dad and I were having

dinner. The dining room windows were

open because it had been such a hot day.

All of a sudden there was a great *swooosh*

of wings—and there, on the window sill,

sat Wol. Before any of us had time to

move, he gave a leap and landed on the

floor beside my chair. And he hadn't come

empty-handed. Clutched in his talons was

an enormous skunk. The skunk was dead,

but that didn't help matters much because,

before he died, he had managed to soak

himself and Wol with his own special

brand / of perfume.

Questions

1. How did the pet owl come into the house?
   (*Through the window.*)
2. What was the owl carrying?
   (*A dead skunk.*)
3. What had the skunk done before he died?
   (*Sprayed the owl with his odor.*)

Words:	100
Errors:	____
Error quotient:	1.0
Accuracy:	____ %
Self-corrections:	____
Time:	____min. ____sec.
Rate:	6,000/sec. = ____wpm
Comprehension:	____/3

3

(*cont.*)

APPENDIX 2.2. *(cont.)*

Score Sheets (for the Examiner)

Fourth-Grade Passage

From Eve Bunting's *Blackbird Singing*, p. 1. Copyright 1980 by Eve Bunting. Used by permission of Simon and Schuster.

Introduction

Artists sometimes paint pictures outside. Read this passage.

I stood behind Mom, watching her paint.

She had set up her easel in her favorite

place, with the house behind her and the

stand of trees in front. Fred Johnson, our

fat black cat, lay at her feet, his tail moving

just enough to make the tasseled grass

sway. The smell was horrible here, so close

to the foulness of the droppings under the

trees.

   Mom's picture was only partly

finished, and I knew she was waiting for

the birds.

   Her head tilted back, then swung

expectantly toward the west, and I heard

them coming, too, heard them before / I

saw them.

Questions

1. Who is Fred Johnson?
   (*A black cat.*)
2. Why was the smell so horrible in the grass?
   (*Bird droppings.*)
3. What did they hear coming?
   (*The birds.*)

Words:	100
Errors:	____
Error quotient:	1.0
Accuracy:	____ %
Self-corrections:	____
Time:	____min. ____sec.
Rate:	6,000/sec. = ____wpm
Comprehension:	____/3

4

(cont.)

APPENDIX 2.3. Scoring Examples for the Spelling (Phoneme Awareness) Task

Spelling word	1 point	2 points	3 points	4 points	5 points
bike	B, BRRW	BK, BC, BKE, BI	—	BIK, BIC, BICK	BIEK, BICKE
fill	F, FA	FL, FE, FLA, FLE	—	FEL, FELL	FIL
plate	P	PT, PA	PAT	PLAT	PLAET, PLAYT
mud	M, MT	MD	—	MOD	MUDD, MUDE
flat	F	FT, FA, FTA	—	FAT	FLATE
bed	B	BD, BA, BE	—	BAD	BEDD, BEDE
drive	J, G, D	JV, GRV	JIV, GIV	JRIV, DRIV	DRIEV, DRIAV
chop	H, C, CA	CHP, CP, HP	HOP	CHIP	CHOPP, CHOPE
wish	Y, W	YS, WS, WE	WES, WEH	WESH, WIS, WICH, WHIS	WISHE
step	C, S	SP, CP, SA, CA	SAP, CAP, CEP	STAP, SDAP	STEPP, STEPE
plant	P	PT, PA	PAT, PAN, PATE	PLAT, PLAN	PLANTE
dress	J, G	JS, GS, GA, DS	JAS, GAS, DAS	JRAS, DRAS, JRES	DRES, DRESE
stuff	S, C	SF, CF, SO, SDF	SOF, COF	STOF, CTOF	STUF, STUFE
chase	H, C	HS, CHS	HAS	CHAS	CHAIS, CHACE
wise	Y, W	YS, YZ, WS	—	WIS, WIZ, WHIS	WIZE, WHISE
shopping	S	SP, SPN	SIPN SOPN	SHOPEN, SHIPING	SHOPING
train	T, CH	TN, CHN, TA	TAN, CHAN, CHRAN	TRAN	TRANE, TRAINE
cloud	C, K	CD, KD, KLD	COD, KOD	CLOD, CLODE	CLOWD
thick	F	THC, THK	—	THEK, THEC, THECK	THIC, THIK
float	F	FT	FOT	FLOT	FLOTE, FLOET

From *The Howard Street Tutoring Manual: Teaching At-Risk Readers in the Primary Grades* by Darrell Morris. Copyright 1999 by The Guilford Press. Permission to photocopy this appendix is granted to purchasers of *The Howard Street Tutoring Manual* for personal use only (see copyright page for details).

APPENDIX 2.4. "Katie" Sentences for the Word Awareness Task

Katie is walking in the rain.

She sees a big dog.

The dog shakes water on Katie.

APPENDIX 2.5. Randomized Alphabet Letters for the Alphabet Recognition and Production Tasks

A	F	P	W	K	Z	B
C	H	O	J	U	Y	M
D	L	Q	N	S	X	I
G	R	E	V	T		

---

a	f	p	w	k	z	b
c	h	o	j	u	y	m
d	l	q	n	s	x	i
g	r	e	v	t		

CHAPTER 3

Atticus, the Emergent Reader

To emerge means "to crop up or come into existence." Atticus, a 6-year-old beginning his second month in first grade, will serve as our prototype of an *emergent reader*. The classroom teacher is concerned about Atticus's reading progress. She says:

> Atticus is one of my lowest readers. He knows most of his letters and he tries very hard. However, he is having difficulty learning and holding onto sight words. I'm not sure he is benefiting from even the slow-paced instruction I provide to the low reading group in my classroom. I really think he is a good candidate for one-to-one tutoring.

I. SUMMARY OF INITIAL READING ASSESSMENT

	Word recognition (graded lists)		Oral reading	
	Flash (%)	*Untimed (%)*	*Accuracy (%)*	*Rate (wpm)*
Emergent	—	—	(Could not read emergent passage independently)	
Preprimer	0	0	—	—
Primer	—	—	—	—

Spelling: No. of words spelled correctly—List 1(0 of 10)
Developmental characteristics—Could represent beginning consonant in 4 of 10 words

Atticus could not identify any of the words on the preprimer word list. He did not venture a response for most of the words. With the examiner's help, Atticus was partly successful in finger-point reading the emergent-stage passage, *The*

Storm. However, after reading a line of text, he could not go back and identify an individual word when the examiner pointed to it. On the spelling task, Atticus could write down the beginning consonant letter for only 4 of the 10 words on the first-grade list.

These assessment results profile a child possessing minimal reading skill. Therefore, the examiner administered the optional *alphabet knowledge* task. Atticus identified 19 uppercase letters and 16 lowercase letters; he also wrote to dictation 15 letters of the alphabet.

Although Atticus is definitely at an early or emergent stage in learning to read, he is not a "blank slate" in terms of reading-related knowledge. We know from linguistic research that this 6-year-old possesses a sizeable spoken vocabulary (5,000+ words) and is able to sequence these words, with little or no conscious effort, in a variety of sentence types. When a story was read to Atticus at the end of the assessment session, he became very attentive, showing an interest in the pictures and the story line. He also seemed to understand that the print, not the pictures, carried the story's message. Finally, he could write his first name and identify a number of the letters in the alphabet. What Atticus *lacks*, along with letter–sound knowledge, is a stable concept of word in text. Until he grasps the significance of the spoken word–written word match, allowing him to finger-point read simple written passages, he will make little progress as a reader. The tutor's job will be to get Atticus into text right away, to support fully his initial efforts to read, and to instill in him the firm belief that he *will* become a reader.

II. TEACHING STRATEGIES

Contextual Reading

In the emergent-reader stage, books are divided into 12 difficulty levels, with each level 2 through 11 containing approximately 20 books (see Appendix 3.1).

Book difficulty is primarily determined by predictability of text, amount of print on each page, and number of new vocabulary words. The 12 book levels correspond to traditional basal levels in the following manner:

Book levels	Basal levels
Levels 1–4	Preprimer 1
Levels 5–6	Preprimer 2
Levels 7–8	Preprimer 3
Levels 9–10	Primer
Levels 11–12	Late first grade

Atticus will begin by reading Level 1 and 2 books, short stories written in predictable, natural-sounding language. Initially, each page in a book will contain a colorful illustration with only *one or two lines* of text.

The tutor begins by "sharing the story" with Atticus, asking him to comment on the pictures and the story line as the pages are turned. Next, the tutor returns to page 1 and tells Atticus to watch closely as she models a finger-point reading of the sentence on that page. Then the child attempts a finger-point reading of the same sentence. If he goes off the track in finger-pointing (e.g., on a two-syllable word), the tutor may want to provide some feedback or model another reading of the sentence. Several pages of the book are read in this "echoic" manner until Atticus has had a chance to recognize the predictable sentence patterns in the story.

1. The little chick had lost her mother.
2. "Have you seen my mother?"
3. "No," said the frog, and he hopped away.
4. "Have you seen my mother?"
5. "No," said the duck, and she waddled away.
6. "Have you seen my mother?"
7. "No," said the snake, and he slithered away.
(And so on.)

At this point, Atticus is encouraged to finger-point read the remaining pages in the book by himself, with the tutor providing help as needed.

With supported reading practice of the kind described here, Atticus will eventually come to a crucial understanding. He will begin to see that words are separate units in text, bounded by white spaces on either side. He may still "trip up" on small function words, for example, saying "And he" when he points to *And* in the phrase *And he waddled away.* However, using spacing between words, and initial consonants, to anchor himself in lines of text, he will become more and more adept at matching spoken word to written word in the act of reading.

A result of Atticus's establishing a concept of word in text will be his acquisition of a small sight vocabulary. As he finger-point reads and rereads the short texts, he will begin to recognize and commit to memory individual words. Maybe only two or three words will be gleaned from an eight-page book. Still, over a few weeks' time, a dozen or more words will enter Atticus's sight vocabulary. He will recognize these words immediately when the tutor points to them in context, and he will also recognize the words when they are presented in isolation on small index cards. These first "sight words" should be put on cards, charted, and reviewed each session to the accompaniment of much tutor praise for a job well done.

Atticus's advancement through the book levels will be a strong indicator of his reading progress. If all goes well, he should reach *at least* Levels 9 and 10 (primer level) by the end of his first-grade year.

Word Study

Word study at the emergent-reader stage will include work on the alphabet, beginning consonants, and, eventually, short-vowel word families.

Alphabet

Every printed word in English is composed of a specific subset of the 52 upper- and lowercase alphabet letters. Therefore, accurate, automatized knowledge of the alphabet is an important foundation for learning to read and write (Ehri & Wilce, 1985; Adams, 1990). Because the initial assessment showed that Atticus could recognize only 19 uppercase and 16 lowercase letters, we must devote some tutoring time to helping Atticus increase his alphabet knowledge.

A good place to begin alphabet work is with the child's own name. For example, though Atticus can write his first name correctly, when he is asked to identify the letters in his name, beginning with the *s* and working backward toward the *A*, he is unable to identify (name) the letter *u*. Furthermore, when his last name, *Johnson*, is written on a sheet of paper, we find that Atticus cannot identify the letters *J*, *h*, or *n*. Thus, the child's own name immediately provides four possibilities for alphabet work (Atti<u>c</u>us <u>Joh</u>n<u>s</u>on).

There must be as many informal techniques and games for teaching children the alphabet as there are kindergarten and first-grade teachers. The following teaching suggestions represent only one of many possible ways to proceed, and these suggestions can and should be modified to fit individual tutoring situations.

A first step might involve working with four letters, upper- and lowercase, in Atticus's name. Using small cardboard letter chips, the tutor can mix up the letters and have Atticus put each lowercase letter with its uppercase match. As he performs this task, he should be naming the letters, receiving tutor assistance when required.

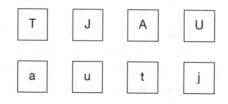

Next, the tutor can reinforce Atticus's recognition of these four alphabet letters by playing a memory game, Concentration. The tutor mixes up and places the eight letter chips (four uppercase, four matching lowercase) *face down* in a 3 × 4 array.

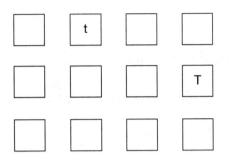

The tutor then explains the rules of the game to Atticus:

1. Turn over a card and name the letter. Then turn over a second card and see whether you have a match (e.g., *t–T*).
2. If you do have a match, pick up the two cards and go again. If you don't have a match, turn the cards back over and let the other player have a turn.
3. The game is over when all the cards have been picked up. The winner is the player who has made the most matches.

Children enjoy the Concentration game, and their memory for the spatial location of the letter cards is often superior to that of an adult tutor's. One thing to remember is that the child must name the letter correctly while turning over the card; otherwise, he/she loses a turn.

It is also important that Atticus learn to write the alphabet letters. Following the Concentration game, Atticus should write the four letters (*a, t, j,* and *u*) to dictation. If he cannot remember how to form a given letter, the tutor should write the letter and have Atticus trace over it; Atticus then writes the letter two more times.

Once Atticus has learned to name and write the first set of letters, he can begin work on mastering new letters. In his case, the last name offers two more learning opportunities: Jo<u>hn</u>son. For other children, learning the alphabet letters in a friend's name, a teacher's name, the tutor's name, or another name, is a viable alternative. The tutor can refer to the initial assessment of alphabet knowledge to identify the specific letters Atticus needs to work on.

The same teaching activities (matching upper- and lowercase letter pairs, playing Concentration, writing the letters to dictation) can be used with each new set of letters to be learned. In introducing new letters, however, it is important to include some "old"—known—letters in the set. For example, if Atticus is to learn *h* and *n*, then the four-letter set for game activities might include the previously mastered *a* and *u*. The mix of the old with the new will keep the learning task from seeming overwhelming to the child, as well as provide an opportunity for correct responses right from the beginning stages of the activity.

Beginning Consonants

The word-initial or beginning consonant is a very useful word recognition cue for the emergent reader, as in the following example:

> Me and my uncle use night crawlers to catch f___.
> Saturday, we c_____ nine fish.
> They were little. W_ threw them back.

In this dictation example, it is easy to see how the beginning consonant letters, *f*, *c*, and *W*, could aid a child's contextual recognition of the words *fish, caught,* and *We*. In fact, the use of beginning consonants along with sentence context has long been considered an effective word recognition strategy (McKee, 1966; Clay, 1991b).

Beginning consonant letter–sound instruction is almost universally stressed in kindergarten and first-grade reading programs, and most children learn these basic phonic relationships at that time (e.g., (/b/ as in /bit/ is represented by *b*; /r/ as in /rat/ is represented by *r*; and so on). Atticus, however, is lacking this elemental letter–sound knowledge; indeed, he does not even recognize all of the consonant letters. Over the first month of tutoring, Atticus will increase his alphabet knowledge and begin to see words as individual, nameable units in memorized text. At that point, he will be in position to benefit from beginning consonant letter–sound instruction.

Getting Started

There are many ways to teach beginning consonant sounds to children. In this manual we will adopt a categorization or *word sort* teaching format. Again, the tutor is cautioned to make sure that the child has demonstrated at least a rudimentary concept of word in text before introducing beginning consonant instruction. By first ensuring that the child has some conscious understanding of what a word is, we can be more confident about that child's "readiness" to focus on a given phonemic element in the word—that is, the beginning consonant.

Step 1. The tutor accumulates five or six picture cards (2″ × 3″) for each of the following consonants: *b, c, d, f, g, h, j, k, l, m, n, p, r, s, t, v, w,* and *z*. For *b*, pictures such as these might be used:

Step 2. The tutor selcts approximately 15 picture cards representing the consonants *b*, *m*, and *s*, then presents the cards one at a time, asking the child to name the pictures. The tutor should provide help when it is needed.

Step 3. The tutor places 3 of the 15 picture cards (words) in a horizontal array across the top of the table and the remaining 12 cards in a deck below.

The tutor should then say to the child,

> We are going to be listening for words that begin alike, that have the same sound at the beginning. All the words down here [pointing to the deck] either begin like *boat*, like *monkey*, or like *sock* [pointing to the three picture cards at the top]. We are going to put these words [pointing to the deck again] in the correct column. Watch, I'll do the first one.

The tutor picks up the picture card *soap*, places it under *sock*, and pronounces both words, emphasizing the beginning sound.

> *Soap* goes under *sock* because they begin alike. Now, you do the next one.

Suppose the child happens to sort the next word in the deck, *bicycle*, in the wrong column—under *monkey*, for example. The tutor says,

> Listen: *monkey—bicycle*. No, those two words do not have the same beginning sound.

The tutor then moves *bicycle* into the correct column, under *boat*, and pronounces both words for the child.

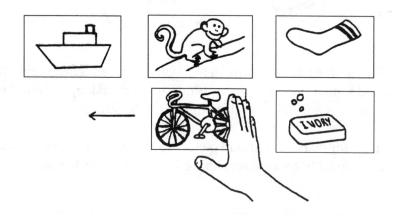

It is the tutor's turn again. This time he/she sorts *seal* under *sock* and *soap*.

The child and tutor continue to take turns sorting the words by beginning consonant sounds until the deck is depleted. Each time a word is sorted in a particular column, all the words in that column (starting at the top) are pronounced to determine whether they contain the same beginning consonant sound.

The word sort or picture sort activity described here is designed to help the child focus on the beginning consonant sounds in spoken words. Word sort is essentially a concept development task in which (1) the tutor models correct responses (examples of the concept) and (2) the child receives immediate feedback as to the correctness of his/her own responses. In a very real sense, this is a problem-solving endeavor, a game in which the child must figure out the rules through inductive reasoning.

Word sorting can be an exciting way for the child to learn and for the tutor to teach. Over time, the observant tutor will be able to see a clear progression in the child's mastery of the concept. For example, the child may initially be totally in the dark as to why a word is sorted in a given column. His/her responses will seem to be random guesses. Later, the concept of categorizing words by beginning consonant sound will start to emerge. The child's responses may be slow and halting at this point, but they will be purposeful. For example, in sorting the word *saddle*, the emergent reader may methodically test the beginning consonant sound, /s/, against an exemplar in each column before deciding that *saddle* belongs under *sock, soap,* and so forth. Finally, after extended practice, the child will sort the words quickly, accurately, and with confidence. This signals the tutor that the concept has been learned and that it is time to move ahead.

After the first three beginning consonant *sounds* have been internalized through the sorting procedure, it is time to draw the child's attention to the relationship between a beginning consonant sound (e.g., /m/) and its corresponding alphabet letter (*m*). To introduce this understanding, the tutor again places the three picture cards on the table in a horizontal array. This time, however, a "letter card" is placed above each picture.

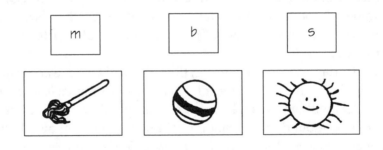

Pointing to the first picture card, the tutor explains:

> If we were to write the word *mop*, the first letter would be an *m*. The letter *m* stands for the first sound in *mop*. [Now pointing to the remaining pictures and letters] The letter *b* stands for the first sound in *ball*, and the letter *s* stands for the first sound in *sun*. Now, let's sort these words [pointing to picture cards in the deck] under the right letters.

The tutor begins by sorting the first card, *basket*, in the *b* column.

> See, *basket* goes here because the letter *b* stands for the first sound in *basket*.

The child sorts next, and the turn taking continues until there are at least three picture cards sorted under each letter. Each time the child sorts, the tutor calls his/her attention to the letter at the top of the column.

In performing this sorting task, it is possible that the child will continue to sort by beginning consonant *sound* (taking a cue from the picture cards already in the column) and thereby pay insufficient attention to the letter–sound relationships. If this happens, the tutor may want to vary the activity by removing each picture after it is sorted under a given letter.

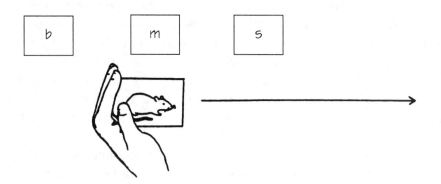

Once *mouse* has been sorted under *m*, the picture card is removed and the other player takes a turn. This procedure requires that the child relate the beginning consonant sound in a word to a corresponding alphabet letter.

Writing letters should also be introduced into the beginning consonant work. After a column sort, the tutor can dictate six sounds (e.g., /b/, /s/, /m/, etc.) or six words (e.g., "bear," "sock," "moon") and have the child write the corresponding letter for each.

After several days of column sorting, the child will become accurate and confident in manipulating the beginning consonant letter–sounds: *b, m,* and *s.* At this point, a great deal will have been learned. Not only will the child have mastered three specific letter–sound correspondences, but he/she will also have learned the more general concept that *a word can have a beginning element—a consonant sound that can be separated off, attended to, and in some cases even categorized.*

With this foundation laid, the next set of three consonants (*c, f, l*) can be introduced. The same task sequence applies:

- Column sorting by beginning consonant sound
- Column sorting by letter–sound match
- Writing letters to dictation

The child's learning rate will usually be faster on this second set of consonants. Nonetheless, there is no need to rush, and the tutor should ensure that the child is making fluent, accurate responses before moving on. A possible order for introducing the remaining consonants is as follows:

b, m, s
c, f, l
t, g, r
j, p, v
k, n, d
w, z, h

Awareness of beginning consonants in isolated words is an important starting point; however, it is the *application* of this knowledge in contextual reading that is the ultimate goal. During a tutoring session, if Atticus hesitates on or misreads a word in sentence context, the tutor has available a simple, effective teaching option. *Without saying a word, she can point (with pencil or index finger) to the beginning consonant in the misread word, signaling the child to use this cue as he attempts to read the word.* On occasion, the tutor may have Atticus return to the beginning of the sentence and use the sentence context *plus* the beginning consonant cue to help identify the target word. Although easy to use, this teaching strategy is extremely important. It demonstrates to the child, within a contextual reading situation, that his beginning consonant knowledge can be a helpful word recognition aid. The child's adoption and consistent use of this strategy will lead to growth in reading.

Word Families

After Atticus has successfully worked through the beginning consonant letter–sound sorts and is consistent in using beginning consonant cues in reading and writing words, he will be ready for the next stage in word study: *short-vowel word families*. Over a few months' time, he will (1) sort short-vowel words into rhyming categories (*cat, mat, hat*; *wig, pig, dig*; etc.), (2) commit a good number of these words to sight memory, and (3) develop competence in spelling these patterns. This next phase of word study will be a long and important one. But, for now, let us consider how to introduce the initial word family lesson to Atticus.

Getting Started

The tutor begins with the short *a* word families. In preparation, she accumulates four word cards (2″ × 3″) for the -*at* family (*cat, mat, bat*, and *sat*) and four for the -*an* family (*man, ran, pan*, and *fan*). The tutor arrays *cat* and *man* on the table and places the other six cards in the deck (as shown).

cat   man

DECK

Next, the tutor asks Atticus to read the exemplars. If he can read both *cat* and *man*, the word sort can begin. If he can read only *cat*, the tutor has to teach *man* before proceeding. (Drawing a small stick figure in the upper right-hand corner of the *man* word card is often helpful.)

Rule 1: *The student must be able to read the exemplars (top cards) before the sort begins.*

Next, the tutor explains that the words in the deck can be sorted under *cat* or under *man*. The tutor slowly picks up the top word in the deck, *ran*, and places it under *man*. She then reads the two words aloud.

cat	man
	ran

It is Atticus's turn. Picking up the next word in the deck, *sat*, he hesitates before looking up at the tutor with a shrug. "Which column does it go in?" asks the tutor. Atticus moves *sat* into the *-an* column under *man* and *ran*. The tutor pauses for a moment and then says, "No, that one doesn't go there." She moves *sat* into the *-at* column, and reads the two words aloud, "cat"—"sat."

cat	man
	ran
◄——————— sat	

The tutor and the student each take two more turns before the activity ends.

cat	man
sat	ran
bat	pan
mat	fan

Rule 2: *Sort no more than four words in a column.*

After just one lesson, Atticus is still uncertain about why the words go in the different columns. However, he does demonstrate one promising ability. When asked to read down a column of words, he is tentative but successful ("cat," "s—at," "b—at; bat"). This shows that in this structured context, he is capable of using his beginning consonant knowledge and rhyming ability to decode *new* words.

What is being learned in this simple word family sort? To what features is the student learning to attend? In sorting word families containing the same short-vowel sound, it is the *final consonant* that actually cues the child as to which words belong in a given column.

cat	man
sat	
bat	

Bat goes under *cat* and *sat* because the words share the same final consonant letter–sound. Thus, the word family sort forces the student to attend consistently to the end of the word, a first-time experience for many beginning readers.

After several lessons of sorting the same eight *-at* and *-an* words, the tutor should introduce the Concentration game. Following a column sort, the tutor shuffles the eight cards and arrays them face down on the table, as shown.

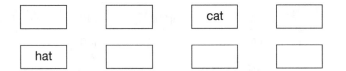

The game begins with Atticus turning over two cards, reading them aloud, and checking for a word family match (e.g., *cat* and *hat*). If there is a match, he can remove the two words from the table and take another turn. If there is not a match, he turns the cards back over, and the tutor takes a turn. The game is over when all the words have been removed from the table.

The Concentration game is a perfect reinforcement activity. The format not only randomizes the words, requiring the student to read them out of column context, but it also encourages the student to hold the short *a* patterns in visual memory while searching for matches on the table.

Spell checks are a second way to review and reinforce the short *a* word families. The procedure is simple. After completing a column sort or game, the tutor scoops up the cards, leaving only two exemplars on the table.

<u>cat</u>   <u>man</u>

The tutor then proceeds to dictate four or five spelling words. As Atticus writes the words, he is allowed to use the exemplars on the table as a pattern reminder. On completion of the test, the tutor and student review the spellings and correct any mistakes.

mat
ran
sat
~~pat~~   pan

The spell check will be an integral part of our word study lessons because it provides an alternative route or process for securing target patterns (in this case, short *a* word families) in memory.

Rule 3: Use the Concentration game and spell checks to review the word patterns under study.

Once the student is comfortable in sorting, reading, and spelling the *-at* and *-an* families, a third family, *-ap*, can be added.

hat	man	cap
rat	fan	lap
sat		
	tap	

And once these short *a* families have been mastered, a second set, short *i* word families, can be introduced.

hit	pin	big
fit	win	pig
sit	tin	wig
bit	spin	twig

Now and again a given child may have trouble progressing through the word family lessons. The emerging reader may have difficulty attending to the individual letter–sounds within the short-vowel words, or may have difficulty committing the pattern words to sight memory. In either case, a "drop-back" teaching strategy is to have the child build and take apart short-vowel words using individual letter chips. This *Make-a-Word* activity is described in detail in Chapter 4 (pages 129–132).

Mastery of the short-vowel word families—the ability to read and spell the words in isolation as well as in context—will be a major goal in Atticus's tutoring program. Instruction will not be rushed but, instead, carefully paced to Atticus's individual learning speed. (See *Word Study* in the next chapter, pages 125–133, for further explanation of the word family instructional sequence.)

Sentence Writing

In the early 1970s, linguist Carol Chomsky (1971) stated that young children should "write first, read later." In analyzing preschoolers' written messages, Chomsky observed that young children often construct or spell words by attending to the sequential sounds in the words. Thus, a precocious 5-year-old might write:

I	YET	FOR	A	RID	EN	DA	KR
(I	went	for	a	ride	in	the	car.)

Chomsky reasoned that early writing can be an important precursor to reading acquisition because it provides prereaders with purposeful experience in analyzing the sequence of sounds in spoken words and in matching appropriate letters to these sounds (see also Clay, 1991b).

Following Chomsky's logic, we will make writing an important part of Atticus's tutoring program. During each lesson Atticus will write a sentence of his own choice, with the tutor providing support as needed. In the rest of this section, let us consider how the writing lessons might evolve over the first few months of tutoring.

Getting Started

To facilitate writing in the first few weeks, the tutor uses various sentence starters:

> I can . . .
> I like . . .
> After school, I . . .

Atticus's task each day is to complete the sentence orally and then write it down in his Writing Book. After several lessons, the tutor encourages Atticus to come up with his own sentence. Topic possibilities are unlimited, including friends, pets, hobbies, family activities, school activities, and so on.

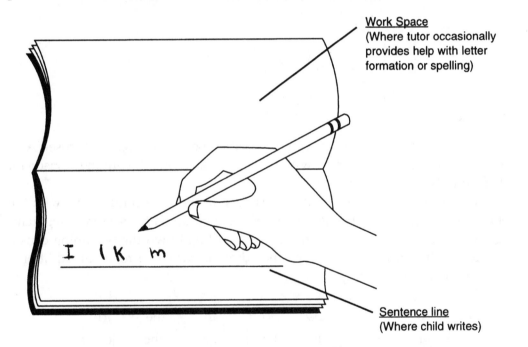

Work Space
(Where tutor occasionally provides help with letter formation or spelling)

Sentence line
(Where child writes)

Once Atticus has a sentence in mind, the tutor has him repeat it orally *two times* to seat it in memory. As the child begins to write, he pronounces each word slowly, trying to attend to its beginning sound. *It is critical that Atticus (not the tutor) say each word*; he needs to feel his own articulatory movements, hear his own pronunciation, and search independently for the initial sound. In *September* Atticus can represent only a few beginning consonants in his sentence writing attempts:

M	D	is*	A	B	hound*	D.
(My	dog	is	a	big	hound	dog.)

*Throughout, an asterisk indicates that the tutor assists the child in spelling the word correctly.

In the preceding example, the tutor probes for the initial sound in each word ("What sound do you hear at the beginning, Atticus?"). Atticus is hesitant, but he is able to write the beginning letter for four of the five words. When he stops on *is* (a high-frequency word), the tutor writes the word and lets Atticus copy it into his sentence. When Atticus is unable to "hear" the beginning consonant in *hound* (a low-frequency word), the tutor simply writes this word into the sentence.

With the writing completed, the tutor copies the sentence (correctly spelled this time) onto a sentence strip and has Atticus finger-point read it.

> My dog is a big hound dog.

Next, the sentence strip is cut into word units, and the word units scrambled. Atticus's final task is to reassemble the sentence and finger-point read it.

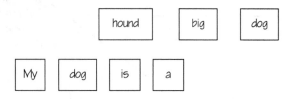

Note that each of the subtasks in this September writing lesson focused Atticus's attention on word units within the sentence and beginning consonant letter–sounds in the words.

Three weeks later, in *mid-October*, Atticus has become comfortable with the sentence-writing routine. He has no trouble coming up with a sentence, segmenting the spoken sentence into word units, or writing down the beginning consonant for each word. At this point the tutor decides to probe for additional letter–sounds in the writing.

I	W(T)	TO	T(?)	in*	the*	J(P).
(I	went	to	town	in	the	jeep.)

In the preceding sentence, the tutor probes for the ending sound in *went, town,* and *jeep* ("Atticus, say the word again and tell me what sound you hear at the end. Good! 'Went' does have a *t* at the end."). Atticus is able to perceive the ending consonant sounds in *went* and *jeep*, but not in *town*. He spells *to* correctly from sight memory and receives help from the tutor on the words *in* and *the*.

Another 4 weeks go by. Atticus's sentence-writing ability is progressing nicely. He now knows several high-frequency spellings (e.g., *the, is, my, like*, etc.) and consistently writes the beginning and ending consonants in words. In *November,* his tutor decides it is time to probe for medial vowels.

MY   DAD   T(A)KS   ME   TO   SKL   IN   HZ   J(?)P.

(My   dad   takes   me   to   school   in   his   jeep.)

In this sentence, the tutor probes for the long-vowel sounds in *takes* and *jeep*. First, she sketches a "sound box" on a piece of paper:

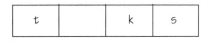

TUTOR: [Pointing to the sound box] Atticus, you got the beginning and ending letters in "takes." Say the word slowly, and try to hear another sound in the middle.

ATTICUS: t—a—ks; t—a—. It's an A.

TUTOR: Good! Why don't you change your spelling? [Atticus changes the spelling TKS to TAKS.]

Atticus is led through a similar routine with *jeep,* but this time he is unable to perceive the medial vowel sound. The sound box provides a visual representation of the spoken word, in effect freezing the word's sequential speech sounds for analysis (Clay, 1993; Elkonin, 1973). The success of this teaching strategy depends on the student's developmental readiness to perceive medial vowel sounds. The issue cannot be forced. If the strategy does not work the first time it is tried, patience is called for. More reading, writing, and word study will eventually ready the student for vowel awareness, a crucial step forward in reading acquisition.

Sentence writing is an important part of the emergent reader's tutoring program. It allows the child to develop sound awareness and letter–sound knowledge in the context of purposeful writing. Sentence writing at this stage is not uncomplicated, but requires concentrated effort from the child and thoughtful, moment-to-moment support from the tutor. Still, it is worth the effort. Over time, the daily Writing Book (unedited) will provide the clearest and most persuasive evidence of the emergent reader's growth in word knowledge. Note Atticus's development in the few examples cited earlier:

September

M   D   is*   A   B   hound*   D.

October

I   WT   TO   T   in*   the*   JP.

November

MY   DAD   TAKS   ME   TO   SKL   IN   HZ   JP.

The Lesson Plan

Atticus's tutor follows a set lesson plan (see Invernizzi et al., 1997; Morris, 1995; Pinnell, 1989; Santa & Hoien, 1999). In its outline, the 35-minute tutoring lesson includes four parts:

1. *Rereading books* (14 minutes). Atticus rereads two or three short, natural-language books, with the tutor offering support as needed. The books are graded in difficulty from Level 1 (early-first grade) to Level 12 (late-first grade). At the beginning of the year, the student rereads eight-page books (Levels 1 to 3) that contain only one to two lines of print per page and a repetitive text pattern.

2. *Word study* (8 minutes). Atticus, depending on his level of word knowledge, works on the alphabet, beginning consonants, short-vowel word families, or vowel patterns.

3. *Sentence writing* (8 minutes). Each day Atticus writes a sentence of his own choice. At the beginning of the year, he requires close tutor support in this activity. However, with consistent practice in reading, word study, and writing, Atticus's sound awareness and letter–sound knowledge will improve, and he will become more independent in the sentence writing.

4. *Introducing a new book* (5 minutes). During the last part of the lesson, Atticus reads a new book. After previewing the book with the tutor (surveying the pictures and identifying difficult vocabulary), Atticus returns to page 1 and attempts to finger-point read the new story. The tutor provides assistance as needed. (*Note*: This new book will be reread in part 1 of the next day's lesson.)

The four parts of Atticus's lesson plan are interrelated. The knowledge gained through finger-point reading the simple texts (e.g., attention to the spoken word–written word match, beginning consonants, sight vocabulary, etc.) is applied in the sentence-writing activity. Conversely, the letter–sound knowledge that is exercised in sentence writing is applied in the book reading. Even the seemingly isolated work on alphabet letters, beginning consonants, or word families (part 2) is immediately put into practice each time the student finger-point reads a book or invents spellings in sentence writing. The result is an integrated tutorial lesson that melds whole-to-part and part-to-whole learning in a meaningful way.

III. REPRESENTATIVE TUTORING LESSONS ACROSS THE YEAR

In this section we examine how instruction for Atticus might evolve across the first 3 months of tutoring. The first person (I) will be used in referring to the tutor.

Lesson 1 (September 22)

1. **Rereading books.** I begin by bringing out *The Chocolate Cake*, a Level 1 book. (*Note*: Because this is the first lesson, each book is new to Atticus; tomorrow

he will begin rereading them.) Atticus and I page through *The Chocolate Cake* (see illustration), naming the characters in the pictures and commenting on the story line.

The Chocolate Cake (Level 1) by J. Melser (1981, pp. 2–3). Copyright 1981 by Shortland Publications. Reprinted by permission.

Then we return to page 1 and begin *echo reading*. That is, I finger-point read a page or two, and then Atticus finger-point reads the same pages. In this easy book, Atticus is successful in matching the spoken words to the printed words as he reads. After the book has been read, I return to page 7 and ask Atticus to read the sentence "It's all gone." He cannot do so. We echo read the sentence, and then I point to the middle word, *all*, asking Atticus to identify it. Significantly, he responds with "all gone."

Atticus and I read a second book, *The Ghost* (Level 2), in the same manner. Again, with my support, he is successful in finger-point reading the simple text. However, after the reading he is inconsistent in identifying individual words in the text when I point to them.

2. **Word study.** On the initial screening, Atticus identified only 16 of the 26 lowercase alphabet letters. I decide to teach him a few more consonant letters before starting work on beginning consonant sound–letter relationships.

In this first lesson I array four tagboard chips on the table:

As I point to each letter card, Atticus identifies *A* and *T* but not *J* and *N*, two letters that, incidentally, are found in his last name, *Johnson*. After a little practice on the four uppercase letters, I bring out their lowercase matches:

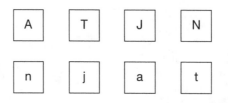

Atticus and I take turns matching upper- and lowercase letter pairs (see the preceding illustration). Then we turn the letter cards face down on the table and play a quick game of Concentration (see page 71).

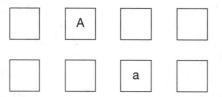

Atticus enjoys playing Concentration. He is accurate in identifying one of the two "new" letters (*j*), but requires my assistance on the other (*n*).

3. **Sentence writing.** I begin the sentence-writing activity by asking Atticus what he does after school.

ATTICUS: I go down to the creek with Tom.

TUTOR: Is Tom your friend?

ATTICUS: Nope, he's my dog.

TUTOR: Say your sentence again, Atticus.

ATTICUS: I go down to the creek with Tom.

TUTOR: Good! Let's write your sentence [handing Atticus the pencil]. What word should we write first? I—go—down . . .

ATTICUS: I. [Atticus writes *I* on the paper.]

TUTOR: What comes next?

ATTICUS: Go.

TUTOR: Okay, let's leave a space, and you can write 'go' right here [pointing to the appropriate spot on the line].

Unfortunately, Atticus has difficulty remembering the letter that represents /g/. Therefore, I write, *go*, at the top of the page and have Atticus copy the word into his sentence (*Go* is a high-frequency word that I want him to learn).

On the next word, *down*, Atticus again hesitates.

TUTOR: Say the word again, Atticus. What do you hear at the beginning?
ATTICUS: "Down"—"d." I hear a D.
TUTOR: Good! Write it down.

I   go   D

I ask Atticus to go back and finger-point read what he has written thus far (see the preceding illustration). On the remaining words, he is able to write the first letter in *to, creek,* and *Tom*. He is unable to write the first letter in *with* and requires help in spelling *the*.

I	go*	D	T	the*	K	w*	T.
(I	go	down	to	the	creek	with	Tom.)

Atticus's completed sentence is an example of "beginning consonant" writing. That is, on four of the words he is able to represent the beginning consonant letter in his spelling. Atticus seems reasonably pleased with his effort, and I congratulate him on a job well done. (*Note*: Before moving on, I quickly write Atticus's sentence in correct spelling at the bottom of the page. This will allow me to return to the sentence a few days, weeks, or even months later and make sense of Atticus's writing.)

Next, I copy Atticus's sentence (using correct spelling) onto a sentence strip, cut the sentence strip into words, and then mix the words. Atticus is successful in reassembling the sentence. Requiring little assistance, he uses the beginning consonant letters as a guide in resequencing the words.

4. **Introducing a new book.** Atticus and I preview the amusing eight-page book *Yuck Soup* (Level 2) (see illustration). On each page, we examine the pictures and name the unusual items (snails, feathers, toothbrushes, etc.) that are being placed in the large soup pot.

On several pages, I draw Atticus's attention to the printed word that represents the items in the picture (e.g., snails, feathers).

Next, we return to page 2 of *Yuck Soup* and begin to read. On page 2 (see the following list), I model a finger-point reading of the sentence and then Atticus attempts to finger-point read. Pages 3 and 4 are read in the same manner.

(p. 2) In go some snails.
(p. 3) In go some feathers.
(p. 4) In go some thistles.

On reaching page 5, I urge Atticus to continue finger-point reading *by himself*.

In go some snails.

In go some feathers.

Yuck Soup (Level 2) by J. Cowley (1983, pp. 2–3). Copyright 1993 by The Wright Group. Reprinted by permission.

(p. 5) In go some toothbrushes.
(p. 6) In go some socks.
(p. 7) In go some shoes.
(p. 8) Yuck!

Relying on the sentence pattern and the picture cues, Atticus finger-point reads page 5 correctly. On page 6, he gets going too fast and fails to match spoken word to printed word as he reads. I have him reread page 6, and this time he is successful; he also finger-point reads page 7 correctly. After he hesitates on page 8, I supply the word "Yuck," and Atticus smiles in agreement.

Commentary

Atticus is off to a good start. Two strengths are his ability to finger-point read simple texts and his emerging ability to attend to the beginning consonant sound in spoken words. Atticus lacks a stable concept of word in text. In echo reading a short sentence, he can point to the words left-to-right, but he is unable to go back and identify a single word in the line of print when asked to do so.

Atticus's next tutoring lesson will build directly on what was accomplished today. That is, Atticus will reread three books to begin the lesson, *Yuck Soup* being the third to be reread. He will work on the same four alphabet letters (*J, A, T,* and *N*). He will dictate a new sentence and assist the tutor in writing it. Finally, Atticus will read a new book after previewing it with the tutor.

Lesson 5 (October 6; 2 Weeks Later)

1. **Rereading books.** Atticus does a nice job finger-point reading two Level 2 books and one Level 3 book. When he occasionally goes "off the track," mismatching a spoken word to a printed word, he self-corrects by going back and rereading the line. After he finishes reading a book, I point to individual words on several pages. Atticus cannot identify the words immediately; however, he is able to return to the beginning of the line and successfully finger-point over to the target word. This is something we have been working on.

2. **Word study.** After four lessons of alphabet work, Atticus knows most of the consonant letters (*q, x,* and *z* can wait). I decide it is time to introduce beginning consonant sorts. I know Atticus is ready for this instruction because he is already showing the ability to attend to beginning consonant sounds in his sentence writing.

I bring out 12 picture cards representing the beginning consonants, *b, m,* and *s.* After having Atticus name the pictures, I array three cards across the top of the table and place the remaining nine cards in a deck below.

I say to Atticus:

> We are going to be listening for words that begin alike, that have the same beginning sound. All the words down here [pointing to the deck] either begin like *boat,* like *mouse,* or like *sock* [pointing to the three picture cards at the top]. We are going to put these words in the right column. Watch, I'll do the first one.

I pick up the picture card *soap,* place it under *sock,* and pronounce both words carefully.

> *Soap* goes under *sock* because they begin alike. Now, you do the next one.

Atticus sorts the next word in the deck, *bell*, in the correct column—under *boat*. I tell him to pronounce both words and decide whether they have the same beginning sound. He pronounces the words and nods affirmatively.

Atticus and I take turns sorting the remaining words in the deck. His sorting responses are slow but accurate. He is definitely able to attend to the beginning consonant sound in the words.

3. **Sentence writing.** In response to my query, "What did you do over the weekend?" Atticus produces the following sentence:

We*   P   K   aNd*   R.
(We   played   cops   and   robbers.)

Atticus writes the W in *We*, but cannot hear the second sound. I write *We* in the work space, explaining to Atticus that this is a small word that we will meet many times in our reading (Atticus adds the *e* to his spelling). Atticus quickly puts down a *p* for *played* and is ready to move on. I intervene:

TUTOR: Atticus, say "played" one more time and see if you can hear the ending sound.

ATTICUS: "Played" [shakes his head without responding].

TUTOR: That's okay. Read back what you have written and let's go to the next word.

ATTICUS: [Finger-pointing] "We played cops . . ."

Atticus proceeds to write *K* for *cops*, *N* for *and* (I help him with this high-frequency word), and *R* for *robbers*. He then finger-point reads his completed sentence.

Next, I copy the sentence (with correct spelling) onto a sentence strip, cut up the sentence into individual words, and have Atticus reassemble it. He has no trouble with this task.

4. **Introducing a new book.** As Atticus and I preview the eight-page book (Level 3), I call attention to a few picture cues and pronounce a couple of difficult

words (*away, farmer*). In going back to read the text, we echo read the first three pages and then Atticus proceeds to read the last five pages of the book independently. We have a little extra time, so I let him finger-point read the whole book one more time before we close the lesson.

Commentary

Over the first five tutoring lessons, Atticus's concept of word in text has stabilized. He is finger-point reading with accuracy, and he can now use a contextual or "rerun" strategy to identify an individual word when I point to it in a line of print. Atticus still uses only beginning consonants in his writing, but he is quicker and more confident in using this strategy.

Lesson 11 (October 21; 3 Weeks Later)

1. **Rereading books.** Atticus rereads three Level 3 books today. His finger-point reading is steady and accurate, indicating that he is attending to each word unit as he reads. After each book (of eight pages) is read, I go back and point to individual words in the text. Interestingly, Atticus identifies several of the words *immediately*, almost as if they were sight words. The others he identifies by using sentence context.

On two occasions I call Atticus's attention to the use of picture and beginning consonant cues, as in the following example using *Our Street* (see illustration).

This is a tall house.   This is a tent house.

Our Street (Level 3) by J. Cowley (1986, pp. 5–6). Copyright 1986 by The Wright Group. Reprinted by permission.

Tutor: [Pointing to *tent*, a word in the text] What is this word?

Atticus: [Returns to the beginning of the sentence and finger-points over to the target word.] This—is—a—tent. "Tent."

Tutor: How can you be sure that it's "tent"?

Atticus: There's a tent in the picture.

Tutor: How else?

Atticus: It starts with a T.

Tutor: Good.

2. **Word study.** Atticus is just finishing work on his third set of beginning consonants. He has no trouble segmenting the beginning consonant from other sounds in a spoken word, and the lessons at this point are simply providing a review of the consonant letter–sound relationships. Within 2 weeks, Atticus should be ready to leave beginning consonant sorts and begin work on the short-vowel word families.

3. **Sentence writing.** Atticus has a sentence ready today: "We took my rabbit to the doctor." I have him repeat the sentence two times, and then he begins to write. What follows is a word-by-word account of the interplay between child and tutor during the sentence-writing activity.

(*We*)

Atticus: [Writes *we* correctly, but with a lowercase *w*.]

Tutor: The first word in a sentence has to have what?

Atticus: [Erases the lowercase *w* and writes the uppercase form.]

(*took*)

Atticus: [Writes *t* and stops.]

Tutor: Okay, you got the first letter. Say "took" again; what do you hear at the end?

Atticus: Too—k. I hear a K.

Tutor: Good, write it down.

Atticus: [Writes down *k*.]

Tutor: Now go back and read what you have written so far.

Atticus: [Finger-point reads, "We tk," leaves a two-finger space, and proceeds to write the next word.]

(*my*)

Atticus: [Writes *m* and stops.]

Tutor: [Goes up to the work space and writes *my*.] Atticus, this is a word we are going to use a lot.

Atticus: [Copies the *y* onto his sentence line.]

(*rabbit*)

ATTICUS: [Writes *r* and stops.]

TUTOR: Say "rabbit" slowly; what else do you hear?

ATTICUS: Raa—bit. I hear a B.

TUTOR: Put it down. [Atticus writes a *b*.] Now, say "rabbit" again and tell me what you hear at the very end.

ATTICUS: Ra—bit—t. T? [He writes the *t*.]

TUTOR: Very good.

    (*to*)

ATTICUS: [Writes *to* quickly and confidently.]

TUTOR: That's a word you have learned.

    (*the*)

ATTICUS: [Hesitates, seems frustrated that he doesn't know how to begin this familiar word.]

TUTOR: [Goes up to work space and writes *the*.] You'll learn this word soon, Atticus. Look at each letter; *th* makes the /th/ sound. Copy it down here [pointing to Atticus's sentence].

ATTICUS: [Writes *the*.]

    (*doctor*)

ATTICUS: [Writes *d*. Pauses, and then repeats the word slowly, emphasizing the end, "d—o—c—d—r—r." Writes an *r*.]

TUTOR: Excellent, Atticus. I like the way you listened for the ending sound. Now read your whole sentence again.

We	TK	My	RBT	TO	the*	DR.
(We	took	my	rabbit	to	the	doctor.)

After Atticus finger-point reads his sentence, I rewrite it, cut it into word units, and he reassembles the sentence.

4. **Introducing a new book.** After the preview, Atticus requires very little assistance in reading the new Level 3 book. He uses both picture and beginning consonant cues to identify new words. He seems ready for Level 4 books.

Commentary

There has been a qualitative change in Atticus's concept of word. In reading, he now clearly sees printed words as *units in text with a recognizable beginning letter–sound*. In spelling, he consistently represents the beginning consonant sound in words and shows some ability to attend to ending consonants. He is building a firm foundation for future word knowledge growth.

Gains in word knowledge notwithstanding, when beginning readers like Atticus are exposed to a steady diet of predictable books (Levels 1 to 4 in this program), they sometimes overrely on picture cues and repetitive sentence patterns, thereby paying too little attention to the individual printed words (see illustration of *Our Street*).

This is a big house.

***Our Street* (Level 3)**

This is a big house.
This is a small house
This is a tall house.
This is a tent house.
This is a bus house.
This is our house,
the just-right-for-us house.

Our Street (Level 3) by J. Cowley (1986, pp. 2). Copyright 1986 by The Wright Group. Reprinted by permission.

One way to counter a beginner's overreliance on context is to start a *word bank*. For example, after Atticus has read a given book several times, I go back and point to individual words in the text, making notes of which words he can identify immediately.

Later, I write these "known" words on small cards (2″ × 3″) and review the words with Atticus at each lesson. This review—presenting the word cards one at a time—serves two purposes. First, the isolated presentation of each word forces Atticus to attend to the letters in the word; there is no context to rely on. Second, as the number of known words in the "bank" increases, there will be a corresponding increase in Atticus's confidence as a reader. It is true that he may be able to identify a specific word one day but not the next. In this case, the unknown word is simply dropped from the bank. The important point is that the overall number of *known* words in the bank continues to increase, even if it does so at a gradual pace.

Lesson 19 (November 24; 4 Weeks Later)

1. **Rereading books.** Atticus's finger-point reading of two Level 4 books (for example, see illustration of *Two Little Dogs*) and one Level 5 book is controlled and accurate.

Two Little Dogs (Level 4) by J. Melser (1982, pp. 4–5). Copyright 1982 by Shortland Publications. Reprinted by permission.

The few times he does miscall a word, I do not intervene but let him read on. Each time, Atticus stops, goes back, and self-corrects the error. This is a good sign, for it shows he is attending to both meaning and letter–sound cues as he reads. After each book is read, I quickly go back and point to individual words in the text; some are words we have been working on, some are new. Of the four new words, Atticus identifies three immediately and the other one by using sentence context.

Following the book reading, Atticus reviews his *word bank*. I present the word cards one at a time, and he reads 15 of 16 correctly: *go, cat, said, little, my, jump, and, like, look, ran, fly, it, big, we,* and *house.* Next, I make new cards for *down, into,* and *some,* the three words Atticus identified immediately following today's book reading. He can read *down* and *into* in isolation but not *some,* so two new words are added to his word bank today.

2. **Word study.** Atticus began working on short *a* word families 2 weeks ago (see pages 77–80 for a description of how to introduce word families). Today we are working on a three-column sort of short *a* words. I array three exemplars on the table and have Atticus read them:

cat   man   tap

Atticus proceeds to sort nine short *a* words as I hand them to him one at a time. His sorting is accurate and confident, and he has no difficulty reading down the columns of rhyming words.

cat	man	tap
mat	ran	lap
bat	pan	cap
hat	fan	map

With the words still in column format (as in the preceding lists), I point randomly to several words (*man, cap, fan, bat,* and *lap*). Atticus reads each of the words without hesitation.

Atticus wins the Concentration game that follows, again showing his ability to read the short *a* words in isolation.

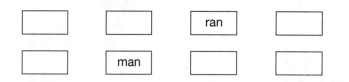

He also has no difficulty spelling five short *a* words from dictation (*mat, ran, tap, fan,* and *hat*).

3. **Sentence writing.** Today Atticus chooses to write about a recent accident:

I	R(O)D	MY	B(I)C	IN	THE	DH.
(I	rode	my	bike	in	the	ditch.)

He spells four of the high-frequency words (*I, my, in,* and *the*) correctly. When he writes RD for *road,* I decide to probe for the vowel sound.

TUTOR: [Pointing to the sound box (see above)] Atticus, you have written the beginning and ending sounds in "road." Say the word again and see if you can hear the middle sound. Say it slowly.

ATTICUS: R—od, r—o—. Is it O?

TUTOR: Yes, it is. Good job! [Tutor writes an *o* in the sound box.] Now you can change your spelling.

ATTICUS: [In his sentence, changes his spelling from RD to ROD.]

I use the same "sound box" strategy in helping Atticus to hear the /$\bar{i}$/ sound in *bike*. I decide to save *ditch*, a short-vowel word, for another day.

After the writing, I copy Atticus's sentence, cut it up, and let him reassemble it. However, the cut-up sentence task is providing little challenge at this point in the year, and I will soon drop it from the tutoring lessons.

4. **Introducing a new book.** We echo read only the first page today. Atticus reads the remaining seven pages of the Level 4 book independently, requiring my assistance on only two words. I have him reread the story, and this time his performance is more fluent and error-free.

Commentary

Over the first 2 months of tutoring, Atticus has established an important reading foundation. At this point he can steadily track each word as he reads text, self-correcting mistakes when necessary. He can represent both beginning and ending consonants in his spellings and is showing some awareness of the medial vowel. Maybe most noteworthy is the fact that he is acquiring a sight vocabulary. As he reads and rereads simple texts, he is beginning to store a set of known words in permanent memory. This is a key to future reading progress, and there is little doubt that Atticus is on his way to becoming a reader.

Lesson 26 (December 17; 4 Weeks Later)

1. **Rereading books.** Today Atticus rereads three Level 6 books. At Level 6, there are more words on a page and more pages per story; however, the sentences, although longer, are still predictable in pattern (see illustration from *Grandma's Memories*).

Despite the increased complexity of the text, Atticus actually requires less support as he finger-point reads. His sight vocabulary and emerging decoding skill combine to make him more independent. In fact, at certain points, I purposely withhold word recognition assistance, forcing Atticus to problem-solve

When my grandma reads me
a story,

she remembers reading
without her glasses.

When my grandma makes me
a cake,

she remembers mixing
with an old eggbeater.

Grandma's Memories (Level 6) by V. King (1989, pp. 2–5). Copyright 1989 by Mimosa Publications. Reprinted by permission.

an unknown word by coordinating sentence context, picture, and letter–sound cues.

Two weeks ago, when Atticus's word bank reached a total of 25 words, we celebrated with red lollipops. Then we discarded the old word bank and started a new one. With two new words added from today's reading, the new word bank now contains 13 words.

2. **Word study.** Atticus has advanced successfully through the short *a* and short *i* word families. Today, he works on a combination sort (/ă/ versus /ĭ/):

hat	cap	sit
sat	lap	fit
mat	clap	hit
flat	tap	bit

Atticus has no difficulty with this task. He reads most of the words quickly, *before* sorting them into columns. When he hesitates briefly on the blends (*clap* and *flat*), I point to the first two letters and he is able to sound out these words.

We quickly play Concentration, and then I administer an eight-word spell check. This is a good test for Atticus, for it forces him to attend to the medial vowel sound in these one-syllable patterns (e.g., *sat* versus *sit*; *hat* versus *hit*).

3. **Sentence writing.** With the Christmas break only 4 days away, the holiday is on Atticus's mind. Without pausing, he writes the following sentence:

I	AM	GOEN	TO	GANPAS	HOS	ON	CRSMS.
(I	am	going	to	Grandpa's	house	on	Christmas.)

After congratulating Atticus on writing a fine sentence, I decide to probe on three words.

(going)

TUTOR: Atticus, look at your spelling of "going." Remember how we write "-ing" at the end of a word.

ATTICUS: [Quickly erases EN and writes ING.]

(Grandpa's)

TUTOR: You did a great job on "Grandpa's." You heard almost all the sounds. Let's say the first part of "Grandpa." Atticus, say "grand."

ATTICUS: "Gran."

TUTOR: Okay, look at the sound box for "grand."

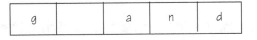

g		a	n	d

You wrote the G, the A, and the N. And there's a D at the end that is hard to hear. Now, look at the empty box. There is a sound right after G.

ATTICUS: Grr—an; g—r—r. It's R. [He proceeds to write an *r* in the sound box and then in his spelling on the sentence line.]

(*Christmas*)

TUTOR: Look at this sound box for the first part of "Christmas."

Say "Cris-" slowly and see if you can hear the vowel sound.

ATTICUS: Cr—is; Cr—i—i; It's an E.

TUTOR: Okay, it sounds like an E. But what is another letter that makes the /ĭ/ sound?

ATTICUS: I?

TUTOR: Excellent! Like in "hit," right? How do we spell "hit"?

ATTICUS: H-I-T.

TUTOR: Good work.

Following the sentence writing, I do *not* rewrite Atticus's sentence with correct spelling and cut it up into words. This activity, having served its developmental purpose, was dropped from his lesson plan 2 weeks ago.

4. **Introducing a new book.** In the book introduction, I focus on three words that may cause difficulty (*gorse, grandfather,* and *nibble*). I identify and define the first word and help Atticus sound out the other two. He then finger-point reads the entire 16-page book by himself, needing my help in only two places.

Commentary

Atticus is on his way to becoming a reader. His sight vocabulary is growing with each lesson, as is his ability to decode new words using sentence context and letter–sound cues. He is progressing nicely through the word study sequence, and his attention to medial vowel sounds in his spelling attempts (HOS for *house* and GANPAS for *Grandpa's*) is a very positive sign. Most important, Atticus feels good about himself as a reader and writer. He can sense his growing competence, and this makes him all the more willing to try hard in the tutoring lessons.

Atticus, the Second Half of the School Year

Atticus's reading ability advanced fairly steadily during the second half of the year. He did stall, or plateau, upon reaching Level 8 in book reading (preprimer 3). After 2 weeks of lackluster lessons, the tutor decided to drop back to Level 6 and 7 books in order to rebuild the child's reading fluency and confidence. The strategy worked, for when Atticus eventually returned to Level 8 books, he was successful.

Atticus's lesson plan changed a bit over the final few months of school. At Level 7 (January), the word bank was dropped. At Level 9 (early April), sentence writing was discontinued. The final lesson plan, used in April and May, included supported oral reading of two books, with a brief word study lesson sandwiched between them.

Lesson Plan
(May 2, 1998)

1. Guided reading: New Level 10 book (15 minutes)
2. Word study: *-at*, *-ake*, *-ar* (10 minutes)
3. Easy reading: Reread Level 9 book (10 minutes)

By the end of the year, Atticus had reached Level 10 in book reading (primer level). In word study, he could read and spell short-vowel patterns and showed some understanding of the "silent-e" long-vowel pattern (e.g., *take*, *side*, *rose*, etc.).

IV. ASSESSMENT OF PROGRESS

How does one know that a child is making adequate progress in a tutoring program? This is an important question, because both the tutor and the child want and need to know whether their work is producing gains in learning. With an emergent reader like Atticus, the assessment path will be clearly marked by a series of developmental milestones:

1. Learning to recognize and write the alphabet letters
2. Developing a concept of word in text
3. Becoming aware of individual sounds within words
4. Acquiring an initial sight vocabulary
5. Using letter–sounds as a word recognition aid in contextual reading and as a word production aid in writing.
6. Advancing through a graded series of first-grade-level reading books

Although there is a rough developmental sequence implied by the 1–6 ordering in the preceding list, in truth these abilities or understandings will to some degree overlap one another in the learning-to-read process. For example, sound awareness (milestone 3) is a multilayered, slowly emerging skill. Atticus may become aware of the beginning consonant sound in words before he develops a concept of word in text. However, he will need to establish a stable concept of word (and probably a small sight vocabulary) before he will be able to attend fully to the sequence of sounds within a *word* (particularly to the medial vowel). Acknowledging this overlap phenomenon, let us consider these early reading–writing abilities one by one to show how they can be assessed over the course of tutoring.

Informal Assessment during the Course of Tutoring

Alphabet Knowledge

A *formal* assessment of alphabet knowledge can be made at any time during the year. To assess *recognition*, the tutor asks Atticus to name the alphabet letters as she points to them in random order. To assess *production*, the tutor has the child write the letters as she dictates them in random order. Such a formal assessment might be carried out after several months of focused work on learning the alphabet.

Alphabet knowledge can be assessed *informally* in a number of tutoring situations. For example, if Atticus hesitates in reading a word in sentence context, the tutor might point to the initial consonant in the word as a word-recognition prompt. If he still hesitates, the tutor can check to see whether he can name the consonant letter. The writing process will also afford opportunities to assess Atticus's alphabet knowledge, specifically his ability to produce (or recall) the alphabet letters. For example, Atticus might well stop in the midst of writing a word and say, "I don't know how to make a *g*." The tutor has to keep track of Atticus's alphabet learning so that, over time, specific, not-yet-mastered letters are targeted for instruction.

Concept of Word in Text

Because supported contextual reading is a major part of Atticus's tutoring program, there will be ample opportunity to assess his developing concept of word in text. A child demonstrates a concept of word when he/she can point accurately to individual words as he/she reads and, after reading a few lines in this manner, can go back and identify target words in the text. With practice, Atticus will become more accurate and fluent in his finger-point reading, and a written record of this improvement should be kept by the tutor, as in the following example:

Lesson 6
October 30

Plan	*Evaluation*
1. Echo read *The Lonely Bear* (Storybox—Level 2)	1. We echo read 2 lines at a time. Atticus did a good job finger-pointing, self-correcting his own errors without my help.

Phoneme (or Sound) Awareness

If an emergent reader is to learn to map letters to sounds in the effort to decode words, he/she must first become aware that a spoken word is composed of a sequence of sounds (/ran/ = /r/ + /ă/ + /n/). Only when Atticus comes to understand that the word *ran* includes three different sounds will he be able to make the connection that the individual letters in the written word (*r, a,* and *n*) correspond to the sound units in the spoken form of the word.

Research has shown that for some children the development of phoneme, or sound, awareness is a gradual process, depending in part on a child's early experiences with written language (Liberman & Liberman, 1992; Morris, 1993b; Perfetti, Beck, Bell, & Hughes, 1987). Thanks to clinical observation and some developmental studies, we also know the sequence children follow in becoming aware of the sounds within words. Beginning readers become conscious first of the beginning consonant sound; later, of the beginning and ending consonants; and, finally, of the medial vowel sound within a syllable. First graders' spelling attempts during the first few months of school often reflect this developing sequence of phoneme awareness.

	Sept.	Oct.	Nov.
back	B	BK	BAC
mail	M	ML	MAL
jump	G	JP	JOP

Atticus's spelling will provide the tutor with clear, ongoing evidence of his developing phoneme awareness. As he attempts to sound out words in the daily sentence-writing activity, he will visibly (and audibly) indicate which sounds he can percieve in spoken words.

Initial Sight Vocabulary

There are several steps involved in assessing sight vocabulary in the emergent reader stage. After Atticus has read a book several times, he can be asked to read individual words in the story when the tutor points to them. If Atticus can identify a given word *immediately*, the tutor prints the word on a 2″ × 3″ card and puts the card into a sight word deck or *word bank*. The word bank cards are then reviewed every few days to assess retention of the sight vocabulary. Although Atticus will forget a few sight words now and then, a steady increase in the number of words in his bank will be an important indicator of reading progress.

A simple thermometer chart can be used to provide a visual record of Atticus's sight word growth.

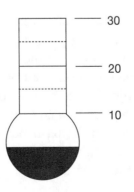

When the goal of 30 sight words is reached, 20 known words are put aside, and Atticus begins work on filling a new thermometer. The word bank is usually discontinued when the child reaches Level 7 or 8 (preprimer 3) in the book-reading sequence.

Using Letter–Sound Knowledge as a Word Recognition Aid and as a Word Production Aid

Once a child knows the alphabet letters and can "hear" or perceive individual sounds within words, he/she is in a position to exploit the alphabetic code of written English. That is, the child can use letter–sound cues in his/her attempts to read words, and sound–letter cues in attempts to write words. The tutor can monitor such letter–sound use in several contexts:

- Does Atticus sometimes self-correct word-reading errors by attending to letter–sound cues (as in the following example)?

the ✓

Up,   up   came   little   spider

- On meeting a new word in sentence context, does Atticus "sound" the beginning consonant letter as an aid in identifying the word?
- When practicing reading his word bank cards, do some of Atticus's errors indicate his attention to both beginning and ending consonants in the word? For example, does he read "bike" for *back*, "cap" for *cup*, or "fast" for *first*?
- In contextual reading, does Atticus eventually make conscious attempts to "sound his way through" new words in a left-to-right manner (e.g., s—a—d for *sad*)?
- In spelling, does Atticus progress through a developmental sequence in representing the sounds within words (e.g., *side* spelled S, then CD, and later SID or even SIED)?

Advancement through a Graded Series of First-Grade-Level Reading Books

Atticus's advancement through the 12 book levels (early- to late-first grade) will be a strong indicator of his reading progress. At a given level (e.g., Level 4), he may need to read all the books before moving forward. At another level (e.g., Level 5), he may need to read only one half or two thirds of the books before advancing. When to move Atticus up to a new book level is a judgment call for the tutor. Valuable time is wasted when a child is kept at a difficulty level he has already mastered. On the other hand, no purpose is served, and no progress made, by pushing him up to a level that is too difficult.

Beginning at Level 6, the tutor can use "accuracy checks" to decide whether to move Atticus to a book at the next level of difficulty. As Atticus reads the first 100 words in a story, the tutor records his errors (see "Oral Reading" in Chapter 2). If, over several stories, Atticus makes 7 or fewer errors (93% accuracy) on his first rereading of a story, it may be time for him to move up to the next book level. Although word reading accuracy is important, Atticus's fluency, decoding ability, and self-correction behavior should also be considered. In short, he should be "in control" of the reading process at a given level before he is asked to tackle more difficult material.

Beginning-of-Year / End-of-Year Assessment (Atticus)

PRETEST (SEPTEMBER)

	Word recognition (graded lists)		Oral reading	
	Flash (%)	*Untimed (%)*	*Accuracy (%)*	*Rate (wpm)*
Emergent	—	—	(Could not read emergent passage independently)	
Preprimer	0	0	—	—
Primer	—	—	—	—

Spelling: No. of words spelled correctly—List 1(0 of 10)
Developmental characteristics—Could represent beginning consonant in 4 of 10 words

POSTTEST (MAY)

	Word recognition (graded lists)		Oral reading	
	Flash (%)	*Untimed (%)*	*Accuracy (%)*	*Rate (wpm)*
Emergent	—	—	—	—
Preprimer	80	90	97	—
Primer	60	80	94	45
1-2	35	65	84	36

Spelling: No. of words spelled correctly—List 1 (3 of 10); List 2 (0 of 10)
Developmental stage—Phonetic

The posttest results above show that Atticus is, at year's end, a solid *primer-level* reader. His word recognition score (60%—flash) and oral reading score (94%) clearly meet the primer-level criteria. Atticus also showed some ability to read Level 1-2 words (35%—flash; 65%—untimed), although he failed to meet the oral reading accuracy criterion of 90% at this level.

Atticus's posttest spellings (see the following list) show that he has moved into the *Phonetic* stage of spelling development.

Spelling word	Atticus's spelling
bike	BIK
fill	FIL
plate	PLAT
mud	MOD
flat	FLAT (c)
bed	BED (c)
drive	DRIV
chop	CHOP (c)
wish	WESH
step	STAP
plant	PLAT
dress	DRES
stuff	STOF
chase	CHAS
wise	WISS
shopping	SHOPING
train	TRAN
cloud	CLOD
thick	THIK
float	FLOT

He is now able to represent the beginning consonant, vowel, and ending consonant in his spellings. On closer look, he shows good knowledge of consonant blends and digraphs (DRIV for *drive*; CHAS for *chase*), but inconsistently represents short vowels (FIL for *fill*, but WESH for *wish*) and shows little awareness that long vowels are marked with an extra vowel letter (PLAT for *plate*; FLOT for *float*). Overall, Atticus's posttest spelling performance is very encouraging. Keep in mind that on the September pretest he could write only 15 letters of the alphabet and was unable to represent even the beginning consonant sound in his spelling attempts.

The pretest–posttest comparison indicates that Atticus has made significant progress in learning to read and spell during the year. However, a skeptic might point out that after a year of tutoring, Atticus is still only two-thirds of the way through the first-grade reading program. In responding to such a statement, at least three factors must be considered: (1) What kind of knowledge or "readiness" did Atticus bring to the learning-to-read process in September? (2) How quickly was he able to pick up basic understandings about the reading process? (i.e., what was his initial rate of learning?), and (3) How much reading progress would he have made without the tutoring? Let us consider these factors one by one.

Atticus was a virtual nonreader at the beginning of the school year. He possessed little or no sight vocabulary, he could name only 16 letters of the alphabet and could write even fewer, and he showed little awareness of word units in text or of beginning consonant sounds in spoken words. In teaching Atticus to read, his tutor was forced to start *at the beginning*.

Not only did Atticus lack what some might term "prereading skills" (alphabet knowledge, concept of word, beginning consonant awareness), but in the early tutoring lessons he was slow to develop these abilities. Several weeks went by, for example, before Atticus showed any consistency in finger-point reading memorized texts. His learning of the alphabet letters and beginning consonant sounds also proceeded slowly. Moreover, a full 2 months, or 19 hours, of tutoring passed before he could recognize just 17 sight words. Thus, the initial steps in learning to read were painstakingly slow for Atticus (and for his tutor). At the same time, these steps were crucially important ones, for they laid the conceptual foundation for future growth. During the last 4 months of the school year, Atticus did progress at a faster rate, and this is what enabled him to score as high as he did on the posttest assessment (primer reading level).

How much reading progress would Atticus have made *without* one-to-one tutoring? Such a question requires speculation, of course, and readers of this manual are free to draw their own conclusions. However, given Atticus's meager readiness skills in September and his initial slowness in acquiring basic understandings even with one-to-one support, one can argue reasonably that he would have made minimal reading progress during the year in the absence of tutoring. Here we have a child whose special needs in the area of written language learning are very difficult to meet in a crowded first-grade classroom. Nonetheless, effective one-to-one tutoring can offer such a child a "lifeline" to literacy; that is, it can get the emergent reader off to a good start in learning to read and write. The seemingly modest pretest–posttest reading gains that began this section should be viewed in this context.

APPENDIX 3.1. Books for Atticus Listed by Difficulty Level

The following book list is used in Early Steps, a first-grade reading intervention program (Morris, 1995; Santa & Hoien, 1999). The 12 book levels correspond to traditional basal reader levels in the following manner:

Book level	Basal level
1	Emergent
2	
3	Preprimer 1
4	
5	Preprimer 2
6	
7	Preprimer 3
8	
9	Primer
10	
11	1-2 (late-first)
12	

Title	Level	Author/Series	Publisher
At the Zoo	1	PM Starters	Rigby
Big Things	1	PM Starters	Rigby
Birthday Cake, The	1	Sunshine	Wright Group
Chocolate Cake, The	1	Storybox	Wright Group
Dad	1	PM Starters	Rigby
Little Brother	1	Sunshine	Wright Group
Mom	1	PM Starters	Rigby
Pets	1	PM Starters	Rigby
Toy Box, A	1	Literacy 2000	Rigby
All of Me	2	Literacy 2000	Rigby
Bicycle, The	2	Storybox	Wright Group
Big Hill, The	2	Storybox	Wright Group
Ghost, The	2	Storybox	Wright Group
Go-Carts, The	2	Storybox	Wright Group
If You Meet a Dragon	2	Storybox	Wright Group
In the Mirror	2	Storybox	Wright Group
Little Seed, A	2	Smart Start	Rigby
Little Things	2	PM Starters	Rigby
Look at Me	2	PM Starters	Rigby
Moms and Dads	2	PM Starters	Rigby
Our Baby	2	Literacy 2000	Rigby

(*cont.*)

APPENDIX 3.1 (*cont.*)

Title	Level	Author/Series	Publisher
Painting	2	Storybox	Wright Group
Playing	2	PM Starters	Rigby
Sharing	2	Literacy 2000	Rigby
Skier, The	2	PM Starters	Rigby
Time for Dinner	2	PM Starters	Rigby
Tree House, The	2	Sunshine	Wright Group
We Go Out	2	PM Starters	Rigby
Yuck Soup	2	Sunshine	Wright Group
Ball Games	3	PM Starters	Rigby
Dreaming	3	Smart Start	Rigby
I Can Jump	3	Sunshine	Wright Group
I Love My Family	3	Sunshine	Wright Group
Ice Cream	3	Storybox	Wright Group
Little Brother	3	Sunshine	Wright Group
Little Pig	3	Storybox	Wright Group
Lost	3	Storybox	Wright Group
Monster Sandwich, A	3	Storybox	Wright Group
My Accident	3	PM Starters	Rigby
Nighttime	3	Storybox	Wright Group
Our Street	3	Sunshine	Wright Group
Packing My Bag	3	PM Starters	Rigby
Pencil, The	3	PM Starters	Rigby
Photo Book, The	3	PM Books	Rigby
Rock Pools, The	3	PM Starters	Rigby
Shoo	3	Sunshine	Wright Group
Stop	3	Storybox	Wright Group
Trucks	3	Literacy 2000	Rigby
We Can Run	3	PM Starters	Rigby
Where Are the Babies?	3	PM Starters	Rigby
Big and Little	4	Sunshine	Wright Group
Big Kick, The	4	PM Books	Rigby
Bus Ride, The	4	Reading Unlimited	Scott, Foresman
Copy-cat	4	Storybox	Wright Group
Dan, the Flying Man	4	Read-togethers	Wright Group
Danger	4	Storybox	Wright Group
Farm Concert, The	4	Storybox	Wright Group
Fishing	4	PM Starters	Rigby
Hot Dogs	4	PM Books	Rigby
Monsters' Party, The	4	Read-togethers	Wright Group
My Letter	4	Wonder World lll	Wright Group
No, No	4	Storybox	Wright Group
Sally and the Daisy	4	PM Books	Rigby

(*cont.*)

APPENDIX 3.1 (*cont.*)

Title	Level	Author/Series	Publisher
Shark in a Sack	4	Sunshine	Wright Group
Tiger, Tiger	4	PM Books	Rigby
Two Little Dogs	4	Storybox	Wright Group
Under My Bed	4	Smart Start	Rigby
What a Mess	4	Storybox	Wright Group
Along Comes Jake	5	Sunshine	Wright Group
Baby Bear Goes Fishing	5	PM Books	Rigby
Cats and Kittens	5	Reading Unlimited	Scott, Foresman
Father Bear Goes Fishing	5	PM Books	Rigby
Friend for Little White Rabbit, A	5	PM Books	Rigby
Goodbye Lucy	5	Sunshine	Wright Group
Hairy Bear	5	Read-togethers	Wright Group
Haunted House, The	5	Storybox	Wright Group
Horace	5	Storybox	Wright Group
Hungry Kitten, The	5	PM Books	Rigby
In a Dark, Dark Wood	5	Read-togethers	Wright Group
Lion and the Rabbit, The	5	PM Books	Rigby
Mrs. Wishy Washy	5	Storybox	Wright Group
Pete's New Shoes	5	Literacy 2000	Rigby
Pumpkin, The	5	Storybox	Wright Group
Seagull Is Clever	5	PM Books	Rigby
Three Little Ducks	5	Read-togethers	Wright Group
Too Big for Me	5	Storybox	Wright Group
Woosh!	5	Read-togethers	Wright Group
Big Toe, The	6	Read-togethers	Wright Group
Blackberries	6	PM Books	Rigby
BMX Billy	6	Literacy 2000	Rigby
Boo Hoo	6	Read-Togethers	Wright Group
Grandma's Memories	6	Literacy 2000	Rigby
Grandpa's Birthday	6	Literacy 2000	Rigby
Jane's Car	6	PM Books	Rigby
Little Bulldozer	6	PM Books	Rigby
Lucky Goes to Dog School	6	PM Books	Rigby
Mr. Grump	6	Sunshine	Wright Group
Mrs. Bold	6	Literacy 2000	Rigby
Obadiah	6	Read-togethers	Wright Group
Red Rose, The	6	Read-togethers	Wright Group
Sally's Beans	6	PM Books	Rigby
Seed, The	6	Sunshine	Wright Group
T.J.'s Tree	6	Literacy 2000	Rigby
Ten Little Bears	6	Reading Unlimited	Scott, Foresman

(*cont.*)

APPENDIX 3.1 (*cont.*)

Title	Level	Author/Series	Publisher
To Town	6	Read-togethers	Wright Group
Where Are You Going, Aja Rose?	6	Sunshine	Wright Group
All By Myself	7	Mayer, M.	Golden
Baby Bear's Present	7	PM Books	Rigby
Brave Tricerotops	7	PM Books	Rigby
Catch That Frog	7	Reading Unlimited	Scott, Foresman
Clever Penguins, The	7	PM Books	Rigby
Fox Who Was Foxed, The	7	PM Books	Rigby
Go Dog Go	7	Eastman, P. D.	Random House
Honey for Baby Bear	7	PM Books	Rigby
Lion and the Mouse, The	7	PM Books	Rigby
Lion's Tail, The	7	Reading Unlimited	Scott, Foresman
Little Kid	7	Literacy 2000	Rigby
Mine's the Best	7	Bonsall, C.	HarperCollins
Only an Octopus	7	Literacy 2000	Rigby
Pat's New Puppy	7	Reading Unlimited	Scott, Foresman
Prince's Tooth is Loose, The	7	Pictureback Readers	Random House
Sally's Friends	7	PM Books	Rigby
Taking Jason to Grandma's	7	Book Bank	Wright Group
Time for School, Little Dinosaur	7	Pictureback Readers	Random House
Who Will Be My Mother?	7	Read-togethers	Wright Group
Yes, Ma'am	7	Read-togethers	Wright Group
Are You My Mother?	8	Eastman, P. D.	Random House
Baby Monkey	8	Reading Unlimited	Scott, Foresman
Brand-New Butterfly, The	8	Literacy 2000	Rigby
Cross-Country Race, The	8	PM Books	Rigby
Great Big Enormous Turnip	8	Reading Unlimited	Scott, Foresman
Hippo's Hiccups	8	Literacy 2000	Rigby
Hop on Pop	8	Dr. Seuss	Random House
Hungry Giant, The	8	Storybox	Wright Group
Just for You	8	Mayer, M.	Donovan
Just Me and My Little Sister	8	Mayer, M.	Donovan
Just My Luck	8	Literacy 2000	Rigby
Me, Too	8	Mayer, M.	Donovan
Mice	8	Literacy 2000	Rigby
Mrs. Spider's Beautiful Web	8	PM Books	Rigby
New Baby, The	8	PM Books	Rigby

(*cont.*)

APPENDIX 3.1 (*cont.*)

Title	Level	Author/Series	Publisher
Pepper's Adventure	8	PM Books	Rigby
Pete Little	8	PM Books	Rigby
Tents	8	Reading Unlimited	Scott, Foresman
This Is My House	8	Mayer, M.	Golden
Three Little Pigs, The	8	Reading Unlimited	Scott, Foresman
Tommy's Treasure	8	Literacy 2000	Rigby
Victor Makes a TV	8	Reading Unlimited	Scott, Foresman
Big Mama and Grandma Ghana	9	Shelf Medearis, A.	Scholastic
Cave Boy	9	Step into Reading	Random House
Happy Faces	9	Reading Unlimited	Scott, Foresman
Hiking with Dad	9	Wonder World lll	Wright Group
How Turtle Raced Beaver	9	Literacy 2000	Rigby
I Was So Mad	9	Mayer, M.	Donovan
Just Me and My Dad	9	Mayer, M.	Donovan
Just Me and My Little Brother	9	Mayer, M.	Donovan
Just Me and My Puppy	9	Mayer, M.	Donovan
Missing Necklace, The	9	Reading Unlimited	Scott, Foresman
Monkey and the Fire	9	Literacy 2000	Rigby
My New Boy	9	Step into Reading	Random House
Nina, Nina, Ballerina	9	Step into Reading	Random House
P.J. Funnybone Camps Out	9	Step into Reading	Random House
Teeny Tiny Woman	9	Step into Reading	Random House
Tiger Is a Scaredy Cat	9	Step into Reading	Random House
Who Will Be My Friends?	9	Hoff, S.	Harper Trophy
Wind and Sun	9	Literacy 2000	Rigby
Abracadabra	10	Reading Unlimited	Scott, Foresman
Annie's Pet	10	Bank Street	General
Danny and the Dinosaur	10	Hoff, S.	Scholastic
Fight, The	10	Bank Street	Bantam
Good Hunting, Blue Sky	10	Parish, P.	Harper Trophy
Half for You, Half for Me	10	Literacy 2000	Rigby
Hello House	10	Step into Reading	Random House
Little Bear	10	Minarik, E.	HarperCollins
Lonely Giant, The	10	Literacy 2000	Rigby
Loose Laces	10	Reading Unlimited	Scott, Foresman
Popcorn Book	10	Reading Unlimited	Scott, Foresman
Pot of Gold, The	10	Reading Unlimited	Scott, Foresman
Red and Blue Mittens	10	Reading Unlimited	Scott, Foresman
Sammy's Supper	10	Reading Unlimited	Scott, Foresman
Show and Tell Frog, The	10	Bank Street	Bantam
You Are Much Too Small	10	Bank Street	Bantam

(*cont.*)

APPENDIX 3.1 (*cont.*)

Title	Level	Author/Series	Publisher
Adie Meets Max	11	Robins, J.	HarperCollins
Best Little Monkeys in the World, The	11	Step into Reading	Random House
Circus Book	11	Reading Unlimited	Scott, Foresman
Days with Frog and Toad	11	Lobel, A.	Harper Trophy
Dinosaur Babies	11	Step into Reading	Random House
Fox All Week	11	Marshall, E.	Puffin
Henry's Choice	11	Reading Unlimited	Scott, Foresman
I Am Not Afraid	11	Bank Street	Bantam
Lion and Lamb	11	Bank Street	Bantam
Little Bear's Visit	11	Minarik, E.	Harper Trophy
Little Knight, The	11	Reading Unlimited	Scott, Foresman
Lizards and Salamanders	11	Reading Unlimited	Scott, Foresman
Monster from the Sea	11	Bank Street	Bantam
Mouse Soup	11	Lobel, A.	HarperCollins
Mouse Tales	11	Lobel, A.	HarperCollins
Mystery Seeds	11	Reading Unlimited	Scott, Foresman
Norma Jean, Jumping Bean	11	Step into Reading	Random House
Sir Small and the Dragonfly	11	Step into Reading	Random House
Slim, Shorty and the Mules	11	Reading Unlimited	Scott, Foresman
Snowy Day, The	11	Keats, E.J.	Scholastic
Whistle for Willie	11	Keats, E.J.	Penguin
Zack's Alligator	11	Mozelle, S.	Harper Trophy
Frog and Toad Are Friends	12	Lobel, A.	Harper & Row
Frog and Toad Together	12	Lobel, A.	HarperCollins
How Kittens Grow	12	Selsam, M.	Scholastic
My Puppy Is Born	12	Cole, J.	Scholastic
Little Red Hen, The	12	Galdone, P.	Viking
Owl at Home	12	Lobel, A.	HarperCollins

CHAPTER 4

Beth, the Fledgling Reader

Beth, our second case study, is 7 years old and a member of the low-reading group in her second-grade classroom. The *American Heritage College Dictionary* (1993) defines *fledgling* as "a young bird that has recently acquired its flight feathers." Beth's performance on the initial reading assessment (which follows) certainly fits the image of a young, inexperienced reader ready to venture out in text, but still in need of some gentle, timely support.

I. SUMMARY OF INITIAL READING ASSESSMENT

	Word recognition (graded lists)		Oral reading	
	Flash (%)	*Untimed (%)*	*Accuracy (%)*	*Rate (wpm)*
Emergent	—	—	—	—
Preprimer	65	75	96	45
Primer	30	40	82	31

Spelling: No. of words spelled correctly—List 1 (2 of 10); List 2 (0 of 10)
Developmental stage—Phonetic (represents beginning, medial, and ending sounds in one-syllable words)

On the *graded word recognition lists* (flash presentation), Beth was able to read 13 of the 20 preprimer words, but only 6 of the 20 primer-level words (see Figure 4.1). The majority of Beth's errors were "no response" or "don't know." However, when she did attempt to read an unknown word, she generally attended to the beginning consonant in the word and, sometimes, to the ending consonant as well (e.g., "bug" for *big*, "duck" for *back*, "ran" for *rain*).

On the *oral reading task*, Beth read the preprimer passage easily but was unable to read the primer passage with acceptable accuracy (82%) and speed (31 wpm).

	Preprimer				Primer	
	Flash	*Untimed*			*Flash*	*Untimed*
1. and	____	____		1. back	O	duck
2. cat	____	____		2. eat	____	____
3. me	____	____		3. sun	____	____
4. is	____	____		4. bird	____	____
5. go	____	____		5. pat	put	✓
6. play	____	____		6. saw	was	✓
7. where	O	O		7. feet	fat	foot
8. like	O	✓		8. lake	like	O
9. thing	O	O		9. hid	O	hide
10. old	____	____		10. cut	____	____
11. your	O	O		11. about	O	O
12. up	____	____		12. one	____	____
13. said	____	____		13. rain	O	ran
14. big	O	bug		14. water	went	O
15. for	____	____		15. two	____	____
16. by	____	____		16. how	O	who
17. dog	____	____		17. window	O	O
18. not	____	____		18. need	O	O
19. who	O	will		19. that's	O	O
20. here	O	✓		20. mother	O	O
% correct	65	75		% correct	30	40

FIGURE 4.1. Beth's performance on preprimer and primer word recognition lists.

Finally, on the *spelling task*, Beth showed Letter-Name stage spelling ability. She was able to sound her way through most of the words, representing the beginning and ending consonants and the vowel element (e.g., BIC for *bike*, JRIV for *drive*). However, she was inconsistent in spelling consonant digraphs, consonant blends, and short vowels; she also showed little understanding that long vowels are usually marked with an additional letter (pla*t*e, tra*i*n).

First-grade list		Second-grade list	
1. bike	BIC	1. plant	PLAT
2. fill	FEL	2. dress	JRES
3. plate	PAT	3. stuff	STOF
4. mud	MOD	4. chase	GAS
5. flat	FLAT	5. wise	WISS
6. bed	BED	6. shopping	SIPEN
7. drive	JRIV	7. train	(no attempt)
8. chop	GOP	8. cloud	KOD
9. wish	WE	9. thick	THEK
10. step	SAP	10. float	FLOT

These assessment results show that Beth is a beginning reader, but one who has acquired some important knowledge about the workings of written language. For example, she can finger-point read and use beginning consonant cues in her attempts to decode words in context. She can consciously attend to the beginning, middle and ending sounds in one-syllable spoken words (see *spelling* in Initial Assessment). Finally, Beth has acquired a rudimentary sight vocabulary, a store of known words she can identify in isolation (see *word recognition* in Initial Assessment). This previously acquired knowledge will serve Beth well as the tutoring lessons begin.

II. TEACHING STRATEGIES

Beth's lesson plan differs a bit from Atticus's (Chapter 3). Notice, in the following chart, that her lesson is 10 minutes longer (45 versus 35) and includes a short *Read-to* segment at the end.

Atticus's Lesson Plan (35 minutes)	Beth's Lesson Plan (45 minutes)
1. Rereading books (14)	1. Guided reading of new material (18)
2. Word study (8)	2. Word study (10)
3. Sentence writing (8)	3. Easy reading (10)
4. Introduce new book (5)	4. Tutor reads to Beth (7)

Whereas supported *oral reading* and *word study* figure prominently in both students' plans, *writing* is not a required activity for Beth. This is because she already possesses the phoneme awareness that sentence writing helped Atticus to develop. With limited time available during the school day for tutoring, oral reading and word study take precedence over writing in Beth's lesson. (If she is tutored *after* school over a longer time period [e.g., 60 minutes], then writing can be included in her lesson.)

What follows is a description of teaching strategies that address the needs of a fledgling reader like Beth.

Guided Reading

As with Atticus, Beth's reading progress will be measured by her advancement through a graded series of first- and second-grade-level books (see Appendix 4.1). Traditional basal levels will be used to designate text difficulty levels.

Text difficulty levels

Preprimer 2
Preprimer 3
Primer
1-2 (final months of first grade)
2-1 (first half of second grade)
2-2 (second half of second grade)

Beth's initial reading assessment (see page 114) showed that she was comfortable reading a *preprimer* passage but struggled on the *primer* passage. Therefore, in her tutoring lessons she will begin by reading preprimer 3 books.

Providing Support

In the *guided reading* segment of the lesson, Beth reads at her *instructional level*; that is, she reads stories that provide challenge in regard to word recognition and sentence structure. Because the text is at the "cutting edge" of her reading ability, Beth will require support from the tutor.

Previewing a story is one way to provide support (see Clay, 1991a). Before reading, Beth and the tutor "preview" the first six to eight pages of the selection, discussing the pictures on each page and making guesses about the story line ("What do you think is happening in this picture, Beth?" [Turning to the next page] "Now, what is happening?"). During the preview, the tutor points to and identifies a few words in the text that Beth may find difficult to decode. Then Beth returns to page 1 and begins to read. Done appropriately, a preview can provide important support. As Beth reads, she is able to "fill in" a mental outline, confirming or modifying hypotheses that were developed during the preview. This reduces anxiety and makes the reading purposeful.

Echo reading is a second way to provide Beth with support. After discussing a story's title and opening page picture, the tutor reads the first page aloud. Then Beth echo reads the first page, pointing to each word. The second page of the story is read in the same manner. After two pages of echo reading, the tutor stops and asks Beth to predict what is going to happen next. From page 3 onward, Beth reads independently, with the tutor providing assistance as needed. Stops are made every three pages or so to check on comprehension and make further predictions. The echo- or memory-supported reading on the first two pages is important, for it gets Beth "into the story," providing her with character names, a sense of the setting, and preliminary information about the plot. Keep in mind that the hardest part of a story, for the beginner or for the mature reader, is the first one or two pages. Providing support at this opening juncture makes excellent sense.

Partner reading is a third way to support Beth in instructional-level material. Basically, it involves the tutor and child alternating pages as they read a story aloud. Partner reading can be used to ease Beth into a story or to provide a respite if she tires (loses concentration) after independently reading several pages of text. The tutor's reading of alternate pages keeps the flow of the story going and also provides the child with a fluent model of oral reading. Moreover, it can send a needed message to Beth that the tutor is a helpful partner in the lesson, willing at times to share the reading load.

The tutor can vary the guided reading by using the support strategies described earlier, separately. For example, the tutor might introduce one story by previewing and the next by echo reading. Or the tutor may favor one type of introduction and use the other only sparingly. At this point, however, let us consider how all three sources of tutor support (previewing, echo reading, and partner reading) might be integrated in a single guided reading activity.

The Pot of Gold (primer level) is a delightful, 14-page folk tale. The tutor might preview the story in the following manner:

TUTOR: The name of this story is *The Pot of Gold.* Look at the picture on page 2. This man's name is *Grumble* [pointing to the word in the text]. Does he look happy?

BETH: No, he's mad.

TUTOR: Look at the next page [page 3]. What's Grumble doing?

BETH: He's looking at the little guy. Grumble's gonna follow him.

TUTOR: That's a good guess. The little guy is an *elf* [pointing to the word in the text]. Do you know anything about elves?

BETH: They can do magic; they can disappear.

TUTOR: Okay, I've heard that about elves. Also, some people say that an elf has a pot of gold. Do you remember the title of this story? [turning back to the title page].

Once upon a time there was a mean man named Grumble.

One day Grumble saw an elf in the woods. Grumble said, "An elf always has a pot of gold. I'll make this elf take me to his pot of gold."

The Pot of Gold (primer) (pp. 2–3). Copyright 1976 by Scott, Foresman. Reprinted by permission.

BETH: [Beth reads the title and her eyes widen.] The man is going to get the elf's gold.

TUTOR: [Turning to pages 4 and 5] What's happening in these pictures?

BETH: The giant's got the little elf. He's telling him he wants the gold.

TUTOR: Do you think the elf is going to give Grumble the gold?

BETH: No.

TUTOR: [Turning to pages 6 and 7] Beth, look closely at page 6. What is the elf doing?

BETH: He's pointing to the tree where the gold is buried.

TUTOR: Do you think the gold is under the tree?

BETH: No. The elf is gonna trick him.

TUTOR: All right, you've made some great guesses. Let's go back and read this story.

Following the *preview*, the tutor turns back to page 2 and says, "Beth, on these first few pages, I'm going to read first and then I want you to read, okay?"

Grumble took hold of the elf.
The elf began to jerk this way and that way. But Grumble didn't let go.

The elf said, "Let me go! Let me go!"
Grumble said, "Take me to your pot of gold. Then I'll let you go."

The Pot of Gold (primer) (pp. 4–5). Copyright 1976 by Scott, Foresman. Reprinted by permission.

The elf took Grumble to a big tree. The elf said, "The gold is under this tree. You'll have to dig deep to get it."

Grumble said, "I'll need a shovel to dig with. I'll go home and get one. But first I'll mark the tree so I can find it again."

The Pot of Gold (primer) (pp. 6–7). Copyright 1976 by Scott, Foresman. Reprinted by permission.

Tutor and child proceed to *echo read* pages 2 and 3. Because *The Pot of Gold* is not written in "predictable" or patterned language, the tutor decides to continue the echo reading on page 4. On reaching page 5, the tutor says, "Beth, try this page by yourself." Beth has no trouble reading page 5 independently. Given her success, she and the tutor proceed to alternate pages, or *partner read*, the rest of the story, stopping now and then to check comprehension and make predictions. (*Note*: Grumble did not get the elf's gold.)

From the preceding example, we can see how a preview, initial echo reading, and partner reading can work together to facilitate Beth's reading of a new text. Keep in mind that these support-reading strategies are to be used flexibly. Depending on the reader's ability and the difficulty of the story, the length of the preview can be increased or decreased, as can the number of pages that are echo read or partner read. The more challenging the text, the more support the child will require.

(*Note*: During at least the first half of the year, Beth will finger-point to the words as she reads. Finger-point reading at this fledgling reader stage enhances perceptual focus and aids concentration [Clay, 1991b]. It also provides the tutor with a concrete means of monitoring the child's reading process.)

Monitoring Oral Reading Behavior

There is an art to listening to and supporting a young child's oral reading. Experienced, effective teachers may seem to do this effortlessly, but their skill has been shaped by hours and hours of teaching practice. As the tutor begins to listen to Beth read aloud, he will invariably have more questions than answers. Should I correct each and every word recognition error? Should I allow Beth to ignore punctuation? Should I let her labor over sounding out difficult words, or should I provide such words quickly? There are no pat answers to these questions. However, adherence from the start to three simple principles can help to guide the tutor in successfully monitoring a child's oral reading behavior:

1. Keep the ball rolling.
2. The reader shall make sense.
3. The reader shall read, for the most part, the words on the page.

1. **Keep the ball rolling** refers to maintaining an adequate pace in the oral reading lesson. If Beth reads in a laborious, word-by-word (or worse, letter-by-letter) manner, she runs the risk of losing the meaning of a sentence by the time she finishes reading it. Frank Smith (1971) has labeled this phenomenon "tunnel vision"; that is, the beginner loses the meaning of the whole by tunneling in on (sounding out) the parts.

Fortunately, the partner-reading format can be a useful antidote to tunnel vision. When the tutor reads alternate pages of the story aloud, this models for the child new vocabulary, correct phrasing, even appropriate intonation. This consistent modeling, story after story, should eventually pay dividends in more fluent reading by the child. A second way that the tutor can facilitate oral reading fluency is to provide difficult words when the child is "stuck." There is nothing to be gained by having a beginning reader labor over sounding out a phonetically irregular word, such as *laugh* or *heard*, when a literate adult is there to help. With experience, the tutor will become more adept at anticipating difficulty and thus quickly providing certain words that would otherwise break the flow of the child's reading.

2. To say that **the beginning reader must make sense as he/she reads** may seem to be an absurdly obvious statement. Nonetheless, many children are perfectly willing to sacrifice sense or meaning as they negotiate their way, word-by-word, through a written sentence. The following oral reading sample was produced by a second-grade girl reading in a diagnostic testing situation.

1. Bob and his father like to work on old cars.

2. Bob is very young, so none of the cars belong to him.
    soon   *his*

3. He would like to have his own car when he gets big.
  works   *the old*

4. Sometimes Bob and his father go to a car show.

Notice that although the reading of lines (2) and (3) makes no sense, the child continues on with little attention to this fact. It is as if her concept of oral reading is to make a conscientious "stab" at the words on the page, rather than to produce a meaningful rendition of the text. How should the tutor respond to such oral reading? The answer is simple. *Demand meaning.*

If a child's reading of a sentence does not make sense, the tutor has several options:

a. Direct the child to try reading the sentence again.
b. Provide support during a rereading by pointing out a letter–sound cue. For example, if the child were rereading sentence (2), at the appropriate time the tutor might simply point to the first letter in *none*, thereby cueing the child to examine the word from left to right. Such beginning consonant cues, when provided in context, can be of considerable help to the beginning reader.
c. Provide support by rereading the text up to a point, and have the child complete the sentence. For example, given the child's inappropriate reading of sentence (3), the tutor might intervene by rereading the sentence up to the word *have*, letting the child complete the sentence. With this contextual support, the child should now be able to read the rest of the sentence correctly.

The most troubling aspect of the four-sentence oral reading sample we have been analyzing is the lack of self-correction by the young reader. One would hope that the child, after reading ". . . so soon of his cars" in sentence (2), would have paused and then gone back to self-correct or "fix up" this nonmeaningful phrase. The fact that she did not do so deserves the tutor's attention. Self-correction is an extremely important behavior in the beginning reading process (Clay, 1991b); its presence is a positive sign, its absence a negative one. Children who do self-correct with some consistency show us that they are monitoring their reading for meaning. They are also taking some personal control over the reading process, correcting errors without the tutor's direct intervention.

Self-correction behavior will develop, however, only if opportunities to self-correct are made available to the young reader. A strong tendency of novice tutors (and some experienced teachers) is to correct each word recognition error "on the spot"—in midsentence—either by providing the misread word or by helping the child to sound it out. Such a teaching procedure does not allow the beginning reader to read past an error, detect by him/herself that an error has been made, and then go back and self-correct it. In fact, one could argue that a tutor's indiscriminate correction of all word recognition errors may actually retard the child's acquisition of an important reading strategy—self-correction.

At this point, the reader of this section may feel that he/she is receiving mixed messages. After all, earlier it was suggested that the tutor provide difficult words immediately to support the child's oral reading fluency. Now we are considering letting the child read past a serious word recogition error with the hope that he/she will independently go back and self-correct the error. However, there is no contradiction here, just different circumstances. Monitoring a child's oral reading is not something that can be done "by the numbers," using a simple formula. Ongoing, active decision making by the tutor is required, and the decision to provide or withhold assistance is always dictated by the situation.

For example, if the child is stuck on the first or second word in a sentence, it is often wise simply to provide the word, because at this point there is little sentence context there to draw upon. On the other hand, if the same child later misreads a midsentence word embedded in a meaningful context, the tutor may want to let the error go and see what the child will do upon reaching the end of the sentence. The flow or rhythm of the child's reading also cues the tutor whether to provide or withhold immediate word recognition assistance. Certainly, it would be prudent to provide difficult words immediately when a young reader is stumbling through a story-opening paragraph, halting awkwardly on one or two words in each line. However, when the same child has gained some momentum and is now reading fairly fluently in the middle of the story, the tutor may decide to let a serious (meaning-costing) oral reading error go by and see what the child does.

To intervene or not? The preceding examples obviously require ongoing decision making by the tutor. The basic principle that must be followed is, *Demand a meaningful reading of the text.* How this is accomplished, however, will vary according to how the tutor chooses to respond to particular reading situations.

3. **The reader shall read, for the most part, the words on the page.** It should be clear from the preceding discussion that when sentence or passage meaning is disrupted because of a misread word, some type of response must be forthcoming; self-correction by the child or intervention by the tutor (e.g., supplying a difficult word or having the child reread the sentence). However, what is the appropriate tutor response when a word recognition error does *not* cost the young reader meaning? Let us turn to a few oral reading samples (see Figure 4.2) that raise this very issue.

Child A

looked ✓
1. She liked him

knows
2. But she knew it wasn't right to keep him.

3. So she opened the door and told him to leave.

4. "Go home, Gus," she said.

did not   *away*
5. Kim didn't want Gus to go, but he went anyway.

Child B

looked at
1. She liked͜ him

And   she   going
2. But she knew it wasn't right to keep him.

3. (So)she opened the door and told him [to leave.]

on
4. "Go͜home, Gus," she said.

away
5. Kim didn't want Gus to go, but he went anyway.

FIGURE 4.2. Two oral readings with a different number of errors.

An examination of the word recognition errors made by Child A and Child B reveals that both children were reading for meaning; that is, their errors for the most part preserved the meaning of the text. But, again, how is the tutor to respond in this situation—when the child produces a meaningful *reading* of a text without *reading* the actual words on the page? In a sense, the very definition of "reading" is at stake here, and, as one would expect, controversy and disagreement abound.

Some reading educators maintain that as long as the child is making sense as he/she reads, the tutor should not focus on word-level errors. To concentrate on harmless, no-meaning-loss word recognition errors, this group argues, is to divert the young reader's attention from comprehension of the text, the real goal of reading. Conversely, a second group of reading educators would have the tutor pay close attention to the young reader's word recognition errors, *even those errors that do not seriously disrupt sentence or passage meaning*. This second group believes that a major goal of beginning reading instruction is to help children develop accurate, automatic recognition of a steadily increasing number of printed words. Hence, they pose a straightforward question to the opposing camp: If children are not required to read the words exactly as printed on the page, how do they come to learn these words?

As with many complex problems, there is legitimate middle ground between the two pedagogical positions. The two oral reading samples (Child A and Child B) can be used to illustrate this middle position. Granting that both children produced a meaningful reading of the passage, the issue is not *quality* of error, but rather *quantity* of error. Child A misread 4 of the 37 words (one error was self-corrected); Child B misread (omitted, inserted, or substituted) 10 of the 37 words. We need not go into a detailed error-by-error analysis. The answer is right there in the raw number of errors made by each child. Child B is "coming off the page" much more than Child A. In a way, Child B is doing a sophisticated job of "translating" the text. Although we can marvel at this child's ability to maintain meaning while misreading one out of every four words, we must ask ourselves what will happen when Child B faces more difficult reading matter. Will the translation process break down (and with it, comprehension)? Will this "translation" reading require of Child B an inordinate amount of mental energy as compared with that of a second child who effortlessly reads the words that are on the page? Certainly, these are significant questions, questions that should trouble Child B's tutor.

How, then, should the tutor respond to word recognition errors that do not cost the young reader meaning? There is no unequivocal answer; again, the specific situation must guide the tutor's response. However, in the examples before us, a reasonable defense can be made for nonintervention on the part of Child A's tutor. Child B's tutor, on the other hand, must begin to focus the child on a closer reading of the text. This may be done by consistently drawing the child's attention to misread words or by having him/her reread certain pages concentrating on word-reading accuracy. Either way, the message must be gotten across that *one should read, for the most part, the words on the page.*

Keep in mind that tutor support during guided reading can take several forms:

- *Comprehension support:* previewing stories, eliciting predictions, checking recall of important information.
- *Contextual reading support:* echo reading and partner reading.
- *Word recognition support:* encouraging word analysis and self-correction, and, if necessary, providing unknown words.

As Beth's reading ability improves over the year, the tutor's support role will change. In September the tutor may have to provide detailed previews of stories and a considerable amount of echo- and partner-reading support. By midyear, the previews may be limited to the story title and opening page picture, echo reading used only on the first page, and partner reading used only now and then to offer Beth a needed break from oral reading. By year's end, it is entirely possible that Beth will be doing almost all the reading by herself; if so, the tutor's major role at this point will be to guide the child's comprehension of the text.

Word Study

The purpose of word study in the fledgling reader stage is to help Beth develop accurate, automatic knowledge of the *short-vowel* patterns. Simple short-vowel words (*hat, bed, job, trip, plum*) best exemplify the alphabetic nature of the spelling system—that is, letters matching to individual sounds:

h	a	t		t	r	i	p
↓	↓	↓		↓	↓	↓	↓
/h/	/ă/	/t/		/t/	/r/	/ĭ/	/p/

The short-vowel patterns (CVC, CCVC, CVCC, etc.) occur frequently in written language and are regular in terms of pronounceability. Moreover, once Beth has mastered them, she will have foundational knowledge against which other vowel patterns can be compared and contrasted (see the following lists).

Short vowels	Other vowel patterns	
mad	lake	tail
let	feet	mean
slip	drive	night
jog	rope	soak
drum	flute	suit

The initial assessment of Beth's reading and spelling ability (see pages 114–115) clearly reveals her need for short-vowel instruction. On the preprimer and primer word recognition lists, she misread the following words:

Word	Beth's response
big	bug
back	duck
pat	put
hid	hide

On the first- and second-grade spelling lists, she misspelled the following words:

Word	Beth's spelling
fill	FEL
mud	MOD
wish	WE
step	SAP
stuff	STOF
shopping	SIPEN
thick	THEK

Beth's short-vowel misspellings are particularly revealing. She perceived the short-vowel sounds in the spelling words, but represented the sounds with non-conventional, phonetically related letters (e.g., E for /ĭ/, O for /ŭ/, and A for /ĕ/). The fact that Beth can "hear" the vowel sounds is a strength; however, she now needs to learn the conventional letter–sound pairings—that is, I for /ĭ/, U for /ŭ/, and E for /ĕ/.

Short-Vowel Word Families

We introduce short-vowel work with a basic short *a* word family sort. In preparation, the tutor accumulates five or six word cards (2" × 3") for each of the following families: *-at, -an,* and *-ap.* For example, *-at* words might include *cat, hat, rat, sat, fat,* and *flat.*

The tutor begins the sort by arraying three known words across the top of the table and the remaining twelve words in a deck below. It is essential that Beth be able to read the three *exemplars* across the top. However, she does *not* have to be able read all the words in the deck at this point.

hat	man	cap

DECK

The tutor begins by pointing out to Beth that the words in the deck can be sorted under *hat, man,* or *cap.* He then slowly picks up the top word in the deck, *pan,* places it under *man,* and reads the two rhyming words aloud.

It is Beth's turn. Picking up the next word in the deck, *lap,* she hesitates.

TUTOR: Where does it go, Beth?

BETH: [Places *lap* under *cap.*] Lap.

TUTOR: Good! [Pointing to the top word in the column] Read both words.

BETH: Cap—lap.

hat	man	cap
	pan	lap

The turn taking continues with the tutor modeling correct responses and Beth receiving immediate feedback as to the correctness of her sorting attempts. Each time a word is sorted, all the words in that column are read aloud, from top to bottom. However, no mention is made by the tutor as to why a word is sorted in a particular category; Beth is left to figure out for herself why certain words go together.

In Lesson 2, the same short *a* words are sorted once again.

hat	man	cap
sat	fan	tap
mat	pan	nap
fat	ran	lap

With the words in column format, the tutor points randomly to individual words, asking Beth to read them (e.g., *hat, pan, lap, ran, sat, tap,* and *fan*). Beth reads each word, hesitating only on *lap*.

To reinforce the short *a* patterns, the tutor introduces the Concentration game. He arrays 12 word cards, facedown, on the table and explains the rules of the game:

1. Turn over a card and read the word. Then turn over a second card and see if you have a match (e.g., *mat—sat*).
2. If you do have a match, pick up the two word cards and go again. If you do not have a match, turn the cards back over and let the other player have a turn.
3. The game is over when all the cards have been picked up. The winner is the player who has made the most matches.

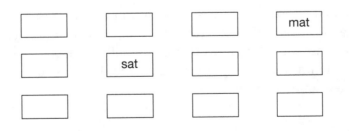

Beth loves Concentration. She has no difficulty reading the short *a* words in isolation and enjoys winning the game (Beth—five matches; tutor—one match).

Lesson 3 introduces a new activity, *spell check*. Following a quick column sort and game of Concentration, the tutor gives Beth a blank piece of paper numbered 1 to 6.

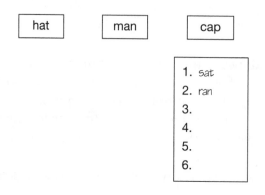

He explains that he is going to dictate some words and Beth is to write them. She can use the word cards on the table (used in the column sort) as a spelling aid. The tutor proceeds to dictate six words (*sat, ran, nap,* etc.). Beth spells each of them correctly without referring to the guide words.

The short *a* word family sorts and accompanying reinforcement activities seem almost too easy for Beth. Nonetheless, the *column sorting* introduces the important idea of categorizing words by pattern; Concentration promotes sight memory of the short *a* words; and *spell check* provides an alternate, visual-motor route for securing the target patterns in memory.

Given Beth's proficiency in reading and spelling the short *a* words over the first three lessons, the tutor may decide to increase the difficulty or challenge level. He can do this by adding a fourth column to the sort (see *-ack* words in the following lists):

hat	man	cap	back
sat	pan	nap	sack
mat	can	clap	
that	plan		

tack?

Another way to increase difficulty is to begin to include consonant digraph and consonant blend words in the sorts (see *that, plan,* and *clap* in the preceding lists). Although the consonant cluster words may initially give Beth some trouble, the word family column sort is a supportive, structured context in which to practice these new letter–sound patterns.

Moving Forward

Once Beth is accurate and fluent in sorting, reading, and spelling the short *a* word families, a second set, short *i* word families, can be introduced.

hit	win	big
fit	pin	fig
bit	tin	dig
sit	chin	twig

The same sequence of reinforcement activities applies to the short *i* word families. When Beth can sort accurately and identify individual words in the columns, the tutor presents the Concentration game. If she is successful in Concentration (i.e., is able to read the short *i* words in isolation), then the tutor begins the spell checks.

When fluency and confidence of response are attained on the short *i* words, the *a* and *i* families are combined in a single sort, as in this example:

cat	fan	hit	big
mat	ran	sit	fig
flat			wig

bit?

Notice that this word family sort above brings vowel discrimination (*a* words versus *i* words) into the process for the first time, foreshadowing the short-vowel pattern work (CVC) that will come later.

At this point in the word sort sequence, the Make-a-Word activity can be used to good effect. The tutor arrays on the table 10 consonant letter cards and the two short vowels (*a* and *i*) that have been introduced thus far.

The tutor begins Make-a-Word by moving down three letter cards to form a simple CVC word:

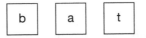

After Beth reads *bat*, the tutor begins to substitute a series of beginning consonant letters (*s, r, n,* and *p*):

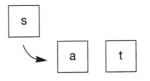

Beth has no trouble reading *sat, rat, nat,* and *pat.* Next, the tutor substitutes a series of ending consonant letters (*pat* to *pan, pan* to *pad, rat* to *rag, rag* to *rap*):

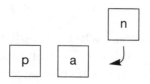

Beth is accurate but a little slower in reading the words resulting from ending consonant changes.

Now the tutor begins to manipulate the vowel letters. With *rap* on the table, he substitutes *i* for *a*:

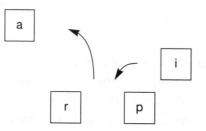

Beth reads *rip* correctly, consciously attending to each letter. The tutor then leads Beth through the following word changes: *rip, rig, rag, lap, lip, fin, fan, bat, lid, pal.* This vowel-changing task forces Beth to attend carefully to each letter in the word; she misreads a few words but overall does well.

The second stage of Make-a-Word involves the tutor saying a word (e.g., *hat*) and Beth moving the letters to form the word. In this "spelling" stage the tutor leads Beth through the same sequence of word changes. That is, first beginning consonants are manipulated ("Beth, make *hat*; now make *mat*"), then ending consonants, and, finally, the vowels.

Make-a-Word can also help Beth with the concept of *consonant blends*. There are 20 two-letter consonant blends that can appear at the beginning of English words. These can be divided into three major groups: *-r* blends, *-l* blends, and *s-* blends:

-r blends	-l blends	s- blends
br	bl	sc
cr	cl	sk
dr	fl	sm
fr	gl	sn
gr	pl	sp
pr	sl	st
tr		sw

Instead of teaching the beginning blends as 20 separate skills, it makes sense to view consonant-blend learning as a conceptual task with three major concepts to be mastered:

- Some consonants blend into -*r* (*br*ag, *cr*ib, *dr*op).
- Some consonants blend into -*l* (*pl*an, *cl*ip, *bl*ock).
- *s*- blends into some consonants (*st*and, *sk*ip, *sp*ot).

Let us consider briefly how Make-a-Word can be used to teach the first of these concepts, -*r* blends.

The tutor begins by placing six consonant letters and two vowels on the table:

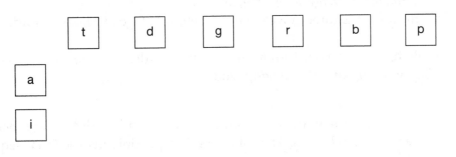

Next, he moves three letters down to form the word *rip*.

After Beth reads *rip*, the tutor moves the *t* card down.

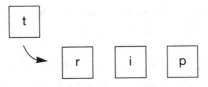

TUTOR: What is this word?

BETH: [Hesitates.]

TUTOR: Beth, we have to blend these first two letters. T-rip [pronounces the word slowly, running his finger under the *t* and *r* as he does so]. Now you try it; point to the letters.

BETH: T-rip [points to the *t* and *r* as she reads the word].

TUTOR: Okay, let's try another one [replaces the *t* with *d*].

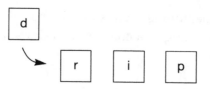

BETH: D-rip [running her finger under the *d* and *r* as she reads].

TUTOR: Good! What about this one? [replaces the *d* with a *g*].

The word making continues with the tutor leading Beth through the following changes: *grip, rap, trap, rag, drag, brag,* and *grab*.

At this point the tutor moves to the "spelling" stage of Make-a-Word.

TUTOR: Beth, now it's your turn to make some words. Make *rag;* now *drag; brag.* Okay, what about *rip*? Now *grip* [and so on].

Obviously, the same Make-a-Word procedure can be used to help Beth decode *-l* blends and *s-* blends. The following is a possible instructional sequence for each blend type:

-*l* blends

Letters needed: *l, p, c, s, f, d, g; a, i*

Word changes: *lap, clap, slap, lip, slip, flip, lad, glad, flag*

s- blends

Letters needed: *s, p, k, m, b, l, n; a, i*

Word changes: *nap, snap, slap, pin, spin, skin, back, nack, snack, smack*

(*Note*: The Make-a-Word sequence described here was borrowed from one of my students, Devery Mock [see Mock, 1996].)

Make-a-Word and *column sorting* are complementary tasks. Whereas column sorting leads Beth to attend to word patterns (*bat, sat, mat, flat*), Make-a-Word leads her to separate words into their individual sounds (*b-a-t, r-a-g, c-l-a-p*). Used together, the two tasks afford Beth needed practice in chunking, taking apart, and then rechunking short-vowel words.

Let us now return to the sequence of word family sorts. After the short *a* and short *i* word families have been mastered, short *o* families are introduced.

hot	top	job
pot	hop	rob
got	mop	mob
shot	stop	Bob

The short *o* and short *i* families are then combined for review:

hot	top	sit	win
pot	hop	fit	tin
not	pop		chin

chop?

The short *u* families are next, followed by the fifth and last set of word families, short *e* (see Appendix 4.2 for a possible sequence of word family sorts).

In Summary. The tutor has led Beth through the short-vowel word families, one vowel at a time (*a, i, o, u,* and *e*). Each vowel has been practiced through column sorting, Concentration, and spell checks. Consonant blends and digraphs were incorporated in the sorts as the child showed mastery of the basic CVC patterns. Make-a-Word was used as needed. Finally, review was provided by overlapping (or combining) a just-taught vowel (e.g., *i*) with a previously taught vowel (*a*).

Individual childen will progress through this short-vowel, word family stage at different rates. There is no need to rush. The tutor must pace instruction so that the child is responding accurately at each level (e.g., *a* and *i*) before moving forward (*o*). Careful teaching at the word family stage will assure a smooth transition to the next stage of word study, *short-vowel patterns.*

Short-Vowel Patterns

Short-vowel words can be categorized in *families* or in *patterns*:

Word family (-at)	Vowel pattern (short a)
cat	cat
mat	bad
hat	tap
pat	ham
flat	plan

In short-vowel word families (see previous section), the vowel and ending consonant remain constant, as does the rhyme. In short-vowel patterns, only the vowel sound (/ă/) and the spelling pattern (CVC) remain constant, thus presenting the child with a more difficult or abstract concept to learn. Difficulty notwithstanding, Beth is ready to study the five short-vowel patterns. She has enough sight vocabulary (known short-vowel words developed through word family sorts) to support learning of the new pattern concept.

Sorting Short-Vowel Patterns

To begin, 18 word cards are needed: six short *a*, six short *i*, and six short *o*. Beth *must* be able to read at least three of the words in each vowel category. The tutor can find these *known* words in previously mastered word family sorts.

Known words	New words
cat	wag
tap	cab
flag	slap
big	hid
win	tip
hit	chin
job	dot
pot	log
mom	drop

The sort begins with the tutor placing three known words on the table to serve as exemplars. He also places three additional known words at the top of the sorting deck.

cat	big	pot

DECK

TUTOR: The words in the deck can be sorted under *cat*, *big*, or *pot*. We are going to try to find words that have the same vowel sound. Okay, you do the first one.

Beth picks up the word *tap*, pronounces it, and places it in the short *a* column under *cat*. The tutor follows by sorting *hit* under *big*; then Beth again, sorting *job* under *pot*. After each sort the tutor points out that words in the same column have the same vowel sound (/ă/, /ĭ/, or /ŏ/). Thus far, no problem; six words have been sorted, and *these were six that Beth could already read*.

cat	big	pot
tap	hit	job

DECK

Now we come to the critical transfer phase of the task. Among the remaining 12 unsorted words in the deck are some *new* words; that is, Beth has either misread them in the past or the tutor suspects that the words may not be in the child's sight vocabulary. As Beth picks up the first new word (*tip*), the following scenario might unfold:

BETH: I don't know this one.

TUTOR: See if you can put it in the right column.

BETH: [Places *tip* under *big*, cueing visually on the *i* in the middle of the word.]

cat	big	pot
tap	hit	job
	(tip)	

TUTOR: [Pointing to *big*] Read down the column and see if that helps you with the new word.

BETH: Big . . . hit . . . t-i-p . . . tip.

TUTOR: Tip—like the tip of your nose. Good!

BETH: [Next, Beth picks up *log* from the top of the deck and quickly places it in the short *o* column.] Pot . . . job . . . l-og . . . log.

TUTOR: Nice going.

Note that the first two words in each column are *known words*. This sets up a situation in which each time the child is faced with decoding a new short-vowel word (e.g., *tip*), she can compare the new word to two known words that have the same visual pattern and vowel sound.

The sort continues, with Beth and the tutor taking turns. Each time a word is sorted, all the words in that column are read aloud. This consistently draws Beth's attention to the spelling–pronunciation relationship, the objective of sorting word cards.

cat	big	pot
tap	hit	job
wag	tip	log
cab	hid	drop
flag	chin	mom

After a few lessons with this three-column sort, the Concentration game and spell check are presented. Concentration is particularly useful at this point. After turning over a word card (see *tip*, in the following illustration), Beth must search her visual memory for matching short *i* words that were turned over earlier in the game. This does require true concentration on short-vowel patterns, albeit within a gamelike activity.

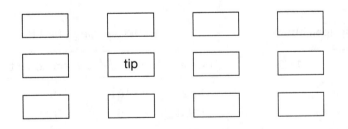

Short *spell checks* provide Beth with auditory–visual–kinesthetic practice with the various short-vowel patterns. After a completed sort, the tutor scoops up the word cards and dictates six or seven spelling words to Beth. Initially, an exemplar for each pattern (e.g., *cat*, *big*, and *pot*) is left on the table to aid the child's spelling. After a few lessons, the exemplars are removed, forcing Beth to spell the short-vowel patterns from memory. Each spell check concludes with the tutor and child correcting any misspellings and then graphing the results (e.g., 6 out of 7 correct) (see Figure 4.3).

Over a few weeks' time, Beth shows some mastery of the *a, i,* and *o* short vowel patterns, and a fourth pattern (*e*) can be introduced. A good way to do this is to contrast the new pattern with two of the old patterns:

hit	top	pet
hid	rob	red
rip	mom	beg
miss	lot	men
swim	drop	less

The introduction of only one new pattern focuses attention on the short *e* words and at the same time allows for important review of the old *i* and *o* patterns.

Finally, it is time to introduce the last short-vowel pattern (*u*). Again, the overlapping of old with new is appropriate:

pot	red	bug
fog	met	rub
mop	hen	bus
spot	bell	cut
lock	mess	club

Up to this point we have seen how the five short-vowel patterns can be taught through column sorting and various reinforcement activities, such as Concentration and spelling. But how does one judge the effectiveness of such instruction? Fortunately, this can be done on a day-to-day basis in several ways:

• *Check speed and accuracy of responses within column-sort format.* After several days' practice with the same column sort, there should be an increase in the speed and accuracy of Beth's sorting responses.

Daily spell check

	11/11/98
1.	ham
2.	~~lod~~ lid
3.	flat
4.	rock
5.	chin
6.	drop
7.	dig

Beth's spelling chart

Date	Number correct		
10/28	⑤	6	7
10/30	5	⑥	7
11/4	5	⑥	7
11/6	5	6	⑦
11/11	5	⑥	7
11/13	5	6	7

FIGURE 4.3. Correcting and charting Beth's spelling performance.

- *Check speed and accuracy of responses within randomized format.* After several days of practice, the tutor can shuffle the 18 or 20 words in a sort and have Beth attempt to read the words in randomized order. The speed and accuracy of her responses will indicate her level of mastery of the specific word patterns being tested.

- *Check transfer to "new" words.* Once Beth seems comfortable sorting a given set of words, the tutor can introduce new words into the sort that fit the same spelling patterns. If Beth is able to sort and read these new words quickly, this is evidence that she is beginning to internalize the spelling patterns.

- *Check transfer to spelling.* Short spell checks following word sorts can also be valuable diagnostically. For example, if, over a few days' time, Beth is consistently accurate in spelling short-vowel words (especially new words not included in a previous sort), this is additional evidence that she is internalizing the target word patterns.

- *Check transfer to contextual reading.* As Beth reads stories aloud, she will come upon many one-syllable short-vowel words in the text. The tutor should watch closely and note the child's success with these words. Accurate reading of short-vowel words in context is, of course, a good sign. Inaccurate contextual reading of these words—especially after considerable word sorting practice—may mean that intervention is needed. For example, after a story or part of a story has been read, the tutor may take Beth back into the text to focus on a short-vowel word (*trap*) that was originally misread. The tutor quickly jots down two known short *a* words (*cap* and *hat*) and has Beth note their similartity to *trap*. The same teaching strategy can be used when Beth misspells a short-vowel word in a writing sample.

The child's mastery of the five short-vowel (CVC) patterns is an important benchmark in learning to read and spell. As she advances through the grades, she will meet these patterns again and again in one-, two-, and multisyllable words found in all types of reading matter (*cap, lad*der, *cat*alyst; *sit; rib*bon, *lit*erate). Mastery at the fledgling reader stage means only that Beth will be able to read and spell the *one-syllable* short-vowel words quickly and accurately. The instructional activities that have been described in this section should lead to this type of mastery.

Easy Reading

Each tutoring lesson, Beth engages in 8 to 10 minutes of "easy" or independent-level reading. Here, she either rereads a previously introduced book or partner reads a new story with the tutor. When easy reading a new book, the tutor adjusts text difficulty by dropping back one *basal* level. For example, if Beth's guided reading level is *primer*, she does easy reading at the *preprimer 3* level; if her guided reading level is *2-1*, she easy-reads at the *1-2* level. The purpose of this activity is to build Beth's sight vocabulary and fluency and to strengthen her confidence as a reader.

The support strategies used by the tutor in *guided reading* (previewing, echo reading, and partner reading) are also appropriate in *easy reading*. However, because the easy-reading text is less difficult in terms of vocabulary load and sentence length, Beth will require less tutor support. A brief story introduction and perhaps one or two pages of echo reading gets Beth started. Partner reading is then used to pace the activity and prevent fatigue (e.g., Beth reads two pages—tutor reads two pages; or Beth reads four pages—tutor reads two pages). Although there are advantages to partner reading, if Beth is "sailing along" in the easy-reading text—reading accurately and fluently—then the tutor should abandon any formulaic sharing strategy and let the child do most of the reading independently.

Easy reading should be an enjoyable, fast-paced part of the tutoring lesson. After selecting a set of books of appropriate difficulty, the tutor may allow Beth to choose the specific stories she wants to read. The child's interest and investment in this activity are important. Easy reading is a time for Beth to orchestrate the reading process, to put the pieces together. It is also a time for her to "shine," to feel the power of her emerging reading skill.

Read to Beth

At the end of each tutoring lesson, the tutor reads to Beth for 5 to 7 minutes. The tutor may read a fairy tale, a fable, a short trade book, or a chapter from a longer book. *Reading-to* serves multiple purposes. First, it rewards Beth for having worked hard during the 45-minute tutoring lesson. Second, the activity allows Beth to extend her language competence (and mental world) by listening to and discussing a text that she cannot read by herself. Third, reading-to can strengthen the interpersonal bond between child and tutor as they share one of life's true pleasures—a well-written story.

Story selection and quality of the tutor's oral rendition of the story are keys to an effective reading-to activity. Story selection, of course, depends on geographic region, culture, community, and the interests of the individual child. Table 4.1 provides a sampling of stories for 7-year-olds that we have used successfully in both urban Chicago and rural North Carolina. (A good children's librarian can quickly come up with many more possibilities.)

The quality of the tutor's oral reading can make or break a reading-to experience. The tutor should choose a story that he/she enjoys, for this will make it easier to read with expression and feeling. As the story is being read, the tutor can stop at times to define unusual words, discuss a picture, or elicit a prediction from the child. However, reading-to is about enjoyment, not recitation, and the tutor should keep this in mind at all times. (*Note*: Some children may prefer that the tutor read content selections [e.g., dinosaurs, the ocean, Native Americans, etc.] instead of narratives. This presents no problem. In fact, the pictures in such content books afford rich opportunities for discussion between child and tutor.)

TABLE 4.1. A Selection of Read-To Stories

Title	Author	Publisher
Beezus and Ramona	Cleary, B.	Dell
Bundle of Sticks, A	Mauser, P.	Atheneum
Dallas Titans Get Ready for Bed	Kuskin, K.	Harper Trophy
Doctor DeSota	Steig, W.	Farrar, Straus, & Giroux
Drinking Gourd, The	Monjo, F. N.	Harper Trophy
How Many Spots Does a Leopard Have?	Lester, J.	Scholastic
John Henry	Keats, E. J.	Dragonfly Books
J.T.	Wagner, J.	Dell
Miss Nelson Is Missing	Allard, H., and Marshall, J.	Houghton Mifflin
Owls in the Family	Mowat, F.	Bantam
Play Ball, Amelia Bedelia	Parish, P.	Scholastic
Random House Book of Fairy Tales, The	Ehrlich, A.	Random House
Robinson Crusoe (abridged)	Lasson, R.	Fearon
Rose for Pinkerton, A	Kellogg, S.	Dial Books
Stone Fox	Gardiner, J. R.	Harper Trophy
Storm in the Night	Stolz, M.	Harper Trophy
Stories Julian Tells, The	Cameron, A.	Random House
Story of Ferdinand	Leaf, M.	Viking
Tailypo, The: A Ghost Story	Galdone, J.	Clarion
Terrible Mr. Twitmeyer, The	Moore, L., and Adelson, L.	Scholastic
Wiley and the Hairy Man	Bang, M.	Aladdin

Writing (Optional)

Writing is an enigma in a tutorial setting. It is obviously an important skill (or language art) for the primary-grade student to work on, but planning for and carrying out meaningful writing activities can be difficult for the tutor. Some children who experience difficulty with reading take to writing "like ducks to water," deriving enjoyment and a sense of pride from their work. Others, however, are so resistant to the writing task that it is not worth the tutor's time and effort to push the activity in the twice-weekly tutoring lessons. Poor spelling ability, a lack of self-confidence, or an unwillingness to share his/her ideas and feelings on paper can all contribute to a child's reluctance to write. Nonetheless, the importance of learning to write cannot be overestimated, and, if time allows, writing should become a part of Beth's tutoring lessons.

One way for the tutor to think about writing in a one-to-one setting is to envision a three-phase process: prewriting, writing, and postwriting.

Prewriting Phase

The prewriting phase involves helping the child to come up with something personally meaningful to write about. Graves (1983) points out that *all* writers, including children, write best when they are drawing on their own experiences or interests. He therefore urges teachers to get to know their children well—their likes, dislikes, and, particularly, their areas of expertise. Interests and areas of expertise will certainly vary from child to child and from time period to time period: for example, pro football to family life, Kung Fu movie characters to baby animals, an airplane trip to New York to a visit by bus to the local zoo. The important point is that a tutor must be knowledgeable about both the sustaining and changing interests of the student over the course of the year.

A helpful strategy in the prewriting phase is the *concept guide*. With the writing topic for the day already selected, the tutor engages the child in conversation on the topic (e.g., visiting the city aquarium). As Beth orally recounts the events in her tutoring group's recent visit to the aquarium, the tutor jots down a few key words on a scratch sheet of paper, as shown here:

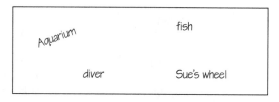

After the prewriting discussion is completed, the tutor hands Beth a fresh sheet of paper and asks her to write a short account of the trip to the aquarium. The scratch sheet with the key words is placed in front of the child, and she is informed that she can use these words, if she wishes, in her story. The concept guide can be very helpful. It can aid the writer in remembering specific events in an experience, and it also provides four "free" spellings, a needed psychological lift for some children.

Writing Phase

Beth writes in an 8" × 11" spiral "writing notebook." The tutor reminds her to write on every other line, for this will make a neater page and leave room for later changes or additions.

As Beth begins to write her story, the tutor also begins to write. The last thing a low-reading second grader (or any other writer) needs is to have an adult looking over her shoulder, inspecting the accuracy of each and every word she puts down on paper. By writing his own story, the tutor not only occupies dead time while the child is writing, but also provides a model of the writing process. For example, out of the corner of her eye, Beth may see the tutor cross through a word, a whole line, or even a paragraph, and begin anew. Or she may see the tutor go back and insert an omitted word in his text by using a caret (^).

The tutor's writing topic should be related to the child's topic, but it need not be identical. For example, instead of writing about the trip to the aquarium, the tutor might write about a remembrance of a childhood trip to a museum. Of course, the tutor does not want to "upstage" the child, so he consciously slows his writing, makes some mistakes and corrects them, and stops now and then to consciously plan upcoming sentences (just as Beth has to do). The tutor's final product is usually longer and better written than the second grader's, but his product should contain ideas, vocabulary, and sentence patterns that Beth can easily understand.

As far as helping Beth in the drafting of her account, the fact that the tutor is writing right along with the child tends to provide a natural barrier to such assistance. However, if Beth does "stop cold" in the act of writing, the tutor can intervene by asking her about her problem. Courses of action might include having Beth reread what she has written up to that point, referring her back to the concept guide, helping her plan a complex sentence, helping her sound through a difficult spelling word, or simply providing the spelling. In any case, the goal is to get Beth back to writing her own story, independently, so that the tutor can return to his.

Postwriting Phase

With the writing sample completed (see Figure 4.4), the tutor asks Beth to read her story aloud. He tells her to feel free to stop and make any changes that seem necessary.

This first reading serves a "proofing" function, as sometimes children will find words that have been omitted (see Beth's insertion of *and* in Figure 4.4) or sentence fragments that "don't sound right."

After Beth has read her story aloud and made any on-the-spot corrections, the tutor immediately responds to the *content* or message in the writing sample, as in the following response:

> I like your story, Beth. You included a lot about our trip to the aquarium. I think the diver feeding the fish was my favorite part of the trip. And I had forgotten that Marvin was the one who reminded us that Sue's car tire was low on air.

I like when we was in the car driveing a rond

it was fun. the fish was swiming in ther

tank. We saw a big fish a little fish. It
$\overset{and}{\wedge}$
was fun when the diver gave the fish there

food and then we had forgot about Sue's whel

and Marvin had told so we went to a

gas stashun.

FIGURE 4.4. First draft of Beth's writing sample.

Positive comments directed to the content of Beth's writing sample are crucial, for such comments let the child know that she has successfully communicated meaning via her writing effort.

After Beth's writing sample has been read and discussed, the tutor reads aloud his sample and asks for comments from Beth. This concludes Day 1 of the writing activity. The prewriting discussion, the actual writing, and a brief sharing of the writing samples can all take place within a 15- to 20-minute time period.

Revision

There should be a purpose for any revision. For example, Beth may want to add information to or improve the clarity of her written account so that it can be shared with other children, taken home to parents, put in the tutoring program's news magazine, or featured in another way. Generally, the tutor allows the child to decide which writing sample, from among two or three, she wishes to revise.

The tutor begins the revision process by having Beth reread her story to see whether she wants to add to or change it in any way (see the original draft). After a quick rereading of her aquarium story, Beth responds, "It's okay." The following dialogue between tutor and child then ensues:

TUTOR: Beth, I have a few questions about your story—some things I'm a little unclear about. In this first part, you say, "I like when we was in the car driving around. It was fun." As a reader of your story, I'm not sure where you were driving to; you just say "driving around."

BETH: We was driving to the Shedd Aquarium.

TUTOR: How could you put that into your story? Where would you put it in?

BETH: [Rereads first two lines.] Up here [pointing to first line]. I could say, "I like when we was in the car driving to Shedd Aquarium."

TUTOR: Good, that makes sense. [Tutor writes *Shedd Aquarium* on a scratch sheet of paper and then hands Beth the pencil.] Okay, Beth, go on and change the first sentence. You don't have to erase, you can just mark through words. [Beth marks through *a rond* and writes *to Shedd Aquarium*.]

Figure 4.5 shows Beth's revisions.

TUTOR: Beth, I've got another question. Down here [pointing to the written story] you say, ". . . it was fun when the diver gave the fish their food and then we had forgot about Sue's wheel and . . ." When did you think about Sue's wheel? When you were watching the fish?

BETH: Marvin's the one who told about Sue's tire being flat.

to Shedd Aquarium
I like when we was in the car driveing a rond

it was fun. the fish was swiming in ther

and
tank. We saw a big fish a little fish. It
^

was fun when the diver gave the fish there

on the way home
food and then we had forgot about Sue's whel
^

and Marvin had told so we went to a gas

stashun. The gas man put aer in the tier and

then we went home

FIGURE 4.5. Example of the revision stage in the writing process.

TUTOR: Okay, but was that when you were watching the fish at the aquarium or when you were heading back home?

BETH: When we were heading home.

TUTOR: Can you make a change to let the reader know that?

BETH: [After rereading] I don't know.

TUTOR: Find where it says, "... we had forgot about Sue's wheel and Marvin told ..." [Beth locates the phrase in the story.] Could we put in, "*On the way home*, we had forgot about Sue's wheel and Marvin told ..."?

BETH: Yeah, yeah.

TUTOR: [Crosses out *and then*, and writes in the phrase, *On the way home*.] Okay, Beth, why don't you read back your story, with the changes, and see if you like it.

BETH: [Reads the story aloud.] I like it better now.

TUTOR: A final question—what happened at the gas station?

BETH: The gas man put air in the tire.

TUTOR: Can you write that sentence at the end? I think readers would like to know that. [Beth writes, *The gas man put aer in the tier and then we went home.*] Good, Beth. Let me read the story back to you, and then maybe you can think of a title. [The tutor reads the revised story aloud.] What would be a good title?

BETH: I know! [And she proceeds to write at the top of the page, *My trip to the Shedd Aquarium.*]

TUTOR: That's a great title. You worked hard on this story today. I think you really improved it by adding more information.

The tutor has been an active participant in the revision process. His questions to Beth regarding story content and his guidance on how to revise were obviously necessary. Even with the revisions, Beth's account of her aquarium trip is far from polished. Nonetheless, the revisions did improve the comprehensibility of the piece, and Beth was led to make most of the changes herself; it is still *her* story expressed in *her* words.

The process of helping a child to revise a piece of writing is not an uncomplicated one. The helping adult must first evaluate the structure and message quality of the child's written account, and then make reasonable suggestions for revision based on the child's cognitive/linguistic capacity to respond to such feedback. In short, things may not go as smoothly as they did in the revision lesson here. Nonetheless, the tutor owes it to a student to tell that child when a piece of his/her writing either is or is not communicating an intended message.

Editing

Editing for correct spelling, punctuation, capitalization, and so forth, is the final step in the postwriting phase. Editing is akin to putting a finish on a well-built piece of furniture. *Not every piece of writing Beth produces needs to be edited, nor should she be held accountable for each and every mechanical error in the pieces she does edit.* Nonetheless, tutor-guided editing of a favorite piece of writing every 2 weeks or so will afford the beginning writer valuable learning opportunities.

The tutor's role in the editing process is twofold: (1) to identify the key skill areas that require work and (2) to put forth specific editing challenges that are within the child's developmental competence. It is not difficult to identify the basic skills a beginning writer needs to work on. The tutor can simply collect three or four writing samples from a given child and then look for *patterns* of error or skill deficiency across the samples. For example, one child may be a fairly good speller but lack knowledge about punctuation. Another may show the reverse pattern—poor speller–adequate punctuation. Still another may be weak in both areas.

Figure 4.6 highlights the errors found in Beth's aquarium story.

Beth misspelled eight words, left out three periods, and failed to capitalize three words. The question facing the tutor is how many errors to include (hold the child responsible for) in a single editing lesson. Obviously, Beth or any other low-reading primary grade student would be overwhelmed by the massive editing assignment suggested in Figure 4.6. To keep editing from becoming a "work camp" experience for the child, the tutor must exercise judgment in selecting items for Beth to edit or correct.

Schwartz (1977) describes an interesting routine for editing. She suggests that the teacher put a check mark (✓) to the left of a line that contains a spelling or punctuation error. The check tells the child that she is to find the error in that line and correct it. For example:

on the way home

1	✓	food ~~and then~~ ‸ we had forgot about Sue's whel
2		and Marvin had told so we went to a gas
3	✓	stashun. *The gas man put aer in the tier and*
4	✓	*then we went home*

The tutor expects Beth to notice and correct the following errors: Line 1, the misspelling, WHEL; Line 3, the misspelling TIER; and Line 4, the omitted period. Correcting three to five errors in a given editing session will provide adequate challenge for Beth.

Initially, Beth may have trouble locating and correcting such errors in her writing. In this case, the tutor needs to intervene with appropriate instruction. With misspellings of "regular" or pattern words, the tutor might provide Beth with a model word to help her with her editing attempt (e.g., provide *keep* as a cue for WHEL, or *fire* as a cue for TIER). With misspellings of "irregular" words (e.g., *our, there*), the tutor may just have to provide the spelling, asking the child to copy it in the text as well as in a special alphabetized writing notebook. In guiding Beth's editing of spelling errors, the tutor should concentrate on basic, one-syllable pattern words (CVC, CVCe, CVVC, CV-r) and high-frequency Dolch-like words (*was, were, come, for*, etc.). These are the word types that will be most useful to Beth in future writing lessons and those that are most likely within her developmental grasp.

After Beth has made her editing corrections, she rereads her rough draft a final time. The tutor then takes the story home with him to type a finished copy. As he types, he corrects any additional spelling and punctuation errors; however, he does not alter Beth's wording. At the next tutoring lesson, Beth draws a picture to go with the typed, finished copy of "My Trip to the Shedd Aquarium."

My trip to the Shedd Aquarium

to Shedd Aquarium
I like when we was in the car driveing ~~a rond~~

it was fun. the fish was (swiming) in (ther)

and
tank. We saw a big fish ‸ a little fish. It

was fun when the diver gave the fish (there)

on the way home
food ~~and then~~ ‸ we had forgot about Sue's (whel)

and Marvin had told so we went to a gas

(stashun.) *The gas man put* (aer) *in the* (tier) *and*

then we went home

FIGURE 4.6. Example of the editing stage in the writing process.

III. REPRESENTATIVE TUTORING LESSONS ACROSS THE YEAR

This section highlights changes in Beth's instruction across a year of tutoring. Again, the first person (I) will be used in referring to the tutor.

Lesson 1 (September 24)

1. **Guided reading.** I choose *Cave Boy* (see illustration), a preprimer 3 book, for our first guided reading lesson. This 26-page book (two to four lines per page) is challenging, but I believe Beth will be able to read it with my support.

Cave Boy (preprimer 3) by C. Dubowski and M. Dubowski (1988, pp. 12–13). Copyright 1988 by Random House. Reprinted by permission.

As we preview the first 13 pages, I explain that Cave Boy is making a birthday present for his chief. Then Beth and I return to page 1 and proceed to echo read the book's first three pages, one page at a time. Beth does well, and I ask her to read the fourth page by herself (i.e., no echoing). She needs help with one word, *What*, but overall seems confident in her ability to read independently. We continue to partner read the book, with Beth taking two pages to my one. I supply difficult words immediately to keep the reading moving along. Beth follows the story line easily and smiles along with the characters at the surprise ending to *Cave Boy*. We are off to a good start.

2. **Word study.** We begin with the short *a* word families (see "Short-Vowel Word Families," page 126). I model the sorting of the first word, *sat*, under *hat*, and then Beth sorts and reads the remaining eight words.

hat	man	cap
sat	ran	tap
mat	pan	lap
flat	plan	map

She has no difficulty with this task, even reading the two consonant-blend words correctly. Next, Beth and I play a quick game of Concentration. Her ability to read most of the short *a* words in this isolated context tells me that we will soon be moving on to short *i* word families.

3. **Easy reading.** Beth reads *Pat's New Puppy*, a preprimer 2 text from the old Scott, Foresman Reading Unlimited series of the 1970s. The natural language, one to two lines of print per page, and supportive picture cues allow Beth to read this story independently.

4. **Read-to.** I read the picture book *Is Your Mama a Llama?* to Beth. She enjoys the riddles that are built into the text as well as the delightful Steven Kellogg illustrations.

Commentary

Beth breezed through this first lesson. Although the guided reading provided some challenge, the word sort and easy reading did not. Over the next few lessons, I will adjust the difficulty level of these activities. The next tutoring lesson will include:

Guided reading: Partner reading *Tiger Is a Scaredy Cat*, a new preprimer 3 tradebook.
Word study: Another short *a* word family sort, reinforced by Concentration and a spell check.
Easy reading: Rereading *Cave Boy*, with Beth doing approximately two-thirds of the reading.
Read-to: Begin reading *Molly the Brave and Me* to Beth.

Lesson 18 (November 24)

1. **Guided reading.** Syd Hoff's *The Horse in Harry's Room*, a primer-level trade book, tells the story of a shy 6-year-old and his imaginary horse (see illustration). Beth and I preview the first 9 pages of the 27-page book and then return to the beginning. We echo read the first three pages and then begin to partner

The Horse in Harry's Room (primer) by S. Hoff (1985, pp. 14–15). Copyright 1985 by Harper Trophy. Reprinted by permission.

read, Beth taking two pages to my one. Beth reads the final seven pages of the story by herself; I provide assistance on two words, *nibbling* and *always*.

2. **Word study.** We begin with a quick Make-a-Word activity (see pages 129–132).

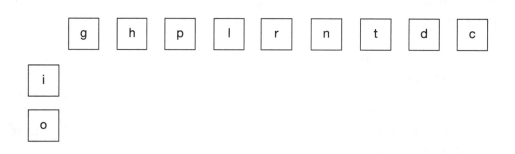

I make the word *hit* and have Beth read it.

Then I change the beginning consonant to produce the following sequence of words: *sit, lit, pit*.

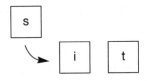

I perform similar beginning consonant changes on the root word *top: pop, hop,* and *chop.* Beth has no difficulty reading these words. Next we work with ending consonant changes. Starting with *hot,* I make *hop,* then *hog;* starting with *lip,* I make *lid,* then *lit.* Beth's responses are a little slower when I change the ending consonant, but she is able to sound through and identify the words. Finally, we move to medial vowel changes: *hip* to *hop,* to *chop* to *chip,* to *lit* to *lot.*

Now it is Beth's turn to make words. I dictate a sequence of words that involve changes in beginning, ending, or medial sounds, and Beth constructs each word by moving the individual letters. She enjoys this activity and is becoming very good at it.

We follow the Make-a-Word activity with Bingo, a variation of column sorting. Each of us has a Bingo card with four columns, as in Figure 4.7.

A player takes a turn by drawing a word card from the deck, placing it in the right column, and reading all the words in that column from top to bottom. "Wild cards" (see smiling faces in the example) can be placed in any column and afford the player another turn. The object of the game is to fill up your Bingo card before your opponent does. Beth eventually wins the Bingo game. She is an excellent player, keeping as close an eye on my Bingo card as on her own.

We conclude the word study with a spell check. Beth spells seven of the eight

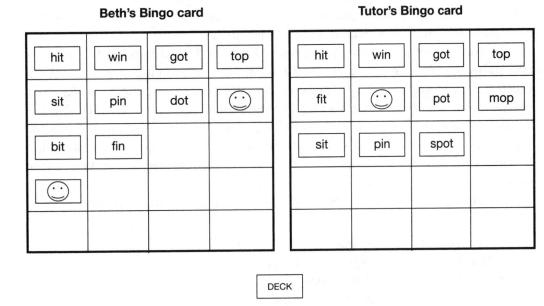

FIGURE 4.7. Example of Bingo game between Beth and her tutor.

short *i* and *o* words correctly, erring only on the consonant digraph, *sh* (CHIP for *ship*).

3. **Easy reading.** Beth reads independently *The Teeny Tiny Woman* from Random House's Step into Reading series. She elects to read by herself and does an excellent job, using picture cues to help with difficult words. When she tires after a dozen pages or so, I read a few pages to give her a break. Then she finishes the last third of the book with a confident flourish.

4. **Read-to.** I read aloud the Southern folk tale *Wiley and the Hairy Man.* We run out of time, and Beth cannot believe that we have to wait 2 days to see how the story will end.

Commentary

Beth is now a solid primer-level reader. Unfortunately, interesting stories written at this mid-first-grade level are hard to find. Complicating matters is the inconsistent readability of the stories found in the new literature basals of the 1990s (see Hoffman et al., 1994). The 1990s basals' deemphasis on word control and word repetition in first-grade stories has produced more lively, literary prose; however, it has created problems for children like Beth who struggle with decoding and sight vocabulary acquisition.

Two factors guide my selection of primer-level stories for Beth—interest and readability. I rely heavily on contemporary trade book collections like Random House's Step into Reading and Harper's I Can Read Books. I also do not hesitate to use older texts from as far back as the 1970s; for example, the Green and Yellow levels of Scott, Foresman's Reading Unlimited, Bowmar's Monster Book series, and Laidlaw's Blue-tailed Horse, a 1980s basal primer.

In guiding Beth's contextual reading, I find that I need to provide less echo- and partner-reading support. Her sight vocabulary is growing steadily, and, on meeting new words in text, she is often successful in sounding them out. At times now, I allow Beth to read past a word recognition error to see whether she will catch her mistake. She usually does so, particularly if the mistake disrupts the meaning of the sentence. This self-correction behavior is a good sign, signaling her growing independence as a reader and her commitment to make it make sense.

In word study, Beth has progressed through the following sequence:

- Short *a* word families (*hat, man, tap, back*)
- Short *i* word families (*sit, win, dig, pick*)
- *a* and *i* families combined (*hat, man, sit, dig*)
- Short *o* word families (*top, job, lot, rock*)
- *i* and *o* families combined (*hit, pick, top, rock*)

The short *e* word families will be introduced next. We are moving slowly but steadily through the short-vowel word family sequence, striving for confident, automatic responding. Column sorts and Make-a-Word are used to introduce new orthographic concepts (vowels, consonant blends, and digraphs); reinforcement games (Concentration, Bingo) and spell checks are used to drive the concepts into memory.

Lesson 34 (February 11)

1. **Guided reading.** Over the past 2 weeks we have been reading selected stories from *Toothless Dragon*, the Level 1-2 book in a 1980s basal reader series (Laidlaw). The stories in this particular 1-2 reader are interesting, and, more important, they feature vocabulary repetition within and across selections.

Today's story, *Kim and Gus*, concerns a little girl who finds a lost dog on her doorstep. Beth and I begin by previewing the first six pages, using the pictures to predict the story line (see illustration). Next, we return to the first page and proceed to partner read *Kim and Gus*, Beth reading two pages to my one. We stop at three points in the well-plotted, 16-page story to check comprehension and make

"Kim and Gus" (Level 1-2) by R. Fairbrother. In W. Eller et al., *Toothless Dragon* (pp. 96–97). Copyright 1980 by Laidlaw Bros. Reprinted by permission.

predictions. Beth's on-the-mark predictions tell me that she is comprehending the story with ease.

Kim and Gus is the fifth story Beth has read in this 1-2 basal, and she is improving with each successive story. I believe that at this stage in her reading development, Beth benefits significantly from the controlled vocabulary and sentence length in this "old" basal reader.

2. **Word study.** Beth has spent several months studying short-vowel words within a rhyming context, as in the following example:

hit	win	pick
fit	pin	sick
bit	tin	lick
kit	spin	stick

Today I introduce short-vowel *patterns* (or nonrhyming words) for the first time. I begin by having Beth read 16 word cards, each containing a short *a*, *i*, or *o* word. She reads 13 of the 16 words correctly, as shown in the following lists:

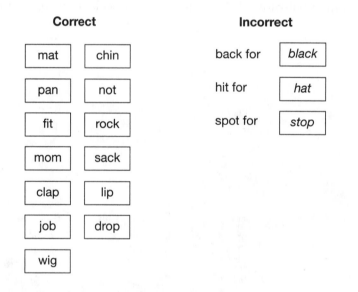

Correct		**Incorrect**	
mat	chin	back for	*black*
pan	not	hit for	*hat*
fit	rock	spot for	*stop*
mom	sack		
clap	lip		
job	drop		
wig			

Next I put three "header" cards on the table (all known words) and explain to Beth that we are going to sort the remaining cards into three columns. I sort the first card (*fit*), and Beth sorts and reads the next two (*pan* and *chin*).

mat	wig	not
pan	fit	
	chin	

After these first three sorts, I stop and ask Beth whether the words in the columns rhyme. She hesitates, and I tell her to read down the short *i* column.

BETH: Wig—fit—chin. No, they don't rhyme.

TUTOR: Right, they don't. Why, then, do we put them in the same column?

BETH: Because they all got an *i*.

TUTOR: Okay. Each of the words has an *i* in the middle. What sound does the *i* make?

BETH: W-i-g. It makes /ĭ/.

TUTOR: Good, Beth. We are sorting these words into a column because they have the same vowel sound. They don't necessarily rhyme, but they have the same vowel sound.

Beth and I continue to sort the words into columns, Beth taking two turns to my one. Interestingly, Beth reads and sorts *back, hit*, and *spot* correctly, each a word that she had misread on the presort flash presentation. Tomorrow we will play Concentration with these short-vowel patterns.

mat	wig	not
pan	fit	mom
back	chin	job
clap	hit	rock
sack	lip	drop
spot		

3. **Easy reading.** Beth reads the first half of Syd Hoff's *Sammy the Seal*, a classic primer-level trade book. She reads independently, needing my help only with a few character names. She loves the book and uses the pictures skillfully to support her oral reading of the text.

4. **Read-to.** We are about halfway through *The Terrible Mr. Twitmeyer*, a chapter book about an apparently heartless dogcatcher in a small town. Beth looks forward to this read-to part of the lesson and is disappointed if we do not get to it because of a lack of time.

Commentary

Beth has made important gains in reading over the past 2 months. She now has a large sight vocabulary, attempts to decode new words in a systematic, sound-it-through manner, and is beginning to read with more fluency and expression. Comprehension is becoming more of an issue as the late-first-grade stories become longer and more complicated. However, the tutor's incidental comprehension checks every few pages ("What do you think will happen next, Beth? Why?") reveal that Beth *is* understanding what she reads.

Beth's guided reading is now divided evenly between trade books and an old 1-2 basal reader (Laidlaw Reading Program, 1980). All basals published prior to 1990 feature controlled vocabulary; what makes the Laidlaw series different is the number of stories at the primer, 1-2, and 2-1 levels that second and third graders seem to find interesting—approximately six to eight per book. Other pre-1990 basals can be used (e.g., Houghton Mifflin Readers [1978] and Holt Basic Reading [1980]); however, one finds that with these programs fewer stories per level (two to four) succeed in capturing the children's interest.

In word study, Beth has progressed to short-vowel *patterns* (e.g., *man, tap, flat; dig, pin, hid*). Given the extensive, systematic work that was put in at the short-vowel *word family* stage (30+ lessons), Beth will in all probability move quickly through the five short-vowel patterns and be ready to take on long-vowel patterns by the end of the school year.

Lesson 54 (April 22)

1. **Guided reading.** *A Girl Named Helen Keller* is a Level 2-1 trade book (44 pages) that does a nice job recounting the story of Helen Keller's remarkable childhood. In lieu of a preview, I read to Beth the first three pages of the book:

> The summer was hot. The year was 1880. Way down south in a little town in Alabama, a healthy baby girl was born. Her parents loved her dearly. Her name was Helen Keller.
>
> Then the baby became ill. She was not yet two years old. Day after day her fever was high. The servants tried to help. Her parents tried to help. The doctor shook his head. "There is nothing more we can do," he said. "The baby may not live."
>
> Helen lived. But she was not the same after the illness. "Something is very wrong," her mother said. At last they found out the truth. The child was deaf and blind.*

With this introduction established, Beth and I begin to discuss the family's predicament.

TUTOR: What does it mean when a child is deaf and blind?

BETH: It means she can't hear or see.

TUTOR: Do you remember how Helen became deaf and blind?

BETH: She was born that way.

TUTOR: Was she?

BETH: No, no. She got real sick and the doctor couldn't help her. And she got deaf.

*From *A Girl Named Helen Keller* (Level 2-1) by M. Lundell (1995, pp. 1–3). Copyright 1995 by Scholastic. Reprinted by permission.

TUTOR: Do you think the fevers might have damaged her brain, the parts of the brain that help us hear and see?

BETH: Yeah.

TUTOR: What kinds of problems do you think Helen will have as she grows up?

BETH: She won't be able to hear her mom, and she won't be able to go outside and see things. And she might trip over things around the house.

TUTOR: What about her parents—will they have difficulty in raising Helen?

BETH: Well, it will be hard to get her to do things, because they can't talk to her. And they might have to guide her around especially when they go outside.

TUTOR: Okay, let's get back to the story. I want you to read the next three pages, Beth.

Beth returns to the story with enthusiasm. In the next few pages, she learns that besides being deaf and blind, little Helen is also bright and spoiled, mimicking her parents' behavior at every chance but refusing to cooperate with their wishes. Beth is hooked! She wants to read the whole story by herself, and I allow her to proceed. We stop a couple of times to discuss Helen's ongoing problems and then put the book down (at its midpoint) after 20 minutes of focused concentration. We will finish the story in our next tutoring session; Beth will make sure of that.

2. **Word study.** Today we continue work on long and short patterns of the vowels *a* and *i*. Beth has little difficulty completing the sort, as shown in the following lists. (*Note*: Each time she sorts a word, I have her read aloud the last three words in that column.)

bad	make	fit	ride
lap	name	big	mine
flat	base	shin	fire
tack	flame	drip	dime
cab	gave	hid	drive

On the spell check, the next activity, Beth spells seven of eight words correctly, erring only on *hid* (her spelling was HIDE).

Beth has been working on these *a* and *i* patterns for three lessons and seems to know them. Today I decide to test her mastery of the patterns with a *timed drill*. To the 20 words in the sort (see the preceding lists), I add 20 more that fit the same patterns. I then shuffle the 40 word cards and flash them to Beth, one at a time, during a 1-minute period. Words read correctly go in one pile, words read incorrectly go in another. In the 1-minute trial, Beth reads 23 words correctly and 4 words incorrectly. We graph the results (as shown here) and agree to take another timed test the next time we meet.

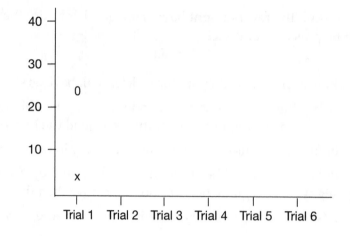

3. **Easy reading.** Beth reads, by herself, "Strange Bumps," an 11-page selection in Arnold Lobel's delightful book *Owl at Home*. She sails through this Level 1-2 story, requiring minimal assistance from me.

4. **Read-to.** No time for this activity today.

Commentary

Beth's reading instructional level is now 2-1. She has sufficient word knowledge to read at this level, although her fluency sometimes falters in reading the early-second-grade stories. The tutor is considering using *repeated readings* during the last month of school to help Beth increase her reading fluency. With this method, Beth will read the *same* instructional-level passage three different times. Each time she will read for 2 minutes, and her goal will be to increase the number of words she reads on successive trials (see Chapter 5, pages 205–208, for a fuller explanation of repeated readings).

At the 2-1 level, the tutor finds it necessary to spend more time on comprehension; simply put, there is more to remember and understand in these longer stories. An informal "predict-read-confirm" strategy is used to help Beth think her way through the text, and, with the tutor's guidance, this comprehension strategy seems to be working well (see Chapter 5, pages 175–187, for an explanation of how to teach comprehension).

In word study, Beth has progressed through the following sequence over the course of the year:

- *Short-vowel word families*: *a, i, o, e,* and *u* (33 lessons)
- *Short-vowel patterns*: *a, i, o, e,* and *u* (6 lessons)
- *Mixed vowel patterns*: short, long, r-controlled:
  — Across A: *a, a-e, ar* (7 lessons)
  — Across I: *i, i-e, ight* (5 lessons)
  — Across A and I: *a, a-e, i, i-e* (3 lessons)

Note that Beth spent well over half of the year (39 of the 54 lessons so far) internalizing the basic short-vowel patterns, including consonant blends and digraphs. With this foundation in place, she has, in the last 2 months, begun to study vowel-pattern contrasts—short versus long versus r-controlled. This vowel pattern study will continue to the end of the school year. With the help of word sorts, reinforcement games, spell checks, and copious amounts of "instructional-level" reading, Beth has made critical gains in word knowledge that will serve her well as she enters third grade in the fall.

IV. ASSESSMENT OF PROGRESS

Tutoring a fledgling reader like Beth can and should be a stimulating, rewarding experience. Feedback to the tutor is ample, for the fledgling reader's behavior—oral reading, story discussion, word sorting, writing, and spelling—is "on the table," visible and consistent from lesson to lesson. This section describes some ways for the tutor to observe, reflect on, and even chart a fledgling reader's progress over the course of a school year.

Informal Assessment during the Course of Tutoring

Contextual Reading

Beth will be doing most of her reading orally, particularly during the first two-thirds of the year, and her lesson-to-lesson oral reading will provide the tutor with ongoing opportunities for assessment. Among other things, the tutor will be observing Beth's reading accuracy, word attack strategies, self-correction behavior, and fluency.

At times Beth may read a word in a sentence by relying on meaning and word-order cues, along with the beginning consonant letter:

> Little mouse ran down to the highway.
>
> *went*
> He wanted to see the cars go by.

Little or no meaning is lost in Beth's reading of the second sentence. Nonetheless, she was not paying close attention to the individual letters in the word *wanted*. The tutor should be conscious of such errors and exercise judgment in responding to them. If meaning-preserving errors of this type occur rather infrequently in Beth's reading, they can be ignored. If, on the other hand, she seems to be overrelying on such a contextually based decoding strategy, her attention should be called to specific words in the text. In some cases, the tutor may stop the reading at the end of a sentence and go back and "lead Beth through" an analysis of a target word. In other cases, the tutor may call the child's attention to given word-reading errors after the entire story has been completed. The point is that Beth must be led to apply whatever letter–sound knowledge she possesses (often demonstrated during word sort activities) to the task of reading words in context.

In the preceding example, Beth's word-reading error preserved the meaning of the text. But what about instances in which her error disrupts passage meaning?

> Tom looked in the paper. "Now I
>
>   who   sū-per
> know how I can surprise Grandma and
>
> Grandpa," he said. "They need a
>
> cookie jar."

Although Beth's reading of the second line in this passage made no sense, she read on, paying little attention to this fact. How is the tutor to respond? The simple answer is, *demand meaning*. If a child's first reading of a sentence does not make sense, the tutor asks the child to reread the sentence. Often, she will be able to *self-correct* her word recognition error on the second reading; if not, the tutor can then provide assistance.

One way to measure improvement in Beth's oral reading ability over time is to consider the *amount of tutor support* she requires in reading instructional-level text. Here, the support-reading cycle (echo, partner, and independent reading), described earlier in reference to instruction, becomes important diagnostically. Suppose Beth has just advanced from a 1-2 to a 2-1 reading level. Initially, the new second-grade stories prove challenging, and the tutor finds that he and Beth need to *echo read* the first four pages of each story before *partner reading* the remaining pages. After a couple of weeks at the 2-1 level, the tutor finds that Beth needs echo-reading support on only the opening one or two pages of a story, and that in the partner-reading phase she can read two pages to the tutor's one. A month later, the tutor notices that Beth can now read a 2-1 story *independently*, requiring only comprehension guidance and occasional help with a difficult word. This dimunition of tutor support over time—or, put another way, Beth's increasing independence at the 2-1 level—is a solid sign of progress. (*Note:* During any lesson throughout the year, the tutor can check Beth's oral reading ability by scoring her reading of a 100-word passage taken from a guided reading selection. If Beth is placed at the appropriate level, she should read with 92% to 95% accuracy and adequate fluency [see "Scoring" under "Oral Reading," Chapter 2, pages 28–33]).

Word Knowledge

Short-vowel patterns were the focus of Beth's word study program. She began her study of short-vowel words by working in a word family or rhyming context (*hat, sat, flat*); next she progressed to patterns, or nonrhyming words (*hat, fan, trap*); and, finally, she learned to contrast short-vowel patterns with other vowel patterns (*hat, sad* versus *made, late* versus *car, hard*). It is important to remember that consonant digraphs (*ch, sh, th,* and *wh*) and consonant blends (*bl, cl, dr, tr, sm, st*) are an integral part of word study at this short-vowel stage.

As a fledgling reader works through this short-vowel sequence, the *word sort* teaching approach, with its accompanying games and spell checks, affords the tutor continuing opportunities to assess the child's progress. The tutor looks for increasing accuracy and automaticity as the child sorts words by pattern, reads them in isolation, and spells them. After a given set of word patterns has been *mastered* (see short *i* word families in Figure 4.8), the word set should be recorded on a wall chart, giving both the child and tutor a sense of what has been accomplished and what comes next.

When the word family chart has been completely filled in, a short-vowel chart can be presented, signaling a new stage in the word study program. In Figure 4.9 are representative wall charts for short-vowel patterns and long-vowel patterns.

Writing–Spelling

If Beth has had little opportunity or encouragement to write in school using invented (or phonetic) spellings, we should not be surprised if she is initially reluctant to write during the tutoring lessons. Accordingly, the tutor's first task is to get Beth to put pencil to paper, to risk expressing her ideas in writing. The child's

Word Families

A	cat	man	mad	back
	mat	ran	dad	tack
	bat	fan	had	sack
	flat	plan	glad	black
I	sit	win	big	sick
	kit	tin	wig	pick
	fit	pin	pig	lick
	hit	twin	twig	stick
O				

FIGURE 4.8. Charting mastery of short-vowel word families.

Short-Vowel Words

short a	short e	short i
cap		big
sat		hit
fan		win
clap		trip

short o	short u
top	
hot	
job	
rock	

Long-Vowel Words

long a	long e	long i
make	meet	ride
name	week	bike
race	seen	mile
plate	sleep	slide

long o	long u
rope	
coke	
home	
wrote	

FIGURE 4.9. Charting mastery of short- and long-vowel patterns.

willingness to do so can be assessed in several ways. The tutor can note the following factors over the course of a few months:

- Beth's verbal and nonverbal responses, positive and negative, to writing tasks.
- Her desire to choose her own topics for writing versus consistent reliance on the tutor for writing ideas.
- Her feelings of pride and ownership ("Can I take this one home?") regarding certain pieces of writing.
- Her tendency, over time, to produce longer and longer pieces of writing (e.g., increasing from a one-sentence writing sample during the first week of tutoring, to a three-sentence sample 6 weeks later, and finally, to a full-page, six-sentence sample at year's end).

Closely related to Beth's willingness to write is the amount of support she requires to complete a piece of writing. Such tutor support may be required at different levels in the writing process. As noted earlier, Beth may need help in choosing a topic. She may also require assistance in sequencing a series of ideas (What should I say next?), in turning a single thought into sentence form (How can I say it?), or in spelling certain words. The tutor will want to monitor, in the lesson plan evaluations, changing patterns over time in the child's need for such writing support.

Because writing, unlike reading, leaves a permanent product, Beth's spelling attempts across writing samples will provide a rich source of data for tutor assessment. Three areas of spelling assume special importance at this fledgling reader stage:

- *Beth's ability to commit to "spelling memory" a growing number of high-frequency function words* (e.g., *the, is, at, to, it, was, in, and,* etc.). Beth's internalization of these frequently occurring spellings will speed her writing and free up mental effort for other areas of the process.
- *Her growing mastery of the regular one-syllable spelling patterns in English* (CVC, CVCe, CVVC). The tutor should monitor closely Beth's short-vowel spelling attempts; does she begin to use the conventional vowel letter (BED for *bed*), or does she continue to use the phonetic substitution (BAD for *bed*)? Later in the year the tutor might watch for the appearance of long-vowel markers in Beth's spellings (SEET for *seat*, RANE for *rain*). This, too, will be an important sign of progress in her spelling development.
- *Her willingness to risk in the spelling of difficult words.* For example, instead of checking with the tutor on the correct spelling of a word like *elevator*, will Beth use her sound awareness and letter knowledge to risk an invented spelling of the word (e.g., LAVATR)? Such risk taking will not only lessen her dependence on the tutor, but will also exercise and extend her ability to "spell by ear."

Punctuation, capitalization, and appropriate sentence structure (absence of sentence fragments and run-on sentences) are also potential areas for writing assessment in the fledgling reader stage.

An 8½″ × 11″ spiral notebook of 50 pages or so can be an excellent vehicle for organizing and preserving a sequential record of Beth's writing. Over a few months' time, Beth will doubtless begin to derive a sense of pride from the amount of writing she has done in her notebook. Each piece of writing should be dated, and the tutor, by referring to specific "past" and "present" writing samples, can make Beth aware of her improvement in such visible areas as length of individual writing samples, quality of handwriting, appropriate use of capitalization and punctuation, and accurate spelling.

On occasion, perhaps once a month, Beth may decide to "publish" one of her writing samples. This will involve working with the tutor in revising and editing the original draft, copying it over, and providing an illustration. The tutor then types a final copy of the piece and assists Beth in choosing a suitable cover (construction paper) for the typed copy.

Beginning-of-Year/End-of-Year Assessment (Beth)

PRETEST (SEPTEMBER)

	Word recognition (graded lists)		Oral reading	
	Flash (%)	*Untimed (%)*	*Accuracy (%)*	*Rate (wpm)*
Preprimer	65	75	96	45
Primer	30	40	82	31
1-2	—	—	—	—

Spelling: No. of words spelled correctly—List 1 (2 of 10); List 2 (0 of 10)
Developmental stage—Early-Phonetic

POSTTEST (MAY)

	Word recognition (graded lists)		Oral reading	
	Flash (%)	*Untimed (%)*	*Accuracy (%)*	*Rate (wpm)*
Preprimer	95	100	—	—
Primer	85	95	98	77
1-2	75	90	96	75
2-1	55	85	95	66
2-2			92	62
3	30	60	84	48

Spelling: No. of words spelled correctly—List 1 (7 of 10); List 2 (1 of 10)
Developmental stage—Within-Word Pattern

This pretest–posttest comparison shows that Beth has made more than a full year of reading progress. Unable in September to read a primer or mid-first-grade passage, in May she is reading at a solid second-grade level. Beth's flash (and untimed) word recognition scores, along with her oral reading scores, support a 2-1 to 2-2 instructional level.

Beth's posttest spelling performance (shown in the following chart) is also encouraging.

Spelling word	Pretest (September)	Posttest (May)
bike	BIC	BIKE (c)
fill	FEL	FIL
plate	PAT	PLAET
mud	MOD	MUD (c)

Spelling word	Pretest (September)	Posttest (May)
flat	FLAT	FLAT (c)
bed	BED	BED (c)
drive	JRIV	DRIV
chop	GOP	CHOP (c)
wish	WE	WISH (c)
step	SAP	STEP (c)
plant	PLAT	PLAT
dress	JRES	DRES
stuff	STOF	STUF
chase	GAS	CHASE (c)
wise	WISS	WIZE
shopping	SIPEN	SHOPING
train	—	TRANE
cloud	KOD	CLOWD
thick	THEK	THIKE
float	FLOT	FLOTE

The posttest spellings show that Beth has moved into the *Within-Word Pattern* stage of spelling development. She spelled correctly 8 of the 20 words. In her misspellings, she represented short vowels conventionally (FIL, DRES, STUF), marked long vowels (PLAET, TRANE, FLOTE), and showed good knowledge of consonant blends and digraphs. The value of a developmental perspective on learning to spell is quite apparent in this case. Even with Beth spelling fewer than 50% of the words correctly on the May posttest, it is still clear, given the quality of her misspellings, that she has advanced significantly in her conceptual understanding of the English spelling system.

The test results shown at the beginning of this section reveal the solid progress Beth has made in reading and spelling. At the end of first grade Beth was significantly behind her classmates in reading. At the end of second grade she is almost on grade level. With the help of systematic, one-to-one tutoring, she has closed the "reading gap" between herself and her peers. It is true that Beth will enter third grade in the fall reading a little more slowly and a little less confidently than some of her *on-grade-level* classmates. Nonetheless, this child has shown that, given the appropriate conditions, she is capable of making normal progress in reading, one year of achievement for one year of instruction. If—and this is a big *if*—Beth is placed at the appropriate reading level (2-2) and receives adequate instruction in third grade, she should continue to advance at an acceptable rate in learning to read. Such a positive and clearly possible third-grade scenario would highlight the role that timely and focused one-to-one tutoring can play in preventing reading failure in the primary grades.

APPENDIX 4.1. Books for Beth Listed by Difficulty Level

For *preprimer 3* books that Beth might read at the beginning of the year, refer to Appendix 3.1 at the end of Chapter 3 (preprimer 3 corresponds to Levels 7 and 8 in the appendix).

The following are books that range from *primer* through *late-second-grade (2-2)* in difficulty.

Title	Level	Author/Series	Publisher
All Stuck Up	Primer	Step into Reading	Random House
Baby Moses	Primer	Step into Reading	Random House
Chester	Primer	Hoff, S.	Harper Trophy
Clifford, the Big Red Dog	Primer	Bridwell, N.	Scholastic
Clifford, the Small Red Puppy	Primer	Bridwell, N.	Scholastic
David and the Giant	Primer	Step into Reading	Random House
Hello House	Primer	Step into Reading	Random House
Kiss for Little Bear, A	Primer	Minarik, E.	Harper & Row
Noah's Ark	Primer	Step into Reading	Random House
Sam and the Firefly	Primer	Eastman, P. D.	Random House
Sammy the Seal	Primer	Hoff, S.	Harper Trophy
Sir Small and the Dragonfly	Primer	Step into Reading	Random House
Stanley	Primer	Hoff, S.	Harper

(For additional primer-level books, see Levels 9 and 10 in Appendix 3.1.)

Title	Level	Author/Series	Publisher
Addie's Bad Day	1-2	Robins, J.	Harper Trophy
Bike Lesson, The	1-2	Berenstain, S. and J.	Random House
Days with Frog and Toad	1-2	Lobel, A.	Harper Trophy
From Caterpillar to Butterfly	1-2	Heiligman, D.	HarperCollins
Ghosts: Ghostly Tales	1-2	Schwartz, A.	Harper Trophy
Happy Birthday, Little Witch	1-2	Hautzig, D.	Random House
How Kittens Grow	1-2	Selsam, M.	Scholastic
How Puppies Grow	1-2	Selsam, M.	Scholastic
Morris the Moose	1-2	Wiseman, M.	Scholastic
Oscar Otter	1-2	Lobel, A.	Harper Trophy
Small Pig	1-2	Lobel, A.	Harper Trophy
Sword in the Stone, The	1-2	Hello Reader	Scholastic

(For additional Level 1-2 books, see Levels 11 and 12 in Appendix 3.1.)

(cont.)

APPENDIX 4.1 (cont.)

Title	Level	Author/Series	Publisher
Baby Animals	2-1	Podendorf, I.	Children's Press
Beavers Beware	2-1	Brenner, B.	Bantam
Big Cats	2-1	Milton, J.	Grosset & Dunlap
Boney Legs	2-1	Cole, J.	Scholastic
Chang's Paper Pony	2-1	Coerr, E.	Harper Trophy
Clara and the Book Wagon	2-1	Levinson, N.	Harper
Daniel's Duck	2-1	Bulla, C. R.	Harper
Dinosaur Days	2-1	Milton, J.	Random House
Fox and His Friends	2-1	Marshall, E.	Puffin
Fox at School	2-1	Marshall, E.	Puffin
From Tadpole to Frog	2-1	Pfeffer, W.	HarperCollins
Girl Named Helen Keller, A	2-1	Lundell, M.	Scholastic
Greg's Microscope	2-1	Selsam, M.	Harper
Henry and Mudge and the Happy Cat	2-1	Rylant, C.	Aladdin
Hill of Fire	2-1	Lewis, T.	Harper
Jafta's Father	2-1	Lewin, H.	CarolRhoda
Juan Bobo: Four Folktales	2-1	Bernier-Grand, C.	Harper
Little Poss and Horrible Hound	2-1	Hooks, W.	Bantam
Molly the Brave and Me	2-1	O'Connor, J.	Random House
No Good in Art	2-1	Cohen, M.	Dell
Outside Dog, The	2-1	Pomerantz, C.	Harper
Peach Boy	2-1	Hooks, W.	Bantam
Poppy Seeds, The	2-1	Bulla, C. R.	Puffin
Shortest Kid in the World	2-1	Bliss, C.	Random House
Sitting Bull	2-1	Penner, L.	Grosset & Dunlap
Snakes	2-1	Demuth, P.	Grosset & Dunlap
Statue of Liberty, The	2-1	Penner, L.	Random House
Tales of Oliver Pig	2-1	Van Leeuwen, J.	Puffin
Volcanoes	2-1	Nirgiotis, N.	Grosset & Dunlap
Wagon Wheels	2-1	Brenner, B.	Harper
Way Down Deep	2-1	Demuth, P.	Grosset & Dunlap
What's Alive?	2-1	Zoehfeld, K.	Harper
When Will We Be Sisters?	2-1	Kroll, V.	Scholastic
Wiley and the Hairy Man	2-1	Bang, M.	Aladdin
Abe Lincoln's Hat	2-2	Brenner, M.	Random House
Beauty and the Beast	2-2	Hautzig, D.	Random House
Best Friends	2-2	Kellog, S.	Puffin

(cont.)

APPENDIX 4.1 (cont.)

Title	Level	Author/Series	Publisher
Bravest Dog Ever, The: The True Story of Balto	2-2	Standiford, N.	Random House
Christopher Columbus	2-2	Krensky, S.	Random House
Dolphins	2-2	Bokoske, S.	Random House
Drinking Gourd	2-2	Monjo, F.	Harper
Elephant Families	2-2	Dorros, A.	HarperCollins
George Washington's Mother	2-2	Fritz, J.	Grosset & Dunlap
Headless Horseman	2-2	Standiford, N.	Random House
Hungry, Hungry Sharks	2-2	Cole, J.	Random House
Jacques Cousteau	2-2	Greene, C.	Children's Press
Josefina Quilt Story	2-2	Coerr, E.	Harper Trophy
Kate Shelley and the Midnight Express	2-2	Wetterer, M.	CarolRhoda
Keep the Lights Burning, Abbie	2-2	Roop, P. and C.	CarolRhoda
Little Soup's Hayride	2-2	Peck, R. N.	Dell
Little Sureshot . . . Annie Oakley	2-2	Spinner, S.	Random House
Long Way to a New Land, The	2-2	Sandin, J.	Harper Trophy
Mare for Young Wolf, A	2-2	Shelfelman, J.	Random House
More Stories Julian Tells	2-2	Cameron, A.	Harper
Rachel Carson, Friend of Nature	2-2	Greene, C.	Children's Press
Roberto Clemente, Baseball Superstar	2-2	Greene, C.	Children's Press
Stories Julian Tells	2-2	Cameron, A.	Harper
Tornadoes	2-2	Hopping, L.	Scholastic
True Story of Pocohontas, The	2-2	Penner, L.	Random House
Twisters	2-2	Penner, L.	Random House
Warrior Maiden, The: A Hopi Legend	2-2	Schecter, E.	Bantam
Whales: Gentle Giants	2-2	Milton, J.	Random House
Who Eats What? Food Chains	2-2	Lauber, P.	HarperCollins

The following *basal readers,* if they can be located, are recommended for use with Beth. They are listed here in order of priority.

(cont.)

APPENDIX 4.1 (cont.)

1. *Laidlaw Reading Program* (1980). River Forest, IL.
   Primer: *Blue-Tailed Horse*
   1-2: *Toothless Dragon*
   2-1: *Tricky Troll*
   2-2: *Wide-Eyed Detectives*
2. *Houghton Mifflin Reading Series* (1978). Boston, MA.
   Primer: *Honeycomb*
   1-2: *Cloverleaf*
   2-1: *Sunburst*
   2-2: *Tapestry*

3. *Holt Basic Reading* (1980). New York.
   Primer: *A Place for Me*
   1-2: *A Time for Friends*
   2-1: *People Need People*
   2-2: *The Way of the World*

These older basals, although not perfect, contain some good stories written in acceptable language. The books can be ordered from the following used-textbook company. Be forewarned, however, that tutoring programs around the country have bought up many of these particular titles.

Follett Educational Services   www.follett.com
5563 South Archer Avenue
Chicago, IL 60638   Tel. 800-638-4424

APPENDIX 4.2. Short-Vowel Word Families and a Possible Sequence of Word Family Sorts

Short-Vowel Word Families

cat	man	cap	back
mat	can	lap	tack
sat	van	nap	rack
pat	ran	tap	sack
rat	fan	map	pack
flat	pan	sap	black
hat	plan	clap	track

hit	big	win	sick
sit	fig	tin	kick
fit	wig	pin	lick
pit	dig	fin	pick
kit	pig	grin	tick
bit	twig	chin	trick
knit		spin	brick

hot	top	sock	look
pot	pop	rock	book
lot	cop	lock	took
not	hop	block	cook
got	mop	clock	hook
shot	stop	knock	shook
spot	drop		

pet	red	tell	hen
met	bed	sell	pen
set	fed	fell	men
wet	led	well	ten
let	sled	bell	then
jet	shed	shell	when
get		smell	

cut	bug	run	luck
nut	hug	gun	duck
but	dug	fun	suck
hut	rug	sun	stuck
shut	jug	stun	truck
	slug		

(cont.)

APPENDIX 4.2 (cont.)

Possible Sequence of Word Family Sorts

<u>cat</u>	<u>man</u>	<u>lap</u>	
sat	fan	map	← ———— (Sample word family sort)
fat	pan	tap	
mat	ran	cap	
flat	can	clap	

<u>cat</u>	<u>man</u>	<u>lap</u>	<u>back</u>	← ———— (Column headers for next sort)*

<u>hit</u>	<u>big</u>	<u>win</u>	
<u>hit</u>	<u>big</u>	<u>win</u>	<u>kick</u>

Review:

<u>cat</u>	<u>man</u>	<u>hit</u>	
<u>cat</u>	<u>man</u>	<u>hit</u>	<u>big</u>

<u>hot</u>	<u>top</u>	<u>sock</u>	
<u>hot</u>	<u>top</u>	<u>sock</u>	<u>look</u>

Review:

<u>hit</u>	<u>win</u>	<u>hot</u>	
<u>hit</u>	<u>win</u>	<u>hot</u>	<u>top</u>

<u>pet</u>	<u>red</u>	<u>tell</u>	
<u>pet</u>	<u>red</u>	<u>tell</u>	<u>hen</u>

Review:

<u>hot</u>	<u>sock</u>	<u>pet</u>	
<u>hot</u>	<u>sock</u>	<u>pet</u>	<u>hen</u>

<u>cut</u>	<u>bug</u>	<u>run</u>	
<u>cut</u>	<u>bug</u>	<u>run</u>	<u>luck</u>

Review:

<u>pet</u>	<u>tell</u>	<u>cut</u>	
<u>pet</u>	<u>tell</u>	<u>cut</u>	<u>run</u>

Note: Every underlined word on the page (e.g., <u>back</u>) represents a column header for a potential sort. Under <u>back</u> might be sorted *sack, pack, tack, black,* etc.; under <u>lap</u> might be sorted *map, tap, cap, clap,* as shown in the first example sort.

CHAPTER 5

Curt, the Late-First-to Second-Grade-Level Reader

Our final case study concerns Curt, an 8-year-old third grader. In a sense, it is inaccurate to label Curt a "beginning reader," his performance on the initial assessment tasks being clearly superior to that of Atticus (Chapter 3) or Beth (Chapter 4). Still, Curt is among the lowest readers in his third-grade class, and his teacher questions how much he is actually benefiting from the daily reading instruction being offered in a second-grade (2-2) basal reader. The classroom teacher also states that Curt's confidence in himself as a reader is low and seems to be getting lower with each passing week. This child can rightly be called a "reader at risk."

I. SUMMARY OF INITIAL READING ASSESSMENT

	Word recognition (graded lists)		Oral reading	
	Flash (%)	Untimed (%)	Accuracy (%)	Rate (wpm)
Primer	100	—	—	—
Preprimer	95	100	98	68
1-2	75	95	97	65
2-1	50	75	90	44
2-2			84	36
3	20	40	—	—
4	—	—	—	—

Spelling: No. of words spelled correctly—List 1 (6 of 10); List 2 (0 of 1?)
Developmental stage—Phonetic/Within-Word Pattern (correc short vowels; inconsistent marking of long vowels)

Curt's word recognition performance was strong on the three first-grade lists (preprimer, primer, and 1-2). However, he could identify only 50% of the second-grade words on the flash presentation and only 20% of the third-grade words. In addition, his correct word recognition responses were not always automatic. Figure 5.1 shows Curt's word recognition protocols for the 1-2 and second-grade lists.

The word recognition protocols reveal several of Curt's strengths and some identifiable weaknesses. Notice that he made few errors on one-syllable short-vowel words. He also seems to know the beginning consonant blends and digraphs (e.g., *smell, shot, priz,* etc.). On the other hand, Curt's performance deteriorated on the third-grade list, which features multisyllable words. There is also some indication that he has not automatized certain long-vowel patterns ("smell" for *smile,* "got" for *gate,* "priz" for *prize*) and r-controlled vowel patterns ("peefit" for *perfect,* "harcut" for *haircut,* and "father" for *farther*).

Curt's *oral reading* was accurate, but relatively slow (for a third grader, anyway) on the first-grade passages. There was a marked decline in both his accuracy and rate on the 2-1 passage, and he reached frustration on the 2-2 passage. Figure 5.2 shows the coding of Curt's reading of the 2-1 passage.

On the *spelling* task, Curt's errors showed characteristics of both the *Letter-Name* and *Within-Word Pattern* stages of development.

1-2				**Second**		
	Flash	*Untimed*			*Flash*	*Untimed*
1. leg				1. able	old	✓
2. black				2. break	book	brek
3. smile	smell	✓		3. pull		
4. hurt				4. week		
5. dark				5. gate	got	✓
6. white				6. felt	feelt	0
7. couldn't	colder	✓		7. north		
8. seen				8. rush		
9. until				9. wrote		
10. because				10. perfect	peefit	prefik
11. men	man	✓		11. change		
12. winter				12. basket		
13. shout	shot	0		13. shoot		
14. glass				14. hospital	hŏspel	✓
15. paint				15. spill	spell	✓
16. children				16. dug	bug	✓
17. table				17. crayon	carrion	carry-on
18. stand	star	✓		18. third		
19. head				19. taken		
20. drove				20. prize	prĭz	0
% correct	75	95		% correct	50	75

FIGURE 5.1. Curt's word recognition performance on the 1-2 and second-grade lists.

hug-H
A hungry wolf can eat 20 pounds of meat

sing-le
at a single meal. That's like eating one

of
hundred hamburgers. To get all this meat,

hurt
wolves usually hunt big animals like deer

mice
mose
and moose. But a hungry wolf will chase

ĕven ✓
and eat ⓐ rabbit or a mouse. It may even go

fishing! Wolves live in groups called packs.

H
The pack members "talk" to each other with their

Then
bodies. When a wolf is scared, it holds its

ears close to its head. When a wolf is happy,

top
it wags its whole tail. If it wags the tip,

watch out! It is getting / ready to attack.

FIGURE 5.2. Coding of Curt's reading of a 2-1 passage (100 words). From *Wild, Wild Wolves* by J. Milton (1992, pp. 15–16). Copyright 1992 by Random House. Reprinted by permission.

First-grade list		Second-grade list	
1. bike	BIKE (c)	1. plant	PLAT
2. fill	FIL	2. dress	DRES
3. plate	PLAT	3. stuff	STOF
4. mud	MUD (c)	4. chase	CHAS
5. flat	FLAT (c)	5. wise	WISS
6. bed	BED (c)	6. shopping	SHOPING
7. drive	DRIV	7. train	TRANE
8. chop	CHOP (c)	8. cloud	CLOD
9. wish	WICH	9. thick	THIK
10. step	STEP (c)	10. float	FLOT

Curt spelled six of the ten first-grade words correctly, but misspelled all ten second-grade words. In his spellings, he represented short vowels conventionally (FIL for *fill*; DRES for *dress*) and showed good knowledge of consonant clusters (*PLAT*, *TRANE*, and *THIK*). These are characteristics of a speller at the Within-Word Pattern stage. However, Curt reverted to the Letter-Name stage when he failed to mark long vowels in several words (e.g., DRIV, CHAS, and FLOT). Overall, Curt's spellings reveal a sound but still-developing grasp of one-syllable word patterns that is in line with his late-first- to early-second-grade word recognition ability.

These assessment results indicate that Curt is a late-first-grade to early-second-grade reader. He possesses a solid base of first-grade word knowledge, although there is some question as to how fully he has automatized this knowledge. A lack of word recognition automaticity may, in fact, be contributing to this child's slow, potentially debilitating, word-by-word reading style.

Word recognition and reading fluency aside, given Curt's 1-2 to 2-1 reading level, comprehension will certainly be a major instructional focus in his tutoring program. Curt's ability to comprehend what he reads—an area not addressed in this initial assessment—will have to be monitored closely as tutoring begins.

II. TEACHING STRATEGIES

Curt's tutoring program will include work in the areas of (1) comprehension, (2) word study, and (3) reading fluency. Contextual reading, as opposed to skill work, will be the cornerstone of Curt's program. In fact, the tutor's main challenge will be *to guide*, in as skillful a manner as possible, Curt's reading of good stories written at an appropriate level of difficulty. This guided reading will serve to do the following:

- Strengthen Curt's comprehension of narrative and content texts.
- Build his sight vocabulary.
- Increase his reading fluency.

In addition to guided reading, the tutoring program will include specific activities (e.g., *word sort* and *repeated readings*) designed to improve Curt's word recognition ability and reading fluency.

Curt's lesson plan will be similar to Beth's (Chapter 4):

Beth's Lesson Plan (45 minutes)

1. Guided reading of new material (18)
2. Word study (10)
3. Easy reading (10)
4. Tutor reads to Beth (7)

Curt's Lesson Plan (45 minutes)

1. Guided reading of new material (22)
2. Word study (8)
3. Easy reading (8)
4. Tutor reads to Curt (7)

The only difference in the two plans is that in Curt's lesson a few minutes have been borrowed from *word study* and *easy reading* to increase the time allotted to *guided reading*.

This section describes, in detail, teaching strategies that address the needs of a struggling reader like Curt. (*Note:* If writing is to be included in Curt's program, refer to "Writing," Chapter 4, pages 139–145).

Guided Reading

Partner Reading

Partner reading, one form of guided reading, often begins with a preview. That is, before reading a selection, Curt and the tutor "walk through" the pictures on the first four to six pages, speculating on what is happening in the pictures and what may happen later in the story. The child and tutor then return to the opening page and begin to partner read (alternate pages), with the tutor usually taking the first turn.

Partner reading is a safe, comfortable way to begin reading stories with a slow, word-by-word reader like Curt. Basically, it involves the tutor and child alternating pages as they read a story aloud, with the tutor asking comprehension questions now and then. Given that this is the same procedure used with Beth (Chapter 4) in reading *preprimer* stories, why use it with Curt, a child with a good deal more reading skill?

There are several reasons that partner reading is a very legitimate way to begin one's work with a first-grade-level reader. First, partner reading is psychologically appealing to the child (in this instance, Curt) because he can perceive the tutor, from the start, as an equal partner who is willing to share the reading load. Over the course of a few weeks, the tutor may well decide to reduce the amount of reading that she does in the lesson; still, in the beginning sessions, many children benefit from the tutor's being an active and equal participant in the reading. A second and related advantage of partner reading is that the tutor's oral reading of every other page provides a fluent model for the child to emulate. It was noted in the initial assessment that Curt tends to read in a word-by-word monotone. Such a beginning reader can benefit significantly from hearing and following along visually with the tutor's intonated oral reading of the alternate pages of the story. A third advantage of partner reading, although one not restricted to this format, is the fact that Curt is reading aloud, thereby providing important opportunities for the tutor to diagnose his reading skill.

The weakness of partner reading at the first-grade-reader stage is the lack of focus on comprehension. With the fledgling reader, Beth, it was perfectly appropriate to partner read the short preprimer stories, stopping now and then for brief, ad hoc comprehension checks. The story lines were uncomplicated, and, in truth, accurate contextual reading by the child was as important a tutoring concern as comprehension. With Curt, however, we have a different situation. Curt can read the words in the first-grade stories. Therefore, the major goal should be to help him become an active, critical comprehender of the stories he reads—a goal not so easily accomplished through the ad hoc, make-them-up-as-you-go-along questions characteristic of partner reading.

A first step toward helping Curt with his reading comprehension involves making slight modifications in the partner-reading procedure. For example, before reading a story, the tutor asks Curt to make a *prediction* about the story's content based only on the title and the first-page illustration. Then, after reading a few pages, he is asked if he wishes to keep or modify his original prediction, and *why*. The same predict-read-confirm strategy is repeated at subsequent points until the story is completed. The prediction questions, when thoughtfully interjected and followed up ("Why do you predict that, Curt?"), will lead the child to take an active, personal interest in the story being read.

As Curt progresses in his tutoring program, moving from a first- to second-grade reading level, there will be a gradual transition from oral reading to silent reading. Regarding tutor guidance, the aforementioned prediction-oriented comprehension strategy will increase in importance. It is to this strategy that we now turn.

The Directed Reading–Thinking Activity (DRTA)

Russell Stauffer, a famous reading educator at the University of Delaware, coined the acronym DRTA (Directed Reading–Thinking Activity) in the mid-1960s. Reacting to the sterile methods of teaching comprehension in the basal reader programs of his day, Stauffer was searching for a new approach—a teaching approach that would demand active, creative decision making of both students and teacher as they read and discussed a story together. Thus was the DRTA born. Before discussing this teaching strategy, however, let us look briefly at a few of Stauffer's assumptions regarding reading comprehension.

Drawing on the early work of John Dewey (*How We Think*, 1916), Stauffer (1970) conceptualized reading as a thinking activity. He argued that the comprehending reader, either adult or child, is engaged in a cyclical process of (1) constructing hypotheses or anticipations about upcoming ideas or events in a passage, (2) testing these hypotheses as he/she reads further, either confirming, disconfirming, or partially accepting them, and (3) constructing new hypotheses based on information presently available.

Make hypothesis 1 → Read → Confirm/disconfirm/partially accept (hypothesis 1)

Make hypothesis 2 → Read → Confirm/disconfirm/partially accept (hypothesis 2)

Make hypothesis 3 → (and so on)

We can readily see that Stauffer viewed reading comprehension not as a *product* (the passive retention of information read), but rather as a *process* (the active construction of meaning through critical interaction with the author's words).

Anticipating by some 25 years a major trend in reading research, Stauffer also argued that comprehension is, in a very real sense, an individual or personal matter. He believed strongly that individual children bring their own distinctive background experiences and thinking styles to the reading of a given story, and that these personal characteristics play a major role in how a child will comprehend the story. For example, a primary-grade story about a young boy on a fishing trip with his dad might be comprehended quite differently by an inner-city child who has never been fishing than by a rural child who, along with his best friend, visits the local pond almost every Saturday morning. This is not to say that in a class of 25 children, there will be 25 different interpretations of a story's message. Stauffer was pointing out, however, that an effective teacher of comprehension will show insight and flexibility in evaluating the background experiences and thinking strategies of individual readers.

With these ideas—comprehension as *hypothesis testing* and comprehension as *an active interaction between the individual and the text*—firmly in mind, Stauffer developed the Directed Reading–Thinking Activity (DRTA). The key terms are *directed* and *thinking*. The teacher directs or guides the reading in such a manner that the child is led to interact with the story in an active, problem-solving manner. At this point, let us use an actual first-grade story to illustrate the DRTA process.

A Model DRTA Lesson

To the reader of this manual: Read the story in Figure 5.3, "Lita's Plan." As you come to each *stopping point* (/) marked in the text, ask yourself what you are thinking at that moment, specifically what you anticipate happening next in the story.

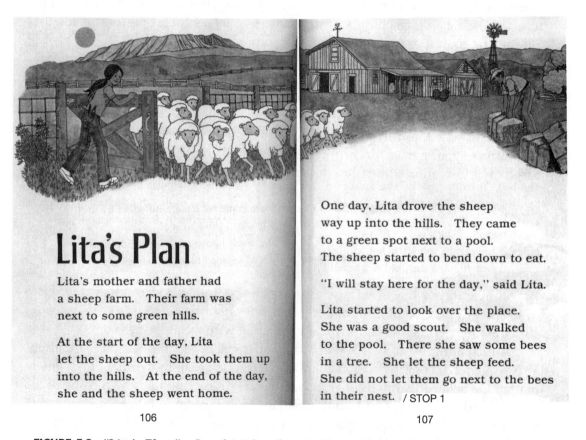

Lita's Plan

Lita's mother and father had a sheep farm. Their farm was next to some green hills.

At the start of the day, Lita let the sheep out. She took them up into the hills. At the end of the day, she and the sheep went home.

One day, Lita drove the sheep way up into the hills. They came to a green spot next to a pool. The sheep started to bend down to eat.

"I will stay here for the day," said Lita.

Lita started to look over the place. She was a good scout. She walked to the pool. There she saw some bees in a tree. She let the sheep feed. She did not let them go next to the bees in their nest. / STOP 1

106   107

FIGURE 5.3. "Lita's Plan," a Level 1-2 basal story. From *Moving On* (1980, pp. 106–111). Copyright 1980 by the American Book Company.

It was a hot day. Not a cloud
was in the sky. Lita sat in the shade
of a tree. Then she took out
her slingshot. To make the day
go by, she shot nuts from the tree
into the pool.

Lita was a fine shot. "I will send
the nuts into the pool," she said.
"One by one! There they go!"

108

As Lita sat with her slingshot,
she saw a big, tan cat. It was
under the tree where the bees had
their nest. The cat wanted to get
at the sheep.

Lita let out a shout, "Go! Go!"
But the cat didn't run. He stayed
still. He was waiting to get
a sheep. Lita had to think fast. / STOP 2

109

In a flash, Lita had a plan.
She took her slingshot. Then she
took a nut. She didn't want
to hit the cat. She wanted
to hit the nest, but she didn't
want to smash it.

110

The nut hit the nest with a
loud crash. The bees came flying
out. They went for the big cat.

Lita shouted with joy as the cat ran off.
She was very proud of the fine shot
she had made. She was proud
of the bees, too! / STOP 3

111

The following dialogue shows how Curt, an 8-year-old inner-city child, might respond to "Lita's Plan" and the comprehension questions accompanying it.

Opening Questions

TUTOR: The title of this story is "Lita's Plan." Can you point to Lita in the picture? [Curt points to the girl in the picture.] Where do you think Lita lives?

CURT: On a farm.

TUTOR: Okay. What kind of plan do you think Lita may have?

CURT: [No response.]

TUTOR: Have you ever had a plan to do something?

CURT: Uh huh. I planned to go on the train to my grandma's house.

TUTOR: Good. Well, it looks as though this young girl, Lita, is going to plan to do something in this story. Do you have any idea what it might be? Look at the picture.

CURT: She might be planning to find a lost sheep.

TUTOR: Could be. I want you to read pages 106 and 107, and we will find out a little more about Lita.

Stop 1

TUTOR: Were you right about where Lita lived? You said on a farm.

CURT: Yes. She lives on a sheep farm.

TUTOR: What is her job each day?

CURT: She looks after the sheep.

TUTOR: How does she look after them?

CURT: She takes them way up in the hills to a swimming pool, but there were some bees there.

TUTOR: You mean a swimming pool with a diving board and lifeguard and everything?

CURT: Yeah.

TUTOR: Would you find that type of swimming pool way up in the hills where sheep graze? I want you to read the top part of page 107 once again to see where Lita took the sheep. [Curt reads the first four lines on page 107.]

CURT: She took them to some green grass near the swimming pool. [Tutor explains that "pool" in this story refers to a small body of water like a pond. It is not a concrete swimming pool like one you would find in the city.]

TUTOR: Curt, you mentioned bees before. What do you think might happen next in this story? Remember, at first you predicted that a sheep was going to get lost. Do you still think that's going to happen?

CURT: I think a sheep is going to go near the bees and get stung, and the girl is going to have to help the sheep.

TUTOR: All right, good prediction. Let's read pages 108 and 109 and see what happens.

Stop 2

TUTOR: Do you want to change your mind about what might happen in this story?

CURT: Yeah! I think the big cat is going to go after one of the sheep and the girl will shoot the cat with the slingshot.

TUTOR: Okay. The cat wants to get at the sheep. Do you think Lita is in danger?

CURT: Yes. If she shoots that cat, he might get mad and come after her. Then she's really in trouble.

TUTOR: By the way, what kind of cat is it?

CURT: A mountain cat. It's big and mean and likes to eat sheep.

TUTOR: All right. The title of the story is "Lita's Plan." Now tell me once again what her plan is going to be.

CURT: When the mountain cat goes after the little sheep, Lita's going to shoot the cat with her slingshot and he's going to run away.

TUTOR: Okay. Let's read to the end of the story and see what happens.

Stop 3 (End of Story)

TUTOR: What was Lita's plan?

CURT: She shot at the bees' nest, and the bees came flying out after the cat, and he ran away.

TUTOR: Was that her plan, or did she hit the bees' nest by accident?

CURT: That was her plan.

TUTOR: Can you read me the sentences that show it was a real plan and not an accident? Look here on page 110. [Child finds the sentences and reads them aloud.] Good. Now do you think it was a good plan?

CURT: Yeah.

TUTOR: Why?

CURT: Because the cat went away.

TUTOR: Okay. But could something have gone wrong?

CURT: Uh huh. She could have missed the nest and hit the cat. Then she'd have been in real trouble.

TUTOR: What else could Lita have done?

CURT: She could have yelled for help, but nobody was around.

TUTOR: What would have happened if she had just tried to take the sheep home?

CURT: The cat would have followed them.

TUTOR: Curt, you really read this story well. One last question—did you like it?

CURT: It was all right!

In analyzing the preceding DRTA dialogue, let us focus on (1) the predictions made by the child, (2) the specific guidance offered by the tutor, and (3) the nature of the dialogue between child and tutor.

Predictions

Curt made three predictions during his reading of the story:

> *Opening prediction:* She might be planning to find a lost sheep.
> *Stop 1 prediction:* I think a sheep is going to go near the bees and get stung, and the girl is going to have to help the sheep.
> *Stop 2 prediction:* When the mountain cat goes after the little sheep, Lita's going to shoot the cat with her slingshot and he's going to run away.

With regard to the actual ending or climax of "Lita's Plan," none of these predictions are correct. However, when we take into account the points at which Curt made the three predictions (at the *beginning* and at *one-third* and *two-thirds* of the way through the story), each of them becomes a perfectly reasonable hypothesis. This is an important point. The tutor, having preread the story, knows how the plot eventually unfolds. However, in evaluating the child's predictions at the various stopping points, the tutor must take into consideration only the information available to the child at a particular point in the story. For example, if the child's prediction at Stop 2 is a logical one based on information read up to that point, it should be accepted, even acknowledged by the tutor as an example of good thinking. If the prediction is illogical ("off the wall," if you will), the tutor can probe for the child's reasons and possibly have him return to the text for a rereading. The major point is that the child should be allowed to read the story "on his own terms" as long as he honors the information in the story line. The tutor's task is *not* to correct the child's predictions; the story line will do this as the child reads on. Rather, the task of the tutor is to listen carefully to the child's answers, to hold him to a reasonable ("within reason") interpretation of the unfolding plot, and to be continually evaluating the quality of the child's thinking.

Guidance

In a DRTA lesson, the eliciting of predictions from the child at various stopping points in the story is one type of guidance offered by the tutor. A second way to guide the reading lesson is to ask a few specific questions at the stopping points that check the child's understanding of key information in the story. These comprehension checks are very important when working with a remedial reader like Curt. Let us examine a few questions in the preceding DRTA dialogue.

Sometimes the child responds quickly and accurately to the tutor's question:

TUTOR: What is her [Lita's] job each day? (Stop 1)

CURT: She looks after the sheep.

TUTOR: By the way, what kind of cat is it? (Stop 2)

CURT: A mountain cat. It's big and mean and likes to eat sheep.

The tutor may choose to acknowledge such correct answers with a nod or a verbal "Okay." In either case, she matter-of-factly moves on, mentally noting that the child is picking up and adequately interpreting important information in the story.

On other occasions, the child's responses to comprehension checks may be incomplete or confused. Consider the following example:

TUTOR: How does she look after them [the sheep]? (Stop 1)

CURT: She takes them way up in the hills to a swimming pool, but there were some bees there.

TUTOR: You mean a swimming pool with a diving board and lifeguard and everything?

CURT: Yeah.

TUTOR: Would you find that type of swimming pool way up in the hills where sheep graze?

CURT: [Silence.]

TUTOR: I want you to read the top part of page 107 once again to see where Lita took the sheep. [Curt reads the first four lines on page 107.]

CURT: She took them to some green grass near the swimming pool. [Tutor explains the alternative meaning of the word *pool*.]

In this example, the tutor posed a question and the child's answer was somewhat lacking. After some probing, the tutor directed Curt to reread a small section of the story to clarify his understanding. Even after this rereading, Curt still did not recognize that the word *pool* referred to a small body of water—a pond. Thus, the tutor provided the needed definition. (Note that when she asked Curt to reread, the tutor designated the page—even the location on the page—where the needed information was to be found. This was to save time and make the important task of rereading less arduous for the child.)

In summarizing this section, there seem to be two distinct types of "guiding" questions in the DRTA. At each stopping point, one or two specific questions related to the story content will induce the child to attend closely to important information as he reads. On the other hand, prediction questions will require him to synthesize the incoming information and make thoughtful projections forward into the story. It is the tutor's skillful, timely use of both types of questions that will produce beneficial comprehension lessons.

The Nature of the Dialogue

The dialogue between tutor and child in a well-run DRTA should be *conversational* in nature—an informal discussion about unfolding events in a story. Such a dialogue cannot be accomplished in a traditional question–answer paradigm:

> Tutor, who knows *the* → Child must produce
> answer, asks a question.   the "right" answer.

In this paradigm, the tutor is the final arbiter of truth. The child ends up reading the story for the tutor's purposes, not his/her own, and an equal, open exchange of ideas does not occur.

Certainly, as we have seen before, direct questions do have a role to play in the DRTA process. Such questions serve as a check on the child's ongoing comprehension of important story information. However, it is the DRTA prediction questions that open up the comprehension lesson. The prediction questions serve as "pivot points" that facilitate discussion between child and tutor. By making predictions about upcoming events in the story, Curt is setting his *own* purposes for reading. The tutor's task, then, is to "climb into the child's mind" and attempt to understand his predictions and the reasoning underlying them. This will lead to honest questions that will inspire trust between the two participants:

TUTOR: What do you think will happen now?

[Child makes prediction.]

TUTOR: Why do you think that, Curt?

[Child gives reasons.]

TUTOR: Okay, I think I see what you're getting at. That makes good sense. Let's read on and see what happens.

One may question why the adjective *conversational* is used in characterizing the optimal DRTA dialogue. Why not a *problem-solving* dialogue or an *open-ended* dialogue? The reason is this: To an outside observer the interaction between tutor and child in a skillfully run DRTA does resemble a conversation, a give-and-take of ideas noticeably lacking in rigidity or authoritarianism. Establishing such a conversational style is not easy. Personality, judgment, and practice all figure into the equation. However, the tutor who is willing to listen carefully to what a child has to say will have a head start toward becoming an effective user of the DRTA.

Planning a DRTA Lesson

The real learning and teaching in a DRTA lesson occurs during the guided reading of the story—in the child's mind as he/she purposefully reads a section of the text, and in the minds of both child and tutor as they dialogue about the unfolding plot. Such learning–teaching cannot be totally prescribed beforehand, because the DRTA process encourages the child to read each story (or section of a story) from his/her own personal perspective. In this way, the reading will always be alive with possibilities, with potential. The spontaneity of the process notwithstanding, a successful DRTA lesson does require a certain amount of *preplanning* on the tutor's part. As we shall see, such planning supplies a needed structure or stage on which the action (learning) can be played out.

The planning process can be described in a straightforward manner:

1. *Read the story through from beginning to end.* This step will take only a few minutes' time.

2. *Go back through the story and choose appropriate stopping points.* Having read the story once (Step 1), the tutor knows the plot. On this second reading, therefore, the tutor should be consciously considering three or four breaks or *stopping points* in the story that lend themselves to questions about what has happened thus far and what might happen as the story continues. Although the choosing of good stopping points is very important, there is no mystery to the task. While reading, the tutor must simply ask, At what point in the story am *I* able to anticipate an important upcoming event or plot turn? Why am I able to do so? What information have I read that is triggering the anticipation?

3. *Plan questions to be asked at the stopping points.* The reasoning involved in choosing a given stopping point (Step 2) should immediately make available to the tutor several questions that can be asked at that stopping point. Therefore, it is suggested that the tutor plan questions for each stopping point as it is sequentially chosen (i.e., choose Stop 1—plan questions for Stop 1; choose Stop 2—plan questions for Stop 2; and so on).

The mechanics of preplanning a DRTA lesson involve (a) marking the stopping points in the text (penciled-in slash marks will do), and (b) writing out possible questions to be asked at each stopping point.

Figure 5.4 provides a useful scheme or design for planning. With slight modifications, this scheme can be applied to the planning and teaching of different types of stories across the grade levels. Notice that in the hypothetical DRTA plan in Figure 5.4 the tutor decided to divide the story into four parts (see Roman numerals I–IV). Such a decision must be based not only on logical prediction points within the story, but also on the story's length. For example, a tutor may believe that a child's motivation and concentration can best be maintained if the reading is stopped every two pages or so for discussion. This would lead the tutor to divide a nine-page story into at least four sections. Over time, as the child's reading fluency and ability to concentrate improve, the number of stopping points in a given story can be reduced.

Having considered the issue of *how many* stopping points to select, let us move through Figure 5.4 from top to bottom, examining the questioning sequence in this particular DRTA plan.

Beginning of Story

In this story, the title and first page picture lent themselves to a global prediction (PQ^1) about the story plot. Be forewarned, however, that not every story title and

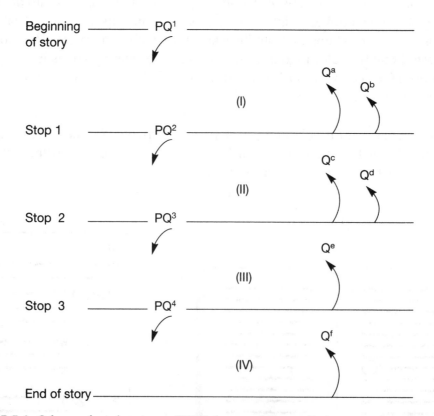

FIGURE 5.4. Schema for planning a DRTA lesson. PQ, prediction question; Q, question back into the story.

opening illustration will be so obliging. Asking a child to predict from such innocuous titles as "Benjie" or "The Bike" can, if one is not careful, create an artificial, uncomfortable beginning to the reading lesson. Therefore, if the title and picture do not lend themselves to an opening prediction, do not press the child to make one. Simply begin reading the story and wait for a more natural point to begin the prediction process.

Stop 1

At Stop 1, after Part I has been read, three questions are planned: Q^a, Q^b, and PQ^2. The first two questions (Q^a and Q^b) seek information about the story setting and the characters that are introduced on the first two pages. The third question (PQ^2) asks the child if he/she wants to keep or change his/her original prediction (PQ^1)—and why or why not.

Stop 2

For Part II of the story, three more questions are planned. Two of these (Q^c and Q^d) check the child's comprehension of plot-relevant information. The third question (PQ^3) asks the child to predict what might happen next in the story.

Stop 3

The questioning at Stop 3 can be handled in two different ways. One way combines a retelling question with a prediction question. Begin by asking the child *to retell* (Q^e) what happened in the section he/she has just finished reading—Part III. If the child's summarization of the events is incomplete, the tutor can probe for further information. If necessary, the tutor can have the child reread parts of the text. With the retelling established, the stage is set for the prediction question (PQ^4); for example, "Based on what you've told me, what do you think will happen now?" Used judiciously, certainly not at every stopping point, the retelling *plus* prediction strategy can be a useful questioning sequence.

An alternative questioning strategy at Stop 3 simply involves asking the child how he/she thinks the story will end (PQ^4). A follow-up question ("Why do you predict that?") may be appropriate, but one does not want to overquestion at this crucial juncture in the story. Elicit the prediction; that is, have the child make an intellectual commitment based on what he/she has read, and then allow the child to read to the end.

End of Story

Questioning at the end of a story can and should be handled in several different ways, depending on the particular story being read. Sometimes a straightforward recap question is called for: "How did it end?" or "Was your prediction correct?"

For other stories a possible "moral" might be pursued. For still others, alternative endings can be discussed, taking into account the logic of and possibilities suggested in the plot. If this course is taken, the tutor often finds that the child's suggestions reflect reasoning and imagination superior to that found in the original story line. One final way to handle end-of-story questions is simply to omit them. On occasion, the tutor will be able to see in the young reader's nonverbal behavior (a smile of satisfaction or a quick look up at the tutor to share the "moment" of comprehension) that the final plot turn has been understood. In such cases, there is good reason to omit preplanned questions that could prove to be redundant and artificial.

The DRTA planning scheme (Figure 5.4) is not intended to be a recipe or set of detailed, sequential steps for planning (and teaching) each and every story. The scheme is systematic only in its broad outline—that is, read the story through one time; go back through the story and choose stopping points; develop questions for each stopping point. In every other respect, flexibility is the key:

- Different stories will have a different number of stopping points (1–5), depending on their length, plot structure, density of ideas, and so forth. Moreover, two tutors could choose different, but equally good, stopping points for the same story. There is no formula to follow at this stage.

- It has been noted that not every story title will lend itself to an opening prediction, nor will every story require a postreading discussion.

- At some stopping points, only a single prediction question may seem appropriate. At others, the tutor may feel obligated to check, via several questions, the child's comprehension of important information in the section just read.

- Although *stopping point* and *prediction* usually go hand-in-hand, there is no ironclad rule that a prediction question must be asked at each stopping point. Within some stories, both good and poor ones, there may be only one or two points where a logical prediction can be made by the reader. Instead of abandoning the story (not enough prediction points), the tutor may choose to designate the customary three to four stopping points, but ask the child to make predictions only at those points in the story where it is reasonable to do so.

- Finally, and possibly most important, the preplanning of questions does not mean that all of them must be asked in the actual teaching of the story. For example, in many cases, a child's response to the first question at a stopping point (Do you want to change your original prediction? Why or why not?) will include the answer to another question that had been planned for that stopping point. Obviously, the tutor will not go ahead and ask a question whose answer has already been supplied. On a more subtle note, it must be reemphasized that the question-and-answer dialogue between child and tutor should be alive with possibilities. If a preplanned question tends to deaden this dialogue, no matter how relevant it appeared to be at the planning stage, that question should be omitted. The decision to omit (or alter) questions must, of course, be made in the act of teaching, and such on-the-spot judgments will improve with experience. Again, the neophyte tutor is urged to pay close attention to the child's verbal and non-verbal behavior during the questioning phase. Take your cue from the child's responses as to whether the preplanned questioning sequence is appropriate. At all costs, do not become a slave to a rigid, preplanned script of questions at each stopping point.

Word Study (One-Syllable Vowel Patterns)

Earlier in this manual we considered the teaching of beginning consonant letter–sound relationships (Chapter 3, "Atticus") and the teaching of word families, short vowels, and consonant blends (Chapter 4, "Beth"). Now we are ready to take up another important aspect of word recognition training—that is, the teaching of high-frequency one-syllable vowel patterns.

Figure 5.5 shows a basic word study sequence for first- and second-grade readers.

Beginning consonants	Word families*	Short vowels*	One-syllable vowel patterns
b	-at	*a* hat	(a) mat
c	-an		lake
d	-ap		car
f	-ack		tail
g			
h	-ed	*e* pet	(e) leg
j	-et		seed
k	-ell		meat
(etc.)			he
	-it	*i* big	(i) kid
	-ing		ride
	-ig		bird
	-ick		light
	-ot	*o* top	(o) job
	-op		rope
	-ock		coat
			born
	-ut	*u* rub	(u) bug
	-ug		mule
	-ub		burn
	-uck		juice

FIGURE 5.5. Sequence of word study instruction. Beginning consonant digraphs (*ch, sh, th, wh*) and beginning consonant blends (*bl, dr, st,* etc.) are introduced at the word-family and short-vowel levels.

In the figure, think of each element in a given column as representing a particular word pattern. For example, -at in the word family column might stand for *hat, mat, cat, sat,* and *rat; big* (short *i*) in the short-vowel column might stand for *big, hit, lid, fin,* and *clip;* and *lake* in the vowel-pattern column might stand for *lake, made, race, name,* and *tape.* It is the teaching and learning of such word patterns that concerns us in this manual.

The sequence of instruction depicted in Figure 5.5 moves from left to right. In fact, a child's learning of concepts further along the continuum (e.g., high-frequency vowel patterns) will depend, in large part, on the child's mastery of concepts introduced earlier (word families, short vowels). To this end, there is overlap built into the instructional sequence that facilitates the learner's movement from one conceptual level to the next. For example, mastery of *beginning consonants* prepares the child for word family sorts. Proficiency in reading and spelling the short-vowel rhyming words (*word families*) leads naturally into work on the five short-vowel patterns. And mastery of the *short-vowel words* ensures that the child will bring important knowledge to the one-syllable vowel-pattern stage.

Over the years scholars have repeatedly stressed the importance of beginning readers internalizing the basic, one-syllable spelling patterns in the English orthography (Calfee, 1982; Fries, 1962; Gibson & Levin, 1975; and Gray, 1960, among others). More recently, Adams (1990) and Perfetti (1992) have argued that automatized knowledge of syllable patterns is *the* central factor in fluent contextual reading. Curt, our first-grade-level reader, has not yet mastered the high-frequency syllable patterns (CVC, CVCE, CVVC, and CV-r); he is not consistently accurate and automatic in reading and spelling them. Therefore, helping Curt to learn and then "overlearn" these patterns will be a major goal of the tutoring lessons.

The word sort or word categorization approach that has been used throughout this manual lends itself nicely to work with vowel patterns. Before moving, however, to a detailed description of how to conduct "vowel pattern" word sorts with a child, let us consider the specific patterns that will be sorted (see Figure 5.6).

	CVC	CVCe	r-controlled	CVVC
(a)	mat	rake	car	rain
	ran	name	hard	mail
(e)	leg	—	—	meet (beat)
	bed	—	—	feel (seal)
(i)	kid	ride	girl	—
	big	like	bird	
(o)	job	rope	born	boat
	not	home	fort	foam
(u)	bug	mule	turn	juice
	rub	cute	curl	fruit

FIGURE 5.6. High-frequency spelling patterns for each of the five vowels.

The preceding chart shows 17 distinct, frequently occurring vowel patterns. It also shows how these patterns are structurally related. For example, looking vertically down the columns, one finds the basic vowel-pattern classifications (CVC, CVCe, CVVC, and CV-r). And looking horizontally across the rows, one sees that for each vowel (a, e, i, o, and u) there are three to four high-frequency patterns. The structural relationships between these high-frequency, one-syllable words are important, for it is the nature of these relationships that will guide our teaching, our sequencing of word-sort lessons over time with the child.

Getting Started: Sorting Patterns of the Vowel A

It is helpful, at the outset, to view vowel-pattern work as proceeding in five phases: sorting word patterns across the vowel *a*, sorting patterns across the vowel *e*, sorting patterns across the vowel *i*, and so on. Therefore, let us begin with the vowel *a*.

Step 1 (Three-Pattern Sort with Tutor Modeling)

The first three *a* patterns to be sorted are CVC (short *a* words), CVCe (long *a* words), and CV-r (r-controlled *a* words). Five to six words per pattern are needed, and *the student should be able to read 75% of these words before the sort begins.* (See Appendix 5.2 for word lists.)

The tutor begins the sort by putting three word cards on the table in a horizontal array:

<u>mat</u>   <u>rake</u>   <u>car</u>

Next, she produces a deck of 15 word cards and explains to Curt that each of the 15 words goes in one of the three categories (under *mat*, under *rake*, or under *car*). The tutor models the sorting of the first word in the deck, *sad*, by placing it under *mat* and reading both words aloud. She then sorts the second word, *name*, in a similar manner.

<u>mat</u>   <u>rake</u>   <u>car</u>

sad   name

Curt picks up the next word in the deck, *hard*, reads it aloud, and places it under *rake* and *name*. The tutor corrects him by simply moving *hard* over to the *-ar* column (under *car*), and again reads the two words aloud. She tells Curt that in sorting the words into columns he must attend both to the way the word "looks" and to the sound that the letter, *a*, makes in the word.

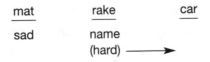

<u>mat</u>   <u>rake</u>   <u>car</u>

sad   name
               (hard) ⟶

It's the tutor's turn again. She sorts *page* under *rake* and *name* in a deliberate fashion, with Curt watching closely now, trying to figure out the rules of this new game.

mat	rake	car
sad	name	hard
	page	

Curt's following play is interesting. Picking up the next word, *can*, he puts it in the *-ar* column briefly. Then he changes his mind, gingerly puts *can* under *mat* and *sad*, and removes his hand uncertainly. When the tutor says, "Good, Curt!" a smile crosses the child's face. He reads aloud the three short *a* words and then eagerly looks to see where the tutor will place the next card.

mat	rake	car
sad	name	hard
can	page	

The tutor and child continue to take turns sorting the 15 words, with the tutor modeling correct responses and also giving Curt immediate feedback as to the correctness of his sorting attempts. By the end of this 5-minute task, Curt is still tentative and inconsistent in sorting the words, but he does seem to be actively involved in the activity.

In the following tutoring session, the word-sort activity is repeated with the same three categories and the same 15 words. As on the first day, Curt's initial sorting responses are slow, deliberate, and sprinkled with errors. However, midway through the activity, following one of his errors that the tutor matter-of-factly sorts in a different category, Curt's eyes light up and he informs the tutor that he has "got it." He has. From that point on, he sorts each word accurately and confidently. At the end of the sort, Curt and the tutor read aloud the words in each column, agree that they are sorted correctly, by vowel sound, and decide that it is time to add something new.

mat	rake	car
sad	name	hard
can	page	start
clap	face	park
rag	made	farm
ham	place	star

Step 2 (Four-Pattern Sort with Reinforcement Games)

Having gained some proficiency at sorting "known" words into the three patterns of the vowel *a*, Curt is ready to add a fourth pattern.

<u>mat</u>   <u>rake</u>   <u>car</u>   <u>tail</u>

The tutor keeps the same 18 words used in the three-pattern sort and adds five *-ai* words (*tail, wait, rain, paid,* and *train*), the first three of which are in Curt's sight vocabulary. Again, the tutor and Curt take turns reading and sorting each word card into one of four categories. Curt shows a little confusion on his first turn (sorting *rain* under *rake*), but he quickly picks up on the new visual pattern (CVVC), and proceeds to sort the remaining words with accuracy and a bit more speed.

To test and extend Curt's confidence in his new-found sorting ability, the tutor reshuffles the word cards and teaches Curt a little game that can be played with the four-column sort.

Column-Sorting Game: Rules

1. The tutor and Curt take turns sorting one word card at a time.
2. If Curt sorts a word in a wrong category and the tutor catches him, the tutor gets 1 point.
3. If the tutor sorts a word in wrong category and Curt catches her, Curt gets 1 point. Conversely, if the tutor sorts a word in a wrong category and Curt does *not* catch her, the tutor gets 1 point.
4. The player with the most points at the end of the sort wins.

One of the advantages of the column-sorting game—aside from the fact that children love to play it—is that in order to win, the learner must concentrate on the vowel patterns within the words not only when it is his/her turn, but also when it is the tutor's turn. Spurred on by the competition, Curt concentrates hard and wins the game by making no errors on his sorts and by "catching" three of the four errors the tutor makes (score: Curt—3, Tutor—1).

At this point in the word-sort sequence the tutor knows that Curt can discriminate between four high-frequency patterns of the vowel *a* (m*a*ke, m*a*t, m*ai*l, and m*a*rk). In fact, he shows some ability to sort correctly new words (*base, brain, last*) that the tutor begins to introduce into the pattern sort. However, Curt needs more practice and reinforcement on these patterns if he is to attain what some have termed "automaticity" of response. To provide such practice, and at the same time to keep the column sorting from becoming rote drill, the tutor introduces new game formats.

Vowel Pattern Concentration: Rules

1. After completion of a column sort, the tutor quickly selects eight matching pattern pairs from the sort (e.g., *man—sat; take—name; rain—tail,* etc.). She randomly places these 16 word cards into four rows of four, *face down* on the table.

2. The first player (usually the child) turns over two word cards. If they are a pattern match (*rain—tail*) and if he can read the words, he can pick them up, place them in his pile, and take another turn. If the two words turned over are not a pattern match (e.g., *mat—cake*), the player must replace them face-down in their original position on the table and allow the other player to take a turn.

3. The game is over when all the word cards have been removed from the table. The winner is the player who picks up the most cards, that is, who finds the most pattern matches.

Vowel Pattern Bingo: Rules

1. Bingo, a variation of column sorting, is fast paced and competitive. Needed materials are (a) two Bingo cards (8½" × 11"), each containing 20 squares, and (b) a deck of word cards containing 32 pattern words and 6 "wild cards." The same *headers* are placed in the top row of both Bingo cards.

Curt's Bingo card

bat	make	car	tail

Tutor's Bingo card

bat	make	car	tail

DECK

2. To begin the game, a player draws a word from the deck. If the player can place it in the appropriate column (e.g., *man* under *bat*), and then read each word in that column, the word is left on the board. If the player misreads the word or places it in an incorrect column (and the other player challenges), then the word is removed from the board. The players alternate turns.

3. If a player draws a wild card from the deck, he/she can place it anywhere on the board and then take another turn.

Curt's Bingo card

Tutor's Bingo card

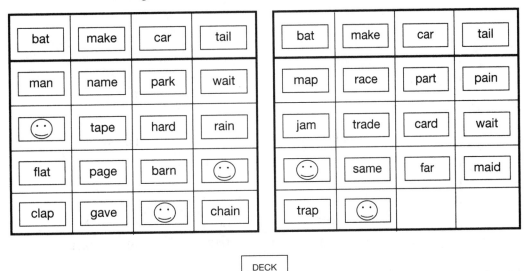

4. The game is over when one of the players fills all the squares on his/her Bingo card.

Timed Trials: Rules

1. Timed Trials is usually the last game or activity to be introduced in studying a set of vowel patterns. Its dual purpose is to strengthen the child's automaticity of response and to provide a concrete measure of this automaticity. Needed materials are (a) 40 to 50 word cards that fit the target patterns (e.g., *sat*, *made*, *hard*, and *rain*), (b) a stopwatch or wrist watch with a second hand, and (c) a progress chart.

2. After shuffling the deck of word cards, the tutor explains to Curt that she is going to "flash" the words to him one at a time. His task is to read correctly as many words as he can in 1 minute.

3. After noting the starting time, the tutor proceeds to present the words one at a time. If Curt reads a word correctly, it goes in one pile; if he misreads the word or hesitates for 3 seconds, it goes in a second pile.

4. When 1 minute has gone by, the trial stops. The tutor counts the words in the "Correct" pile, and Curt counts the words in the "Incorrect" pile. These numbers are then graphed on a progress chart (see Figure 5.7).

Each of the word games described here (Column Sorting, Concentration, Bingo, and Timed Trials) provides the student with needed practice. The games require little advance planning by the tutor, are enjoyable to play, and do a good job of strengthening the child's discrimination of and memory for basic vowel patterns.

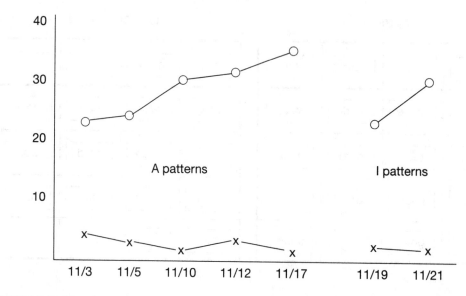

FIGURE 5.7. Number of vowel-pattern words identified in 1-minute trials. ○ = number correct, x = number incorrect.

Another way of reinforcing the *a* vowel patterns is through *spell checks*. After completing a column sort or game, the tutor scoops up all the word cards, leaving only four pattern exemplars across the top of the table:

mat   lake   park   mail

The tutor tells Curt to number from 1 to 8 on a piece of paper in preparation for a spell check. Explaining that each spelling word will follow "one of the patterns we have been working on," the tutor proceeds to dictate eight words (from the word cards she has scooped up), one by one. As Curt spells, he is encouraged to use the exemplars on the table as a pattern reminder. On completion of the test, the tutor immediately goes through the spellings with Curt, having him self-correct any errors.

Step 3 (Four-Pattern Sort with Miscellaneous Column)

Thus far we have been working in what Bear et al. (1996) call a "closed-sort" format. In a closed sort, all of the words being sorted fit neatly into discrete categories (CVC, CVCe, CVVC). However, a closed sort can be modified and made more difficult by adding a *Miscellaneous* or open-ended column.

mat   lake   mail   (Miscellaneous)

In this activity, words that do not fit under the first three exemplars (*mat*, *rake*, and *mail*) are to be sorted in the Miscellaneous column. For example, new *a* patterns (*say, may, day; call, ball, wall*) as well as exceptions to previously learned patterns (*was* vs. CVC; *have* vs. CVCe; *said* vs. CVVC) can be introduced. Although the resulting sort is more difficult, it provides needed challenge for the learner and important diagnostic information for the tutor. This is because true mastery of a concept or pattern requires that the learner be able to determine not only those examples that fit the pattern, but also those that are exceptions to it.

Curt, at this stage in the word-sort sequence, is ready for the challenge of the Miscellaneous column. He experiences some confusion at first, sorting *was* under *mat* and *said* under *mail*, but he quickly learns that he must attend to the vowel "sound" as well as to the spelling pattern. Curt does not have as much trouble sorting *fall, ball, wall, day, may,* and *say,* all of which end up in the Miscellaneous column.

mat	rake	mail	(Miscellaneous)	
tag	name	rain	fall	day
sad	face	wait	say	may
that	made	maid	was	want
clap		tail	said	wall
			ball	

The tutor reshuffles the word cards, and she and Curt play the column-sorting game. There is added challenge with the Miscellaneous words, but Curt's sorting is error-free. As a final task, the tutor asks him whether he can subdivide the Miscellaneous column into three columns. He does this quickly and accurately, the *-ay* and *-all* patterns being easy for him to discriminate at this latter stage in the word-sort sequence.

say	fall	was
day	ball	said
may	wall	want

In the sort just described, Miscellaneous column words contained the same vowel (*a*) as the other three columns. Another way to use the Miscellaneous column is to include word patterns of a different vowel in the sort, as in the following example:

mat	rake	mail	(Miscellaneous)
tag	name	rain	pig
sad	face	wait	ride
clap	made	maid	hit
that			time
			slide

Used in this manner, the Miscellaneous column can actually foreshadow the next phase of vowel-pattern work. Indeed, based on Curt's performance thus far, the tutor may decide to leave the *a* patterns and begin working across the patterns of the vowel *i*.

Sorting Patterns of the Other Vowels—I, O, E, and U

Individual children will require varying amounts of practice to master the patterns of the vowel *a*. Some will do so after three or four tutoring sessions; others will require hours of column sorting and reinforcement games spread out over a 3- to 4-week period. It should be noted that it is not just the specific *a* patterns that the child is learning, but also the more generalized skill of how to search for and detect orthographic structure (spelling patterns) across any set of words. It is this learned tendency to note pattern relationships between words that will transfer to future word sorts—for example, to Curt's sorting of patterns across the vowel *i*.

Step 1 (Three-Pattern Sorts)

The first three *i* patterns to be sorted (CVC, CVCe, CV-r) are identical to those used in the initial *a* sort. Again, five to six words per pattern are needed, and the child should be able to read 75% of these words *before* the sort begins. Once the *i* sort is under way, the tutor may notice that Curt is more accurate, more confident, and somewhat faster in making his sorting decisions than he was at this stage of the *a* pattern sorts. (This is the *transfer phenomenon* that was alluded to earlier.) Accordingly, less time or fewer tutoring sessions may be needed for Curt to achieve proficiency in sorting *i* words into the three major patterns.

big	side	girl
hit	bike	bird
win	time	sir
kid	nine	shirt
swim	slide	first

Steps 2 and 3 (Four-pattern Sorts)

After the fourth pattern of *i* has been introduced (*-ight*) the various reinforcement games can be played (column-sorting game, Concentration, and Bingo).

big	side	girl	night
kid	time	sir	right
win	bite	first	might
swim	nine	bird	sight
hit	slide	shirt	light
	bike		

Finally, in Step 3, the Miscellaneous column can be used.

big	side	girl	(Miscellaneous)	
hit	fine	dirt	kind	nail
win	rice	stir	mind	rain
slip	bike	skirt	wild	wait
hid	smile	third	find	
lick	wide		child	

After Curt has mastered the high-frequency *i* patterns, the tutor may decide to collapse the *a* and *i* patterns into one sort before moving on to another vowel (as in the following example).

hat	lake	hit	like
fan	made	pin	mine
sad	race	dig	kite
rag	sale	sick	time
glad	blaze	lip	slide

A Miscellaneous column added to this sort can contain *a* or *i* words that deviate from the basic CVC and CVCe patterns.

hat	lake	hit	like	(Miscellaneous)
rag	sale	lip	time	hard
glad	place	sick	trike	bird
trap	cane	kid	mice	start
tan	name	trip	pile	shirt
bad				harm

Collapsing a word sort across two vowels allows for a review of previously studied patterns (in this case, *a* patterns), and highlights pattern regularities across the different vowels (*hat* vs. *hit*; *lake* vs. *like*; *hard* vs. *bird*).

At this point, assuming accuracy and fluency in Curt's sorting responses, the tutor can move to a third vowel, possibly *o*. High-frequency patterns of *o* include the following:

top	rope	boat	corn
rob	joke	coal	born
shop	pole	foam	sword
jog	stone	float	torn
mop	code	foal	short

Curt will master this *o* sort in a fairly short period of time because *o* is the third vowel across which he has sorted the same patterns (CVC, CVCe, CVVC, and CV-r). However, the saving of instructional time on later sorts (e.g., *o, e,* and *u* patterns) will be contingent on sufficient instructional time having been devoted to the earlier pattern sorts. Again we see the importance of the tutor's doing a thorough job of teaching the *a* and *i* vowel patterns. It is in these initial sorts that the child learns, or does not learn, an important transferable reading skill—the ability to search for and detect pattern regularities in one-syllable words.

A plan for sorting high-frequency vowel patterns has been illustrated, with *a, i,* and *o* patterns used as examples. Obviously, the *e* and *u* patterns can be sorted using the same basic format. There is no one best sequence or timetable for moving through the vowel-pattern word sorts with a first-grade reader. Children differ in the amount and kind of practice they require to internalize these word patterns. In Appendix 5.2 the tutor will find a proposed sequence of pattern sorts that spans all five vowels. However, such a sequence should be readily adapted by the tutor (specific sorts added, deleted, or modified) according to the needs of the individual child.

Troubleshooting

Word sorting is a thinking person's way to teach word recognition. Tutor and child alternating turns sorting words into columns—on the surface, a simple activity—is, from the tutor's perspective, an exercise in ongoing decision making. As in a game of checkers or gin rummy, the strategy is to make a move, analyze the opposition's following move, and then make your next play accordingly. However, in word sorting the goal is not to defeat one's opponent (i.e., the child), but rather to provide him/her with a series of challenging, yet do-able plays (sorts).

One cannot anticipate and list all the possible decision points that may confront a tutor in a given word-sort activity. Nonetheless, the following situations, presented in question–answer format, will invariably occur as the tutor begins to use the strategy. In a sense, this is a word sort "troubleshooting" reference for the beginning tutor.

Question 1. How should I respond if the child puts a word card in the wrong column?

top	joke	boat	cold
job	hole		
pot	stop		

(Word sorted in wrong column)

Answer. It depends on how much practice the child has had with the specific patterns being sorted. If it is only the first or second time the child has worked with these patterns, the tutor should probably correct the sorting error immediately, thereby providing a model for correct responding. On the other hand, if the child has worked with these word patterns over a number of days, the tutor may choose to ignore the sorting error initially, hoping that the child will later notice and self-correct the error. In fact, the tutor may even wait until the end of the sort and then respond as follows:

> Curt, in the first two columns, two words have been sorted incorrectly. Can you find them and put them in the right column?

top	joke	boat	cold
job	hole	coal	fold
pot	stop	road	hold
box	nose	loaf	
sold	spoke	cloak	

Question 2. What should I do if the child cannot read, or misreads, a word he/she sorts in the correct column?

mat	lake	car	(Miscellaneous)
can	name	hard	say
bag	gate	part	day
clap	shape		ball

(Child reads "ship")

Answer. The tutor should intercede by having the child go back and read the *a-e* column from top to bottom: "lake"—"name"—"gate"—"sh—." Often, the child will now be able to pronounce the word (*shape*) correctly, his/her attention having been refocused on long *a* words having a similar spelling pattern.

Question 3. Is it essential that the child be able to read each word he/she is asked to sort?

Answer. Although, ideally, the child should be able to read all of the words being sorted, in practice this is not always possible. For example, in getting a four-pattern sort started, the tutor may not be able to find five words for each pattern that are in the child's sight vocabulary. If three or four "known" words can be located for each pattern, a knowledgeable tutor can conduct the sort. The tutor's strategy would be to control or manipulate the deck of word cards so that words known by the child are the first to be sorted. When new or unknown words then come up later in the sort, the tutor can encourage the child to attempt reading the new words by comparing their spelling patterns with known words already sorted in the columns. (See the following example.)

hit	ride	night	bird	
dig	like	right	girl	(sight words)
trip	drive	sight		
crib	dime	bright	shirt	
slid	slide		whirl	(new words)

Question 4. Is it always necessary for the tutor and child to alternate turns sorting the word cards?

Answer. Not always. On the third or fourth time through a "new" sort, or on a sort that reviews old patterns, the tutor may decide to let the child sort the deck of word cards by him/herself. However, there are generally several advantages to the tutor's alternating word-sort turns with the child. First, by sorting every other word, the tutor can control the pace of the activity, slowing it down or speeding it up. Other advantages of alternating turns are that the tutor can model correct responses early in a sort, and, if the child is struggling, the tutor can choose to take the difficult words in a sort (e.g., those words beginning with a consonant blend). Finally, taking turns promotes a sense of partnership in the word-sort activity, and this will be very important to some children.

Question 5. How do I make a given sort more difficult or more challenging for the child?

Answer. Two ways come to mind. First, add a *Miscellaneous* column. This will force the child to concentrate on words that do *not* fit the target patterns, as well as on those words that do.

top	rope	boat	(Miscellaneous)
lot	code	coal	coin
flop	joke	toast	boil
lock	pole	float	noise
	broke		comb

Second, add new words to the sort, some of which may not be in the child's sight vocabulary. These new words should come up late in the sort, so that the child can use his/her knowledge of previously sorted known words to predict the pronunciation of the new words (see answer to *Question 3*).

Question 6. How much time should I spend on vowel-pattern word sorts each tutoring session?

Answer. Although word study is important, it must take a back seat to contextual reading in Curt's tutoring program. The tutor should strive to limit word-sort activities, including reinforcement games, to 10 minutes or less per session. A common error made by inexperienced tutors is to try to sort too many words per column; five to six per column will do. It is also important for the tutor to set a brisk pace in moving through both the sorts and the reinforcement games.

Question 7. What should I do when my student begins to tire of a given pattern sort, although I know he/she has not mastered the patterns?

Answer. Word sort, or column sorting, like any other tutoring task, can be "driven into the ground," made repetitious and boring to the child. This is especially true when a youngster is slow in picking up on spelling-pattern regularities and must thus spend considerable time on each pattern sort. The answer is not to abandon teaching the target patterns (e.g., *can, cane, car*, etc.) before they are mastered. Instead, the tutor must vary the presentation to avoid the deadening repetition of the same column sort day after day. Sometimes adding a Miscellaneous (or Mystery) column can spark the child's interest. Or the order of the word-sort tasks can be changed from lesson to lesson. For example, on a given day, the tutor may decide to omit the column sort and go right to a Concentration or Bingo game, followed by a spell check.

Question 8. How do I decide when it is time to move the child to a new sort?

Answer. In Curt's case, for instance, it is time to move on when he shows mastery of a given set of word patterns. The tutor should watch for increases in Curt's accuracy and speed of responding in both the column-sort and game formats. The tutor should also note Curt's ability to read and spell "new" words that are introduced in the sort; success here indicates that he can transfer pattern knowledge to words not originally in his sight vocabulary. Finally, the tutor can use *timed trials* (word recognition against the clock) to provide concrete evidence of Curt's mastery of a given set of patterns.

Word Sorting in Perspective

We are now near the end of a rather lengthy discussion of how to conduct vowel-pattern word sorts. Before leaving the topic, however, three issues deserve mention: (1) inducing versus deducing word patterns, (2) automatizing word recognition responses, and (3) transfering word recognition knowledge developed in isolation (via word sorts) to contextual reading and writing.

1. The word sort approach allows the child to induce the defining characteristics for sorting words into various categories. Note that the child induces *defining characteristics*, not rules. Granting that this is a fuzzy distinction, it is still important to be aware that word sort does not involve the conscious memorization, recitation, or application of phonics rules. Instead, the child learns about the various spelling patterns through self-directed compare–contrast activity. He/she learns *by doing*. By manipulating words first by trial and error, then in a more intentional manner, and, finally, with speed and accuracy, the child gradually comes to internalize aspects of the English orthographic system. (*Note:* This is not to say that the tutor cannot point out to the child a given phonics rule from time to time; for example, "See, Curt? All the words in this column have a silent *e* at the end that makes the *a* long." The point is that the saying of the rule is not as important as the child's having adequate practice sorting words into a column or category that defines the rule in the first place.)

2. The type of word knowledge that is most useful to the young reader is that which affords immediate, effortless recognition of words in the act of reading for meaning. The word sort approach attempts to develop this tacit, automatized word knowledge by having the child sort and re-sort words in various contexts until accuracy, fluency, and generalizability of response are attained. Unlike workbook pages or ditto sheets, word sort cards can be used over and over again in the same sort or in different sorts, depending on the instructional goal. The open-ended nature of the word sort activities allows for the repetition and overlearning that are necessary, but often lacking, in many word recognition programs. At the same time, the child's interest and motivation are not sacrificed to the goal of automaticity, because the gamelike sorting activities are brief, challenging, and, on many occasions, pure fun.

3. A question that confronts every teacher of beginning reading, and every developer of beginning reading materials, is, Will isolated word recognition (or phonics) training transfer to contextual reading? The goal of word sort instruction is to increase the child's knowledge of frequently occurring word patterns so that he/she will have the *potential* to use this knowledge resource when reading or writing for meaningful purposes. If the child's knowledge of word patterns is increased through word sorting and he/she still fails to draw on this resource in contextual reading and writing situations, the tutor must intervene. Note, however, that at this point the tutor's intervention involves calling the child's attention to specific word patterns in text—word patterns that have been introduced, and to some degree mastered, in previous column sorts and reinforcement games. Also note that *prior* to word sorting, such a "calling attention to" intervention would be futile because a sufficient knowledge base for the child to draw upon would be lacking. Figure 5.8 addresses the issue of transfer in graphic form.

Although the arrows in Figure 5.8 depict a one-way direction of transfer, in terms of the child's developing word knowledge, there is obviously an interaction between what he/she learns about words in his/her contextual reading and writing, and what the child learns in the more structured word sort activities.

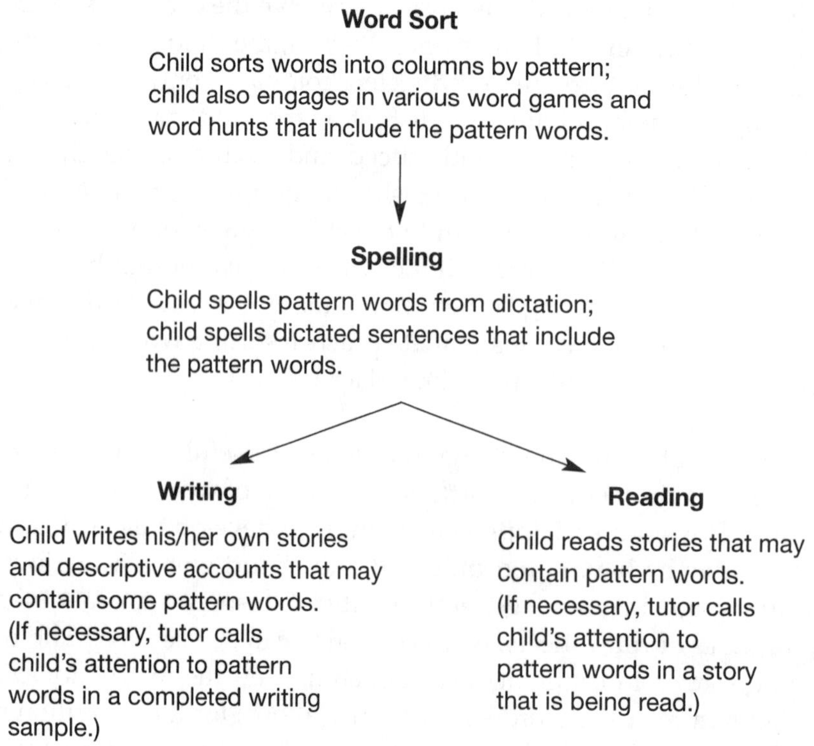

Word Sort

Child sorts words into columns by pattern;
child also engages in various word games and
word hunts that include the pattern words.

↓

Spelling

Child spells pattern words from dictation;
child spells dictated sentences that include
the pattern words.

Writing

Child writes his/her own stories
and descriptive accounts that may
contain some pattern words.
(If necessary, tutor calls
child's attention to pattern
words in a completed writing
sample.)

Reading

Child reads stories that may
contain pattern words.
(If necessary, tutor calls
child's attention to
pattern words in a story
that is being read.)

FIGURE 5.8. Transfer of word knowledge from isolated to contextual reading and writing situations.

Word sort is an instructional process, not an instructional program. For the teacher, it is a flexible framework for presenting word study lessons; for the child, it is a useful compare–contrast setting for making discoveries about the spelling patterns in the language. There are no inviolate rules for using the word sort procedure, and certainly no specific phonics sequence is being prescribed here. Furthermore, not every beginning reader will require intensive instruction in word recognition via the word sort approach. Why, then, one might ask, has so much space been devoted to a description of this approach? The answer is twofold. First, many children who struggle with the task of learning to read *do* need word recognition instruction. Second, word recognition or phonics is not easy to teach. In fact, the mindless application of a rote phonics curriculum, without the individual learner's developmental grasp of words taken into consideration, can potentially bore, frustrate, and even mislead a young reader. Word recognition instruction, then, will be as good as the judgment of the tutor who conducts such instruction. This section of the manual on word sort has attempted to provide background information that will improve the tutor's judgment in this important area.

Building Reading Fluency

Fluent oral reading, even at the first-grade level, is characterized by an adequate reading rate (45 to 60 words per minute) and appropriate intonation. Not all remedial readers require help in this area. Some may read fluently but with poor comprehension. Others may read too rapidly for their own good, ignoring or reconstructing what is actually written on the page. These types notwithstanding, it is safe to say that the majority of low-achieving first-grade-level readers (including the child in our present case study, Curt) are hampered by a slow, monotonous reading style that clearly calls for work in the area of fluency.

But one may ask, "Why worry about fluency or rate if the child is reading accurately and comprehending what he/she reads?" The obvious answer to this question is that rate has always been considered an important aspect of reading skill. A more reflective and honest response, however, must acknowledge that for beginners there is no single optimal rate of reading, but rather a "range of reading rates" that can support accurate word recognition and comprehension. Just as we accept normal interindividual differences in young children's speeds of walking and talking, we must learn to accept normal variation in their oral reading rates. Who, then, requires focused work in reading fluency? The answer is those children at the extremes of the distribution: those who race wildly and unproductively through the text and, at the other end, that larger group who adopt a self-defeating, tortoiselike pace that turns reading into tedious word-calling.

A well-known characteristic of first-grade readers is that they read aloud at about the same speed as they read silently. (The average adult reader reads twice as fast silently.) This leads to an interesting conjecture regarding the possible benefits of increasing a child's oral reading fluency. Let us say that a child is reading text orally and silently at approximately 50 words per minute. If, through fluency training, his/her oral rate increases to 70 words per minute, might not there be a corresponding increase in that child's silent reading rate? Possibly. We cannot deny the importance of silent reading practice in such a situation. However, this scenario does point out that an increase in oral reading fluency could very well have a positive carryover effect on the silent reading mode.

There are several strategies that can be used by a tutor to improve a child's oral reading fluency. In this section, we discuss four of them: *echo reading, easy reading, repeated readings*, and *taped readings*.

Echo Reading

We have met echo reading before in this manual. In its simplest form, the tutor reads aloud one or two sentences and the child attempts to "echo" the tutor's reading. This technique was used extensively in our earlier case studies ("Atticus," in Chapter 3, and "Beth," in Chapter 4) to support the reading efforts of beginners who lacked adequate sight vocabulary and decoding skills.

In the first-grade-reader stage, in which sight vocabulary is not the major concern, echo reading can be used to work on oral reading fluency. For example, on certain parts of a story, Curt may lapse into very slow, expressionless, word-by-word reading. On these occasions the tutor can intervene by saying:

> On this next page, Curt, I'm going to read aloud the first two paragraphs [approximately half the page]; then I want you to go back and read the whole page. Try to make your reading sound like mine.

The tutor proceeds to read the first half of the page with appropriate phrasing and intonation, running her finger under the lines of print as she reads. Then Curt goes back to the beginning and reads.

The echo reading strategy described here can be quite effective. Often, the child not only reads the first two paragraphs (the part modeled by the tutor) more fluently, but is also able to maintain this fluency as he reads the second half of the page. It is as if the momentum gained in echoing the first two paragraphs carries over to the "new" unmodeled text.

Single-sentence or two-sentence sequences can also be echo read. As Curt moves into more difficult reading material (e.g., a second-grade basal), he will confront longer sentences and, possibly, some new grammatical constructions (compound sentences, adjective and adverb clauses). It is not unusual for the young reader to stumble badly on such sentences. When this happens, the tutor may decide, right then and there, to read aloud the "difficult" sentence and have Curt echo her model. For the child, hearing and then correctly producing the new sentence construction can be a first step in gaining control over it.

Echo reading should generally be used when the child is reading at his/her *instructional level*—that is, at a challenging level where word recognition and syntactic demands require the tutor's vigilant support. Keep in mind that at his instructional level, Curt may misread as many as one out of every 12 words.)

Easy Reading

A second, time-honored way to build reading fluency is to do a good amount of reading in "easy" materials—in stories containing words and sentence patterns that are familiar to the child. The instructional goal here is obvious: to increase fluency or speed by having the child experience comfortable, relatively error-free readings of meaningful stories.

Trade books are probably the best sources of material for easy reading. These books generally contain language that is less stilted or formulaic than that found in most first-grade basal readers. Several American publishers have recently put out trade book series that can be used for easy reading at the first- and second-grade levels—for example, *I Can Read Books* (Harper & Row), *Step into Reading (Levels 1 and 2)* (Random House), and *All Aboard Reading* (Levels 2 and 3) (Grosset & Dunlap). Moreover, a trip to a good public library will turn up many more books that are appropriate for easy reading at this stage.

The easy-reading part of the lesson should be pressure-free and enjoyable. Initially, the tutor and child may choose to partner read the text one or two pages at a time. Over a few weeks, as Curt begins to sense his power to read these easy books, he may decide that he wants to read them "all by myself." No tutor, of course, would stand in his way.

Repeated Readings

A third strategy for improving Curt's oral reading fluency is repeated readings (see Samuels, 1979). On the surface, it would appear that there could be no simpler teaching method. The child is directed to read the *same passage* (approximately 150 to 180 words) three times. Each time, he reads for 2 minutes, and the number of words read is recorded by the tutor. With successive rereadings, fluency (or number of words read) increases owing to a practice or familiarity effect. The improvement in fluency is graphed, providing immediate positive feedback to child and tutor alike.

Although repeated readings is a relatively straightforward teaching strategy, several issues arise regarding its actual implementation in a tutoring setting:

- How to choose the passage that the child will read.
- How to determine the number of repeated readings per tutoring session.
- How to monitor the child's oral reading.
- How to graph the results.

1. *A passage chosen for repeated readings should be at the child's instructional level.* Therefore, if Curt is reading for comprehension in a late-first-grade (1-2) reading

book, the tutor can choose a 150- to 180-word passage from a story that Curt has just *finished* reading. This will ensure that the "repeated readings" passage is at the appropriate difficulty level and that Curt will be somewhat familiar with the passage content. With a new story being introduced each day in guided reading, there will be no shortage of passages for repeated readings. Generally, the first 150 words in the story are used for the repeated readings trials. However, any similar-length passage within the story will do.

2. *Two repeated readings trials can be conducted each tutoring session.* A given passage (A) might be read two times on Monday, and then a third and final time on Wednesday, the next tutoring session. Also on Wednesday, a new passage (B) can be introduced for its first reading, with the second and third readings coming the following Monday.

Monday	Passage A (RRs 1 and 2)
Wednesday	Passage A (RR 3), Passage B (RR 1)
Monday	Passage B (RRs 2 and 3)
Wednesday	Passage C (RRs 1 and 2)

(and so on)

There are several ways to introduce a repeated readings trial. In Curt's first trial on a given passage, for example, after locating the appropriate page, the tutor can simply signal Curt to begin reading aloud. Or the tutor can allow him to read the first paragraph or two silently *before* beginning his timed oral reading. In yet another approach, the tutor can model a fluent oral reading of the first 50 to 100 words before having Curt begin to read aloud. Obviously, these three ways of introducing the first repeated readings trial, and later trials for that matter, represent a continuum of support—from no support to a fluent modeling of the task. It is important to keep in mind, however, that even in the first example (no prereading support) the child is already familiar with the story being read.

3. *During the repeated readings trials, the tutor must monitor the quality of the child's oral reading.* Some children may tend to hurry through the text, trying to better their previous "number of words read." In so doing, they may ignore punctuation and omit, insert, and substitute words. How should the tutor respond? Two principles, previously mentioned in this manual, provide guidance:

- The reader shall make sense.
- The reader shall read, for the most part, the words on the page.

If either of these principles is violated, the tutor should intervene by having the child stop and reread the sentence. Because stopping and rereading costs the reader valuable time in a repeated readings trial, after a few such experiences the child will begin to concentrate more closely on his/her oral reading. Regarding the "racing through text" issue, it is important to help the child distinguish between reading fast and reading smoothly. At the beginning of each trial the tutor should remind the child that if he/she reads smoothly, with expression, the number of words read in a 2-minute period will increase.

4. *Graphing results is an indispensable part of the repeated readings method.* A carefully kept graph not only provides the child with immediate trial-to-trial feedback, but it also serves as a permanent record of his/her reading performance over time. Children enjoy reviewing and discussing the graphed results, particularly on days when they reach a new performance plateau. The number of words read should be graphed *after each trial*, two times per tutoring session. If the tutor precounts the words per page (as in the following illustration), this will facilitate a quick tally of the child's performance.

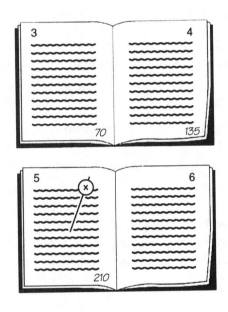

In the trial illustrated here, the child began reading on page 3, and after 2 minutes had reached the (X) mark on page 5. Having precounted the words on each page, the tutor simply tallied the number of words read by the child on page 5 (8 words) and added this to 135, the cumulative word total through page 4. The total number of words read (143) was then graphed (see the last trial, 10/15, in Figure 5.9). Note in the graph that each trial is dated and that information is provided regarding the specific passage being read (title, publisher, level). Such record keeping, aside from its motivational function, is important for several reasons:

- It indicates, over time, how consistently the repeated readings technique is being used.

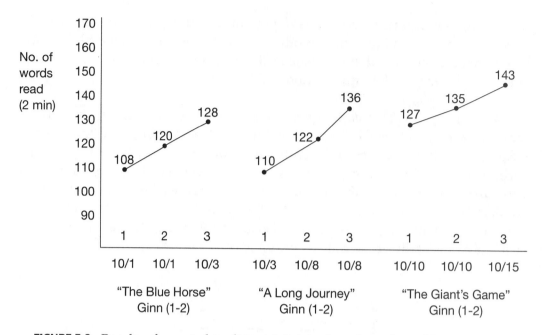

FIGURE 5.9. Results of repeated readings trials (number of words read in 2 minutes).

- It indicates whether and when a change in reading *level* occurs, for example, from 1-2 to 2-1.
- It provides an ongoing visual record of patterns of change in the child's oral reading fluency.

As compared with echo reading and easy reading, repeated readings is a fairly formal way to work on oral reading fluency. Still, the activity has much to offer; it is effective, it is easy to administer, and it is invariably enjoyed by students.

Taped Readings

Taped readings constitute another powerful method for building reading fluency (Carbo, 1981; Chomsky, 1976). With this method, the tutor selects a good story, written at the child's instructional level, and records it on a cassette tape. Then the child, at home or school, practices the story by reading along with the tape.

The recording of a first- or second-grade story (500 to 750 words) is straightforward and takes less than 10 minutes. Nelson and Morris (1987) suggest the following recording procedure for the tutor:

1. Push the RECORD button on the tape recorder.
2. Read the first two pages of the story onto the tape before saying, "Stop."

3. Pause 5 seconds and then read the next two pages before saying, "Stop," once more.

4. Pause 5 seconds and then continue the "Read two pages—Stop" routine until the story is completed.

The tape recorder is never turned off while the story is being recorded. The tutor should read slowly but expressively, pausing an extra moment at phrase boundaries so that, later, the child will have a chance to follow the tape-recorded reading.

With the story recorded, the tutor carefully explains to Curt the "taped reading" procedure:

> Curt, you will listen to or read along with the tape for two pages. When the tape says, "Stop," turn off the recorder and go back and read the two pages. Then restart the recorder and listen to the next two pages until it tells you to stop and reread. When you finish the story, rewind the tape.

The tutor also informs Curt that she will check his tape-recorder "homework" by having him read two or three pages of the story aloud during the following tutoring session.

The taped echo-reading procedure described here can be an extremely important supplement to twice-weekly tutorial instruction. If there is a tape recorder in the child's home, a parent can make sure that 15 minutes are devoted to the task after each tutoring session. If the home setting is unworkable, the child's classroom teacher may agree to monitor the child's tape-recorder reading two times a week. (There can be no more meaningful seat-work task.) In effect, taped reading allows a struggling beginning reader to read, with support, *away from the tutor*. Such opportunities are rare.

III. REPRESENTATIVE TUTORING LESSONS ACROSS THE YEAR

This section describes changes in Curt's instruction across a year of tutoring. The first person (I) is used in referring to the tutor.

Lesson 1 (September 24)

1. **Guided reading.** We begin by previewing Janice Udry's "Alfred," a well-written 1-2 story from an old Houghton Mifflin (1978) basal reader series. After "walking through" the pictures on the first five pages of the story, Curt and I return to the start and begin partner reading. Soon Curt is reading two pages to my one, and I notice that he requires very little assistance with word recognition. We stop a few times to check comprehension, and Curt's responses are right on target.

2. **Word study.** Our first word study lesson involves reviewing three of the five short-vowel *patterns* (*a*, *i*, and *o*). In sorting 12 short-vowel words into columns, Curt shows immediate recognition of all but two of the words and these two, *cot* and *slid*, he is able to decode.

bag	hit	mop
ran	lip	rob
nap	win	doll
plan	pick	cot
sad	slid	drop

We play a quick Concentration game with the words and then move on to easy reading.

3. **Easy reading.** For easy reading, I pick a short selection, "Fox All Wet," from Edward Marshall's *Fox and His Friends*. Curt enjoys this story about a child having to take care of his annoying younger sibling after school. He reads independently, needing my assistance only to pronounce a few character names (*Louise*, *Carmen*, and *Junior*).

4. **Read-to.** I read Irma Simonton Black's *Night Cat* to Curt. This classic picture book, first published in the mid-1950s, describes the nocturnal wanderings of a plump black cat who comes alive when the rest of the family goes to sleep. Curt listens intently as I read and several times comments on the pictures by Paul Galdone.

Commentary

Curt's initial reading assessment suggested a 1-2 to 2-1 *instructional level*. I intentionally started him at the 1-2 level (see "Guided Reading" earlier in this section) to build his confidence and reduce frustration. Nonetheless, Curt's reading of the 1-2 basal story was so strong that next lesson I will move him to the 2-1 level and see what happens. With adequate support (detailed previews and a little echo reading), I believe that he will be able to read early-second-grade material.

In word study, we will spend several weeks reviewing the short-vowel patterns. As we move through the patterns, Curt will also be reviewing consonant blends (e.g., *plan*, *trip*, and *best*) and consonant digraphs (e.g., *chop*, *shut*, *bath*). Presently, he is accurate but not automatic in reading such words. To help him develop requisite automaticity, games and timed trials (see pages 191–194) will be used extensively.

We are off to a good start. Curt is not a nonreader. He is not a huge boulder that must be dislodged from a standing-still position (see the case of Atticus in Chapter 3). Rather, he is a boulder that is rolling slowly and erratically down a very gentle incline. With a little push from behind, this boulder will speed up and roll more consistently.

Lesson 22 (December 10)

1. **Guided reading.** Curt has been reading at the 2-1 level for about 10 weeks. He has read several trade books, along with 8 of the 16 stories in *Tricky Troll*, a 2-1 basal reader (Laidlaw, 1980). Curt's reading fluency and comprehension are steadily improving at the 2-1 difficulty level, and we are in no rush to move forward.

Today Curt reads *Daniel's Duck*, C. R. Bulla's beautiful 2-1 story about rural mountain life (see illustration). We spend a good deal of time discussing the pictures on the first seven pages of the book. We identify the main characters and also talk about characteristics of mountain culture, including quilting and wood carving. These concepts are new to Curt.

As Curt reads aloud *Daniel's Duck*, he requires very little assistance with word recognition. Comprehension becomes the instructional issue, and I stop Curt several times to have him recap information read and make a prediction forward. His responses show that he is following the story line closely, even identifying with the young wood-carver, Daniel. We reluctantly put the book aside after 30 pages, and I promise that we will finish it during our next lesson.

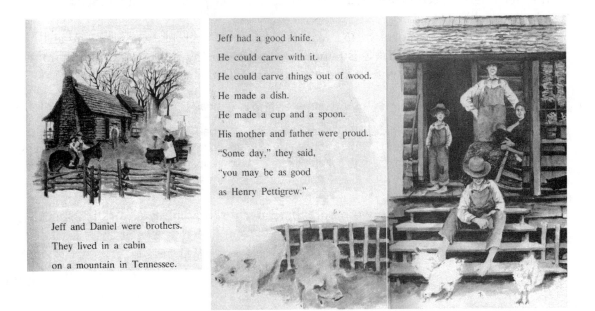

Daniel's Duck (Level 2-1) by C. R. Bulla (1982, pp. 5–7). Copyright 1982 by Harper Trophy. Reprinted by permission.

2. **Word study.** Over the past 20+ lessons, Curt has reviewed the short-vowel patterns and also worked through mixed patterns (short, long, r-controlled) of the vowels *a* and *i*:

- *Short-vowel patterns*: *a, i, o, e*, and *u* (9 lessons)
- *Mixed-vowel patterns*: short, long, r-controlled
  - across *A*: *a, a-e, ar* (5 lessons)
  - across *I*: *i, i-e, ight* (4 lessons)
  - review *A* and *I*: *a, a-e, i, i-e* (3 lessons)

Today I introduce mixed patterns of the vowel *o*. I present 15 word cards to Curt one at a time, asking him to read them. Note his responses in the following list (h = hesitation).

pot		soap	
drop		mom	
note		nose	
boat		float	
lock	(h)	shot	
rope		code	"cod"
coal	"cool"	toast	(h)
spoke	(h)		

Curt reads 10 of the 15 words quickly, as if they are already in his sight vocabulary. He hesitates on three of the words, taking time to decode them, and he misreads two words, *coal* and *code*. His performance indicates that although he has not yet internalized (or automatized) these *o* vowel patterns, with practice he should be able to do so.

Next, I shuffle the deck of 15 cards, lay out three "column headers," and ask Curt to sort the first word. He is familiar with this sorting routine and makes no errors as he places each word in the appropriate column.

pot	rope	boat
mom	nose	coal
drop	code	float
shot	spoke	soap
lock	note	toast

Curt does so well with the word sort that I decide to administer a quick spell check.

1. *mom*
2. *nose*
3. ~~*cod*~~ *code*
4. *shot*
5. ~~*coll*~~ *coal*
6. *rope*
7. ~~*loke*~~ *lock*

Clearly, we have some work to do in learning to spell these *o* vowel patterns.

3. **Easy reading.** Today we reread *A Horse Called Starfire*, a 2-1 story that we completed last week. Curt asked if we could read *Starfire* again, and I readily consented. We start off alternating pages, but soon he is reading independently; I offer only occasional word recognition assistance. Curt's fluency noticeably improves when he is rereading familiar material.

4. **Read-to.** I read aloud the next-to-last chapter in Ann Cameron's *The Stories Julian Tells*. Curt loves this book and, with only one story left, I must look for the sequel, *More Stories Julian Tells*.

Commentary

At this point, Curt is a strong Level 2-1 reader. He has adequate sight vocabulary and decoding ability at this level and, though fluency is still an issue, signs of rhythm or cadence are beginning to emerge in his oral reading. Most important, Curt's confidence in himself is growing with each passing week. He now wants to do all the reading by himself, he wants to sort each word card, and he wants to choose all the books to be read. Although I do not plan to turn the lesson planning over to Curt, I am encouraged by his progress and enthusiasm. After we return from the Christmas holidays, I plan to move him up to 2-2 or late-second-grade reading material.

Lesson 37 (February 16)

1. **Guided reading.** For more than a month Curt has been reading at the 2-2 or late-second-grade level. Today I share with him one of my favorite second-grade trade books, Ann McGovern's *Wanted Dead or Alive: The True Story of Harriet Tubman* (see illustration). I begin by reading aloud the preface, which briefly ex-

Wanted Dead or Alive: The True Story of Harriet Tubman (Level 2-2) by A. McGovern (1965, pp. 4–5). Copyright 1965 by Scholastic. Reprinted by permission.

plains the institution of slavery in the South and why some courageous slaves ran away from their owners to seek freedom in the North. (We quickly refer to a map to locate the southern and northern states and the "freedom line" that separated them). No further background is needed, for McGovern's elegant 60-page narrative provides a clear picture of Harriet Tubman's life and times.

Despite adhering to second-grade readability demands (i.e., high-frequency words and short sentences), *Wanted Dead or Alive* is beautifully written. I want Curt to "hear" the language in this book, so today we we echo read the first two pages and partner read (alternate pages) the next seven. Curt does well; this story is right at his instructional level. We will read this book over several weeks' time; the richness of its content calls for careful, ongoing discussion of the characters' plight and motivation.

2. **Word study.** Over the first two-thirds of the school year, Curt has worked through four of the five sets of frequently occurring vowel patterns. The sequence of instruction is shown in the following list.

Mixed vowel patterns: Short, long, r-controlled

- Across *A: a, a-e, ar, ai*
- Across *I: i, i-e, ir, ight*
- Review *A* and *I: a, a-e, i, i-e*
- Across *O: o, o-e, oa, oo*
- Review I and *O: i, i-e, o, o-e*
- Across *E: e, ee, ea, e* (he, me)

Today Curt and I play Bingo to review the the *o* and *e* vowel patterns.

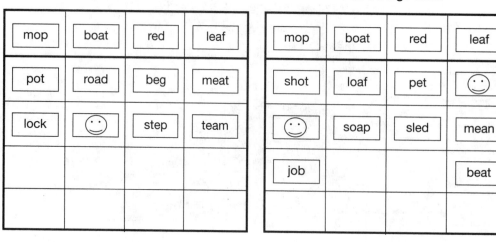

Curt's Bingo card					**Tutor's Bingo card**			
mop	boat	red	leaf		mop	boat	red	leaf
pot	road	beg	meat		shot	loaf	pet	☺
lock	☺	step	team		☺	soap	sled	mean
					job			beat

DECK

The game goes quickly (I win for the first time in two weeks), and Curt begs to play again. I shuffle the word cards and we play a second Bingo game, to Curt's delight.

There is time left for one *timed trial*. I add more words to the Bingo deck and then flash *o* and *e* words to Curt, one at a time for a 1-minute period. He reads 34 words correctly and misreads 2. We graph his performance (see Figure 5.10) and move to the next activity.

3. **Easy reading.** When Curt reached a 2-2 reading level in mid-January, *repeated readings* were introduced in his lesson plan. With this method, the student reads the same passage three times, attempting to increase speed or fluency with each rereading.

Today Curt reads a short passage from a 2-2 book, *The Bravest Dog Ever: The True Story of Balto*, that was previously used for guided reading. Although the passage is familiar, Curt practices reading the opening paragraph silently before beginning his first 2-minute oral-reading trial. On Trial 1, Curt reads 148 words, making only two inconsequential word-reading errors. We immediately graph the results. On Trial 2, he reads 156 words with no errors. This is Curt's best score yet, and he smiles broadly as we graph the result. On Wednesday, Curt will take a third trial on this same passage.

4. **Read-to.** I read *Young Martin's Promise* by Walter Dean Myers. The story describes two incidents of racial segregation from Martin Luther King Jr.'s childhood in Atlanta, Georgia. The story's message of basic injustice is clear, even to an 8-year-old.

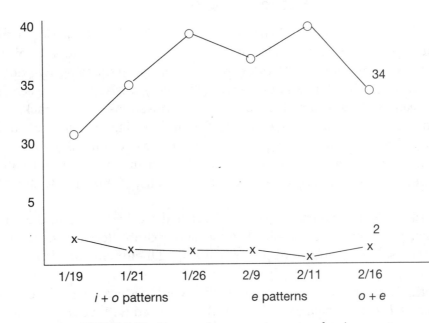

FIGURE 5.10. ○ = number correct, x = number incorrect.

Commentary

Curt now has the requisite word knowledge to read at the late-second-grade level. With continued word study and contextual reading at the appropriate level, his word recognition ability will steadily improve. Of more concern to me at this point in the year are two other areas of Curt's reading—fluency and comprehension.

Curt still reads slowly even though his base reading rate has improved significantly since the beginning of the year. *Repeated readings* is proving to be an excellent vehicle for helping him with his reading fluency. He is motivated by the task, and I can sometimes hear improvement in the flow and rhythm of his oral reading as he rereads the second-grade passages. Within the next week or two I plan to introduce silent reading into Curt's lesson. Initially, he will read only short sections of a story silently, concentrating on comprehension. I am curious as to how his oral reading rate will compare with his silent rate. My guess is that there will be little difference.

Comprehension has always been a strength with Curt. However, the late-second-grade texts we have been reading are providing a greater comprehension challenge. I find myself needing to *preplan* stopping points and questions, whereas this was not always necessary during the first half of the school year. I am also wrestling with the issue of how much to let Curt read before stopping to check his comprehension—one page, two pages, four pages? Obviously, this varies from story to story, even within the same story. Finally, the introduction of silent reading in the lessons will further challenge my ability to facilitate and monitor Curt's comprehension. In the silent mode, the quality of his responses to good comprehension questions will be my only indicator of the quality of his reading.

Lesson 57 (May 6)

1. **Guided reading.** Today Curt reads *Buddy, the First Seeing Eye Dog*, a mid-third-grade book from Scholastic's Hello Reader series (see illustration). This is a true account of the training and work experience of the first Seeing Eye dog in America. Curt reads the first half of the story (23 pages), alternating between oral and silent reading. I stop him three times to ask questions and to track, on a globe, Buddy's travel from Europe (where Seeing Eye dogs originated) to the United States. From his oral reading, I note that Curt has no difficulty with word recognition. His comprehension is also good. We will finish the second half of *Buddy* during our next lesson. (See Appendix 5.1 for a list of third-grade stories.)

2. **Word study.** By the end of March, Curt had worked through the basic, high-frequency vowel patterns—short, long, and r-controlled. He could read these first- and second-grade word patterns and spell them with an adequate degree of mastery.

In April, Curt and I began to study the word patterns in a third-grade spelling book (*Houghton Mifflin Spelling*, 1990). We started with Lesson 7 (the first six lessons review second-grade patterns) and each week have followed a stan-

Every day after that, they walked from Fortunate Fields to the cable car that ran down the mountainside into the village of Vevey.

In town they walked along the twisting streets, with Morris giving directions and Buddy leading him safely through the traffic.

Morris was getting used to the feel of Buddy at the end of the handle. But sometimes he didn't pay attention to the signals she gave him.

One day outside the cable car, Buddy suddenly sat down. But Morris didn't stop. He came crashing down onto some steps.

Morris was angry with Jack for not telling him about the steps.

"I'm sorry if you hurt yourself, Morris." Jack said. "But you must learn to pay attention to Buddy at all times. Your life may depend on it."

Buddy: The First Seeing Eye Dog (Level 3) by E. Moore (1996, pp. 20–21). Copyright 1996 by Scholastic. Reprinted by permission.

dard instructional routine. On Monday, Curt takes a pretest on the 12 spelling words. He then immediately self-corrects any errors by referring to a correct list that I provide. Next, we sort the words into patterns and discuss the features they share (e.g., *bright, sight; tie, die; child, wild*). On Wednesday, we sort the words again, play Concentration, and Curt takes a final posttest. The following week, we move to a new lesson (e.g., Lesson 8).

This week we are working on Lesson 15. Curt self-corrects five errors on the spelling pretest:

1. coin
2. ~~sole~~ soil
3. ~~nosie~~ noise
4. boy
5. ~~ole~~ oil
6. toy
7. point
8. spoil
9. ~~boyl~~ boil
10. join
11. joy
12. ~~soibean~~ soybean

Then we sort the words into patterns:

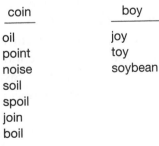

coin	boy
oil	joy
point	toy
noise	soybean
soil	
spoil	
join	
boil	

We note the two spelling patterns of the vowel sound /oi/. Then I ask Curt, "How is the /oi/ sound spelled when it comes at the end of a word? When it comes in the middle?"

We will work with these same /oi/ words again on Wednesday, and Curt will take a posttest.

3. **Easy reading.** Judy Donnelly's *The Titanic: Lost . . . and Found* is not only a good story but also an interesting bit of history written at the second-grade level. Before opening the book, Curt shares with me his knowledge of the *Titanic*:

CURT: It was a big ship that hit an iceberg and sank. Almost everyone died. A few people got rescued. [How?] By a helicopter.

We "walk through" the pictures on the first 15 pages and then go back and partner read, Curt taking two pages to my one. The book is rich in detail, and Curt's enthusiasm for the topic leads to a good discussion. As we read, I have him compare his prereading knowledge (hit an iceberg; almost everyone died; rescued by helicopter) with the information in the text. He enjoys this exercise, learning that one-third of the *Titanic's* passengers survived in lifeboats and were eventually rescued by another ship. We read two-thirds of the book and will finish it next time.

4. **Read-to.** We are in the middle of *J.T.*, a 125-page novel authored by Jane Wagner with pictures by Gordon Parks. This poignant story of an inner-city child's love for an alley cat rings true to both Curt and me.

Commentary

With only a few weeks left in the school year, Curt is now reading at the third-grade level. His word recognition and comprehension are excellent. Reading fluency is still an issue, but this too has improved steadily over the past 2 months. Curt prefers to read orally, but in guided reading he has begun to read at least half of the text silently. Neither his rate nor comprehension declines when he reads in the silent mode; however, he does seem to be in a transitional stage, mouthing many of the words under his breath as he reads.

Over the past 2 months, I have included more content selections in Curt's reading lessons (see *Buddy* and *The Titanic* mentioned earlier). He will face more content or subject-matter reading when he enters fourth grade in the fall, and I want him to be prepared. With content selections, our discussion *prior to* reading becomes very important. Having preread the selection, I am able to ask Curt questions that I know are going to be answered in the text. I jot down his answers or predictions, and then he reads with the purpose of confirming, disconfirming, or modifying his prereading responses.

My year of tutoring Curt is coming to an end. I feel sad about this. However,

I know that he has made important gains, both in reading ability and self-confidence. Curt is "over the hump" and should be able to compete academically as he moves on to fourth grade.

IV. ASSESSMENT OF PROGRESS

As was the case with Atticus (Chapter 3) and Beth (Chapter 4), Curt's growth in reading can be monitored informally throughout the school year. This section highlights some observable behaviors that will warrant the tutor's attention.

Informal Assessment during the Course of Tutoring

Word Recognition

Word sort activities during the year not only serve to deepen and broaden Curt's knowledge of common English vowel patterns (CVC, CVCe, CVVC, CV-r), but also provide ongoing assessment information to the tutor. For example, as Curt and his tutor work through the high-frequency one-syllable patterns, it will become apparent which patterns the child controls in his reading and spelling, and which he still needs to work on. It may be that some simple patterns are known (*map, top, park*) but that their more complex forms are still troublesome (*strap, chop, spark*). Or it may be that a given set of patterns is known but not sufficiently automatized. In any case, the daily word sort lessons (and games) will provide Curt with sustained opportunities to advance his word knowledge, and the tutor with opportunites to assess the child's progress.

Curt's progress through the vowel pattern sorts should be recorded on a large wall chart. After he masters a given set of word patterns, he can circle them on a preprinted chart (see Figure 5.11), or write in the pattern words, himself, on a blank chart provided by the tutor.

In contextual reading situations, the tutor will be interested in how Curt approaches *new* words that he meets. For example, on coming upon a new, unknown word in a sentence (He eyed the large *mustard* jar on the table):

- Does Curt rely on a simple sound-it-out strategy (*m—u—s—t*)?
- Does he use his existing word pattern knowledge to attack the word (*must—ard*)?
- Does he use sentence context and picture cues as word recognition helps?

Note that each of these diagnostic possibilities implies an instructional intervention. That is, Curt could be led, through modeling and discussion, to (1) abandon a letter-by-letter sounding-out strategy, (2) attack new words in syllable chunks, or (3) make use of contextual information when it is available. The daily lesson plan evaluations can be used to record dominant word recognition strategies

A	man	lake	park	mail	day
	bat	name	car	rain	say
	lap	safe	hard	paid	may
	flat	made	farm	wait	pay
	wag	place	start	paint	play
E	leg	feet	team	he	bread
	bed	week	meal	she	deaf
	wet	keep	beat	me	head
	sell	street	steam	we	
	step	cheese	please	be	
I	big	ride	bird	night	find
	tip	mile	dirt	light	mind
	miss	kite	sir	might	child
	fit	mice	shirt	right	wild
	trip	bride	whirl	flight	climb

FIGURE 5.11. Chart illustrating Curt's mastery of various vowel patterns.

used by the child, along with any attempts by the tutor to enhance the child's strategy repertoire.

Reading Fluency

Oral reading fluency is an easy area for the tutor to monitor from lesson to lesson. Each time Curt reads a passage aloud, the tutor can quickly judge the adequacy of his effort in terms of rate, phrasing, use of expression, and so forth. These observations can be logged in the tutor's memory or recorded on the daily lesson plan evaluations.

A more formal documentation of changes in Curt's oral reading fluency over time can be provided by a repeated readings graph. In the repeated readings procedure, the child reads aloud the same passage three times, trying to improve his speed on successive readings. The relevant point here is that Curt's performance—across reading trials on the same passage, and across trials on successive passages—*can be graphed*, thereby establishing a permanent record of his growth in oral reading fluency.

Although the building of oral reading fluency will be an important concern of Curt's tutor, she will also be interested in how such fluency practice transfers to Curt's silent reading. Intonation and phrasing are, of course, impossible to assess when a child is reading silently. However, reading *rate*, a fairly reliable indicator of fluency, can be noted on a silent reading performance. For example, within a guided reading lesson (reading and discussing a 2-1 basal story), the tutor can time Curt's silent reading of a 100-word section of the story. After the tutoring session, the child's silent reading rate in words per minute (wpm) can quickly be computed.

$$\text{wpm} = \frac{60 \times \text{No. of words read}}{\text{No. of seconds}} = \frac{60 \times 100 \text{ words}}{80 \text{ seconds}} = \frac{6,000}{80} = 75$$

By taking such silent reading rate measures every so often (perhaps monthly on two successive stories), the tutor will be in a position to document growth in Curt's silent reading fluency during the year. One pattern that may emerge is the following:

- Early in the year—Oral rate exceeds silent rate.
- Middle of year—Silent rate approaches oral rate.
- Late in the year—Silent rate consistently exceeds oral rate (by 10 to 20 words per minute).

Such a rate pattern, if accompanied by acceptable oral reading accuracy and comprehension, would be a positive sign of reading growth.

Comprehension

Comprehension, the ultimate goal of reading, is not easy to assess. Comprehension *is* an act or event in real time, as anyone who has ever been engrossed in a stimulating novel or short story will testify. However, it is an internal act that is not easily made public. Probably the best means for assessing story comprehension is an informal, open-ended discussion between child and tutor as the story is being read—that is, at designated stopping points within the story. The effectiveness of such an approach depends on a thinking, responsive tutor, one who not only can ask good questions but also can listen actively, make quick judgments about the appropriateness of the child's answers, and probe the child's thinking when necessary.

As mentioned earlier, Curt's comprehension will be assessed at predetermined stopping points in the story. The following indicators will guide the tutor's assessment:

1. *The child's ability to pick up basic plot-related information as he moves through the story.* This includes information about setting, characters, the problem facing the characters, and how they resolve it. Note that comprehension, in this case, can be assessed by using specific, literal questions ("How did John feel when he found his bicycle missing?" [Answer: angry]) or through more general, retelling-type questions ("Tell me what has happened so far").

2. *The child's ability to make logical predictions at key turning points in the story.* It

is not crucial that Curt accurately predict the specific outcome of a story. However, his prediction at a given stopping point should make sense based on the information available to him *up to that point* in the story. Some sample questions for eliciting predictions are, "Based on what you have read so far, what do you think will happen next?" "If you were in John's [main character] place, what would you do now?"

3. *The child's ability to support his predictions with information in the story.* Making a reasonable prediction is not enough. Curt should also be able to support or defend his prediction by referring to information he has come upon in the story. In fact, it is the quality of Curt's reasoning, manifested in his defense of his prediction, that is of true diagnostic import to the tutor. Again, the tutor's questioning can be quite straightforward. After Curt has made a prediction, the tutor might ask, "Curt, why do you think that?" or "What in the story makes you think that?"

4. *After finishing the story, the child's ability to reconstruct the main events in the plot.* Some children benefit from taking part in reconstructions of the stories they read, focusing particularly on the following story elements:

- How the story began (information about main characters and the setting).
- The problem that confronted the characters.
- What action(s) the characters took in response to the problem (and the reasoning behind their action).
- How the problem was actually resolved.

Although at first the tutor may have to assume an active, modeling role in this story recapitulation process, with experience Curt should be able to take on more and more of the responsibility.

Along with the comprehension indicators mentioned earlier, the tutor can look for two other signs of comprehension growth. The first concerns the number of times Curt has to read a section of text before he can demonstrate understanding of the information in that section. For example, some primary-grade remedial readers do not engage their minds with the text as they read. It is as if their concept of "reading" is the accurate mouthing of the words on the page, and no more. These children not only have trouble making predictions, but they may even fail to pick up literal information in the story line. The tutor's only recourse is to have such children reread the section of text one or more times until they can demonstrate at a basic level that they understand what they have read—be it a page, paragraph, or sentence. Neither child nor tutor tends to enjoy these rereading–requestioning cycles; nonetheless, they are sometimes necessary. The positive aspect is that by holding the child accountable in this manner, eventually the child will begin to focus on meaning as he/she reads. The tutor will note this when the child's responses to questions at stopping points become more appropriate, indicating that he/she is reading for understanding the *first* time through the story.

Another sign of progress is the child's ability to read longer and longer passages while still maintaining good comprehension. In the initial lessons the tutor may have to question Curt at the end of every page to ensure that he is concentrating on and understanding what he reads. Over time, however, the tutor should increase the distance between stopping or questioning points in the stories—from one to two to possibly even three pages. If Curt can demonstrate adequate comprehension of these longer passages, this too will be a clear sign that he is becoming a stronger reader.

Beginning-of-Year/End-of-Year Assessment (Curt)

PRETEST (SEPTEMBER)

	Word recognition (graded lists)		Oral reading	
	Flash (%)	*Untimed (%)*	*Accuracy (%)*	*Rate (wpm)*
Preprimer	100	—	—	—
Primer	95	100	98	68
1-2	75	95	97	65
2-1	50	75	90	44
2-2			84	36
3	20	40	—	—
4	—	—	—	—

Spelling: No. of words spelled correctly—List 1 (6 of 10); List 2 (0 of 10)
Developmental stage—Phonetic/Within-Word Pattern (correct short vowels; inconsistent marking of long vowels)

POSTTEST (MAY)

	Word recognition (graded lists)		Oral reading	
	Flash (%)	*Untimed (%)*	*Accuracy (%)*	*Rate (wpm)*
Preprimer	100	—	—	—
Primer	100	—	—	—
1-2	95	100	98	91
2-1	90	95	97	86
2-2			97	85
3	65	90	94	79
4	35	55	86	67

Spelling: No. of words spelled correctly—List 1 (9 of 10); List 2 (5 of 10)
Developmental stage—Within-Word Pattern (correct short vowels; long vowels marked)

The pretest–posttest comparison shows that Curt has progressed at least one full year in reading skill. He entered his third-grade year as a borderline Level 2-1 reader and is leaving as a solid third-grade-level reader. On the posttests, Curt made impressive gains across the board. For example, he raised his second-grade *flash word recognition* score from 50% to 90% correct, and his third-grade flash score from 20% to 65%. Curt's *oral reading* score at the 2-2 level improved from 84% to 97%; moreover, he was able to read the third-grade passage with "instructional level" accuracy (94%).

Much tutoring time was devoted to improving Curt's reading fluency, and the posttest *rate* scores suggest that this instruction was successful. Curt is still a relatively slow oral reader for a child completing third grade. However, his 79 wpm rate on the third-grade passage indicates that he is no longer a halting, word-by-word reader. The tutor is also aware, through observation, that Curt has begun to read a bit faster in the silent mode than he does in the oral.

The spelling posttest in May was almost too easy for Curt.

Spelling word	Pretest (September)		Posttest (May)	
bike	BIKE	(c)	BIKE	(c)
fill	FIL		FIL	
plate	PLAT		PLATE	(c)
mud	MUD	(c)	MUD	(c)
flat	FLAT	(c)	FLAT	(c)
bed	BED	(c)	BED	(c)
drive	DRIV		DRIVE	(c)
chop	CHOP	(c)	CHOP	(c)
wish	WICH		WISH	(c)
step	STEP	(c)	STEP	(c)
plant	PLAT		PLANT	(c)
dress	DRES		DRESS	(c)
stuff	STOF		STUF	
chase	CHAS		CHASE	(c)
wise	WISS		WIZE	
shopping	SHOPING		SHOPING	
train	TRANE		TRAIN	(c)
cloud	CLOD		CLOD	
thick	THIK		THICK	(c)
float	FLOT		FLOTE	

He spelled correctly 9 of the 10 first-grade words and 5 of the 10 second-grade words. When he misspelled a word, he was very close (STUF for *stuff*; WIZE for *wise*; FLOTE for *float*). The word sort instruction during the year seemed to have helped Curt ferret out the various high-frequency long-vowel patterns (see pretest–posttest changes: PLAT to PLATE; WISS to WIZE; TRANE to TRAIN). Note also that in May he represented other orthographic features that had been missing in his September spellings—for example, the ending consonant doublet in DRESS, the preconsonantal nasal (n̲) in PLANT, and the -*ck* digraph in THICK. Overall, Curt's posttest spellings reveal his solid grasp of frequently occurring, one-syllable vowel patterns.

The May posttest results are encouraging. One to 1½ years behind on entering third grade, Curt made more than a full year's gain in reading, thereby closing the achievement/grade-level gap a bit. Now able to read and comprehend text at a solid third-grade level, he will be entering the middle-elementary grades with a fighting chance, academically speaking.

IN CONCLUSION

With the completion of the description of Curt's case, it is time to bring this tutoring manual to a close. In this book, tutoring has been a vehicle for talking about the teaching and learning of beginning reading. At heart, my position has been a simple one. Children who struggle with beginning reading need to be guided skillfully through a graded series of reading books and a graded word study curriculum. To this end, I have suffused the three case study chapters (Atticus, Beth, and Curt) with specific information on book levels, word study levels, and various teaching approaches and techniques.

Still, underlying the specifics in the three case studies has been a developmental perspective on teaching beginning reading: that is, not just *what* to teach and *how* to teach it, but also *when* to teach it and *why*. This developmental perspective is of crucial importance. Successful teachers of at-risk readers are active problem solvers who hypothesize, teach, and reflect within a credible developmental framework. These teachers know precisely where a beginning reader *is presently* and where he/she *needs to go next*. Such teachers, whether they work directly with children or supervise the tutoring efforts of other adults, make a real and lasting difference in literacy learning. They are, every one, worth their weight in gold—and our profession, our society, must commit to producing as many of them as we possibly can.

APPENDIX 5.1. Books for Curt Listed by Difficulty Level

For *second-grade* books (levels 2-1 and 2-2), refer to Appendix 4.1. *Third-grade* books are listed here.

Title	Level	Author/Series	Publisher
Abraham Lincoln	3	Colver, A.	Dell
Amazing Rescues	3	Shea, G.	Random House
Baseball's Greatest Hitters	3	Kramer, S.	Random House
Baseball's Greatest Pitchers	3	Kramer, S.	Random House
Bicycle Rider	3	Scioscia, M.	Harper Trophy
Buddy, the First Seeing Eye Dog	3	Moore, E.	Scholastic
Canada Geese Quilt, The	3	Kinsey-Warnock, N.	Dell
Comeback: Four True Stories	3	O'Connor, J.	Random House
Courage of Sarah Noble, The	3	Dalgliesh, A.	Aladdin
Dolphin Adventure	3	Grover, W.	BeachTree
Five True Dog Stories	3	Davidson, M.	Scholastic
Five True Horse Stories	3	Davidson, M.	Scholastic
Gift for Tia Rose, A	3	Taha, K.	Bantam
Go Fish	3	Stolz, M.	Harper
Hannah	3	Whelan, G.	Random House
Helen Keller	3	Davidson, M.	Scholastic
Hundred Dresses, The	3	Estes, E.	Harcourt Brace
Jackie Robinson	3	O'Connor, J.	Random House
J.T.	3	Wagner, J.	Dell
Lion to Guard Us, A	3	Bulla, C. R.	Harper Trophy
Molly's Pilgrim	3	Cohen, B.	Dell
Moonwalk: The First Trip to the Moon	3	Donnelly, J.	Random House
Most Beautiful Place in the World	3	Cameron, A.	Random House
Mustard	3	Graebner, C.	Bantam
Mystery on October Road	3	Herzig, A.	Scholastic
Pompeii . . . Buried Alive	3	Kunhardt, E.	Random House
Sarah, Plain and Tall	3	MacLachlan, P.	Harper
Shoeshine Girl	3	Bulla, C. R.	Harper
Silver	3	Whelan, G.	Random House
Stone Fox	3	Gardiner, J. R.	Harper
Titanic, The	3	Donnelly, J.	Random House

(cont.)

APPENDIX 5.1 (cont.)

Title	Level	Author/Series	Publisher
To the Top: Climbing the Highest Mountain	3	Kramer, S.	Random House
Trojan Horse, The	3	Little, E.	Random House
Tut's Mummy	3	Donnelly, J.	Random House
Vanished . . . Amelia Earhart	3	Kulling, M.	Random House
Wall of Names, A	3	Donnelly, J.	Random House
Wanted Dead or Alive: The True Story of Harriet Tubman	3	McGovern, A.	Scholastic
Year of the Panda	3	Schlein, M.	Harper
Young Martin's Promise	3	Myers, W. D.	Steck-Vaughn

APPENDIX 5.2. Word Lists from Which to Choose Words for Vowel Pattern Sorts

"A" Vowel Patterns

cat	lake	park	rain
ran	race	car	mail
dad	tape	hard	wait
hat	page	barn	pain
cab	same	card	tail
map	make	far	chain
jam	name	part	paint
flat	take	harm	maid
clap	gave	dart	sail
back	trade	start	paid
trap	shake	shark	stain

day	fall	(Miscellaneous)
say	ball	was
may	tall	have
way	call	what
pay	wall	saw
clay	hall	want
stay	small	

"E" Vowel Patterns

pet	feet	meat	he
red	deep	team	we
beg	meet	lead	she
get	feel	mean	me
bell	free	peak	be
less	green	clean	
nest	seed	beat	
left	need	dream	
ten	queen	beach	
step	jeep	leaf	
sled	bleed	wheat	

head	herd	(Miscellaneous)
lead	germ	been
dead	clerk	these
bread	nerve	there
deaf	serve	the
breath		were
spread		

(cont.)

APPENDIX 5.2 (cont.)

"I" Vowel Patterns

hit	ride	right	girl
lip	nice	night	dirt
win	bike	light	bird
big	five	might	sir
kick	mile	bright	first
hid	side	high	firm
pin	drive		shirt
trip	mine		birth
swim	dime		third
fit	wise		
chin	shine		

wild	by
mind	my
find	fly
child	cry
climb	sky
kind	eye
mild	bye
blind	buy

"O" Vowel Patterns

top	rope	boat	book
job	note	road	good
pot	hole	soap	foot
mom	nose	load	look
dot	coke	coal	stood
drop	hope	loaf	hook
jog	bone	soak	brook
lock	code	coach	wood
stop	stone	toast	
bomb	spoke	float	
shot	close	cloak	

told	go	moon	boil
cold	no	roof	coin
colt	so	pool	soil
gold		boot	point
post		tool	noise
folk		shoot	spoil
sold		tooth	voice
hold		broom	(boy)
ghost		spool	(toy)

(cont.)

APPENDIX 5.2 (cont.)

"U" Vowel Patterns

bug	cute	blue	hurt
cup	rule	true	burn
bus	use	glue	curl
fun	rude	clue	fur
rug	tune		turn
club	huge		purr
sun	June		nurse
mud	fuse		curve
drum	flute		

knew	fruit
grew	suit
new	juice
few	
flew	
chew	
screw	

APPENDIX 5.3. Proposed Sequence of Vowel Pattern Sorts

cat	lake	car
ran	name	park	⟵ (Sample vowel pattern sort)
bad	made	hard
rag	sale	barn
clap	base	start

cat	lake	car	rain	⟵ (Sample headers for next sort)*
cat	lake	car	(Miscellaneous)

bed	keep	he
bed	keep	he	beat
bed	keep	beat	(Miscellaneous)

Review:

cat	lake	bed	keep
cat	rain	bed	beat

hit	ride	girl
hit	ride	girl	night
hit	ride	night	(Miscellaneous)

Review:

bed	keep	hit	ride
bed	beat	hit	night

top	rope	boat
top	rope	boat	book
top	rope	book	(Miscellaneous)

Review:

hit	ride	top	rope
hit	night	top	boat

bug	rule	fruit
bug	rule	fruit	new

Review:

top	rope	bug	rule
top	boat	bug	new

*Note. Every underlined word on the page (e.g., rain) represents a column header for a potential sort. Under rain might be sorted *wait, tail, maid, train,* etc.; under car might be sorted *park, hard, barn,* and *start,* as shown in the example sort at the top of the page.

References

Adams, M. (1990). *Beginning to read: Thinking and learning about print.* Cambridge, MA: MIT Press.

American Heritage College Dictionary. (1993). Boston: Houghton Mifflin.

Barr, R. (1974). Instructional pace differences and their effect on reading acquisition. *Reading Research Quarterly, 9,* 526–554.

Bear, D., Invernizzi, M., Templeton, S., & Johnston, F. (1996). *Words their way: Word study for phonics, vocabulary, and spelling instruction.* Englewood Cliffs, NJ: Merrill.

Beers, J., & Henderson, E.H. (1977). A study of developing orthographic concepts among first graders. *Research in the Teaching of English, 11,* 133–148.

Calfee, R. (1982). Literacy and illiteracy: Teaching the nonreader to survive in the modern world. *Annals of Dyslexia, 32,* 71–93.

Carbo, M. (1981). Making books talk to children. *Reading Teacher, 34,* 186–189.

Chall, J. (1967). *Learning to read: The great debate.* New York: McGraw-Hill.

Chittenden, E. (1983). *Assessment of beginning reading: Error patterns in oral reading performance.* Unpublished report, Educational Testing Service, Princeton, NJ.

Chomsky, C. (1971). Write first, read later. *Childhood Education, 47,* 296–299.

Chomsky, C. (1976). After decoding, what? *Language Arts, 53,* 288–296.

Chomsky, C. (1979). Approaching reading through invented spelling. In L. Resnick & P. Weaver (Eds.), *Theory and practice of early reading* (Vol. 2, pp. 43–64). Hillsdale, NJ: Erlbaum.

Clay, M. (1991a). Introducing a new storybook to young readers. *Reading Teacher, 45,* 264–273.

Clay, M. (1991b). *Becoming literate: The construction of inner control.* Portsmouth, NH: Heinemann.

Clay, M. (1993). *Reading Recovery: A guidebook for teachers in training.* Portsmouth, NH: Heinemann.

Dewey, J. (1916). *How we think: A restatement of the relation of reflective thinking to the educative process.* Boston: Heath.

Ehri, L. (1980) The development of orthographic images. In U. Frith (Ed.), *Cognitive processes in spelling* (pp. 311–338). London: Academic Press.

Ehri, L. (1992). Review and commentary: Stages of spelling development. In S. Templeton & D. Bear (Eds.), *Development of orthographic knowledge and the foundations of literacy* (pp. 307–332). Hillsdale, NJ: Erlbaum.

Ehri, L., & Wilce, L. (1985). Movement into reading: Is the first stage of printed word learning visual or phonetic? *Reading Research Quarterly, 20,* 163–179.

Elkonin, D. B. (1973). U.S.S.R. In J. Downing (Ed.), *Comparative reading* (pp. 551–580). New York: Macmillan.

Flesch, R. (1955). *Why Johnny can't read.* New York: Harper & Row.

Fries, C. (1962). *Linguistics and reading.* New York: Holt, Rinehart & Winston.

Gentry, J. R. (1978). Early spelling strategies. *Elementary School Journal, 79,* 88–92.

Gibson, E., & Levin, H. (1975). *The psychology of reading.* Cambridge, MA: MIT Press.

Gill, J. T. (1992). The relationship between word recognition and spelling. In S. Templeton & D. Bear (Eds.), *Development of orthographic knowledge and the foundations of literacy* (pp. 79–104). Hillsdale, NJ: Erlbaum.

Goodman, K. (1969). Analysis of oral miscues: Applied psycholinguistics. *Reading Research Quarterly, 5,* 9–30.

Graves, D. (1983). *Writing: Teachers and children at work.* Exeter, NH: Heinemann.

Gray, W. S. (1960). *On their own in reading.* Glenview, IL: Scott, Foresman.

Guszak, F. (1985). *Diagnostic reading instruction in the elementary school.* New York: Harper & Row.

Harris, A., & Jacobson, M. (1982). *Basic reading vocabularies.* New York: Macmillan.

Henderson, E. H. (1990). *Teaching spelling* (2nd ed.). Boston: Houghton Mifflin.

Henderson, E. H., & Beers, J. (1980). *Developmental and cognitive aspects of learning to spell: A reflection of word knowledge.* Newark, DE: International Reading Association.

Hoffman, J., McCarthey, S., Abbott, J., Christian, C., Corman, L., Curry, C., Dressman, M., Elliot, B., Matherne, D., & Stahle, D. (1994). So what's new in the new basals? A focus on first grade. *Journal of Reading Behavior, 26,* 47–73.

Huey, E. B. (1968). *The psychology and pedagogy of reading.* Cambridge, MA: MIT Press. (Originally published in New York: Macmillan, 1908)

Invernizzi, M., Rosemary, C., Juel, C., & Richards, H. (1997). At-risk readers and community volunteers: A three-year perspective. *Journal of Scientific Studies in Reading, 1,* 277–300.

Johnson, M., Kress, R., & Pikulski, J. (1987). *Informal reading inventories.* Newark, DE: International Reading Association.

Johnston, F., Invernizzi, M., & Juel, C. (1998). *Book Buddies: Guidelines for volunteer tutors of emergent and early readers.* New York: Guilford Press.

Juel, C. (1988). Learning to read and write: A longitudinal study of 54 children from first through fourth grades. *Journal of Educational Psychology, 80,* 437–447.

Liberman, I. Y., & Liberman, A. M. (1992). Whole language versus code emphasis: Underlying assumptions and their implications for reading instruction. In P. Gough, L. Ehri, & R. Treiman (Eds.), *Reading acquisition* (pp. 343–366). Hillsdale, NJ: Erlbaum.

McKee, P. (1966). *The teaching of reading in the elementary school.* Boston: Houghton Mifflin.

Mock, D. (1996). *Systematic instruction of students with severe reading disability: Two case studies.* Unpublished master's thesis, Appalachian State University, Boone, NC.

Morris, D. (1982). Word sort: A categorization strategy for improving word recognition ability. *Reading Psychology, 3,* 247–259.

Morris, D. (1993a). *A selective history of the Howard Street Tutoring Program (1979–1989).* (ERIC Document Reproduction Service No. 355 473)

Morris, D. (1993b). The relationship between children's concept of word in text and phoneme awareness in learning to read: A longitudinal study. *Research in the Teaching of English, 27*, 133–154.

Morris, D. (1995). *First Steps: An early reading intervention program.* (ERIC Document Reproduction Service No. 388 956)

Morris, D. (1996). Children's development of printed word knowledge in sentence-based reading approaches. *Reading Horizons, 36*, 340–353.

Morris, D. (in press). The role of clinical training in the teaching of reading. In P. Mosenthal & D. Evensen (Eds.), *Rethinking the role of the reading clinic in a new age of literacy.* Greenwich, CT: JAI Press.

Morris, D., & Perney, J. (1984). Developmental spelling as a predictor of first-grade reading achievement. *Elementary School Journal, 84*, 441–457.

Morris, D., Shaw, B., & Perney, J. (1990). Helping low readers in grades 2 and 3: An after-school volunteer tutoring program. *Elementary School Journal, 91*, 133–150.

Morris, D., Tschannen-Moran, M., & Weidemann, E. (1981). An inner-city LEA tutoring program. *Journal of Language Experience, 3*, 9–25.

Nelson, L., & Morris, D. (1987). Echo reading with taped books. *Illinois Reading Council Journal, 16*, 39–42.

Perfetti, C. (1992). The representation problem in reading acquisition. In P. Gough, L. Ehri, & R. Treiman (Eds.), *Reading acquisition* (pp. 145–174). Hillsdale, NJ: Erlbaum.

Perfetti, C., Beck, I., Bell, L., & Hughes, C. (1987). Phonemic knowledge and learning to read are reciprocal: A longitudinal study of first grade children. *Merrill–Palmer Quarterly, 33*, 283–319.

Pinnell, G. S. (1989). Reading Recovery: Helping at-risk children learn to read. *Elementary School Journal, 90*, 161–183.

Read, C. (1971). Pre-school children's knowledge of English phonology. *Harvard Educational Review, 41*, 1–34.

Read, C. (1975). *Children's categorization of speech sounds in English.* Urbana, IL: National Council of Teachers of English.

Samuels, S. J. (1979). The method of repeated readings. *Reading Teacher, 32*, 403–408.

Sanders, M. E., & Buhle, R. (1997). *Paraprofessionals and early intervention in reading: What does it take to make it work?* Position paper, Naperville, IL, School District 203.

Santa, C., & Hoien, T. (1999). An assessment of Early Steps: A program for early intervention of reading problems. *Reading Research Quarterly, 34*, 54–79.

Sarason, S.B. (1972). *The creation of settings and the future societies.* San Francisco: Jossey-Bass.

Schlagal, R. (1992). Patterns of orthographic development into the intermediate grades. In S. Templeton & D. Bear (Eds.), *Development of orthographic knowledge and the foundations of literacy* (pp. 31–52). Hillsdale, NJ: Erlbaum.

Schwartz, M. (1977). Rewriting or recopying: What are we teaching? *Language Arts, 54*, 756–759.

Slavin, R. (1994). Preventing early school failure: The challenge and the opportunity. In R. Slavin, N. Karweit, & B. Wasik (Eds.), *Preventing early school failure* (pp. 1–12). Boston: Allyn & Bacon.

Slavin, R., Madden, N., Karweit, N., Dolan, L., & Wasik, B. (1994). Success for all: Getting reading right the first time. In E. Hiebert & B. Taylor (Eds.), *Getting reading right from the start: Effective early literacy interventions* (pp. 125–147). Boston: Allyn & Bacon.

Smith, F. (1971). *Understanding reading*. New York: Holt, Rinehart & Winston.

Stanovich, K. (1986). Matthew effects in reading: Some consequences of individual differences in the acquisition of literacy. *Reading Research Quarterly, 21*, 360–406.

Stauffer, R. (1970). *The language-experience approach to the teaching of reading*. New York: Harper & Row.

Templeton, S., & Bear, D. (1992). *Development of orthographic knowledge and the foundations of literacy: A memorial festschrift for Edmund H. Henderson*. Hillsdale, NJ: Erlbaum.

Veatch, J. (1959). *Individualizing your reading program: Self-selection in practice*. New York: Putnam.

Vellutino, F., Scanlon, D., Sipay, E., Small, S., Pratt, A., Chen, R., & Denckla, M. (1996). Cognitive profiles of difficult-to-remediate and readily remediated poor readers: Early intervention as a vehicle for distinguishing between cognitive and experiential deficits as basic causes of specific reading disability. *Journal of Educational Psychology, 88*, 601–638.

Wasik, B. (1998). Using volunteers as reading tutors: Guidelines for successful practices. *Reading Teacher, 51*, 562–570.

Wasik, B., & Slavin, R. (1990). *Preventing early reading failure with one-to-one tutoring: A best evidence synthesis.* Paper presented at the annual convention of the American Educational Research Association, Boston, MA.

Wasik, B., & Slavin, R. (1993). Preventing early reading failure with one-to-one tutoring: A review of five programs. *Reading Research Quarterly, 28*, 178–200.

Watson, D. (1989). Defining and describing whole language. *Elementary School Journal, 90*, 129–141.

Zutell, J. (1979). Spelling strategies of primary school children and their relationship to Piaget's concept of centration. *Research in the Teaching of English, 13*, 69–80.

Reading Materials Cited in Text

CHAPTER 3 (ATTICUS)

Cowley, J. (1986). *Yuck soup*. Bothell, WA: Wright Group.
Cowley, J. (1986). *Our street*. Bothell, WA: Wright Group.
King, V. (1989). *Grandma's memories*. Crystal Lake, IL: Rigby.
Melser, J. (1981). *The chocolate cake*. Bothell, WA: Wright Group.
Melser, J. (1982). *Two little dogs*. Bothell, WA: Wright Group.

CHAPTER 4 (BETH)

Bang, M. (1987). *Wiley and the hairy man*. New York: Aladdin Books.
Dubowski, C., & Dubowski, M. (1988). *Cave boy*. New York: Random House.
Eller, W., & Hester, K. (1980). *Toothless dragon* (pp. 96–111). River Forest, IL: Laidlaw Brothers.
Guarino, D. (1989). *Is your mama a llama?* New York: Scholastic.
Hoff, S. (1980). *Sammy the seal*. New York: Harper Trophy.
Hoff, S. (1985). *The horse in Harry's room*. New York: Harper Trophy.
Lobel, A. (1982). *Owl at home*. New York: Harper Trophy.
Lundell, M. (1995). *A girl named Helen Keller*. New York: Scholastic.
Moore, L., & Adelson, L. (1988). *The terrible Mr. Twitmeyer*. New York: Scholastic.
O'Connor, J. (1986). *The teeny tiny woman*. New York: Random House.
O'Connor, J. (1990). *Molly the brave and me*. New York: Random House.
Phillips, J. (1986). *Tiger is a scaredy cat*. New York: Random House.
The pot of gold: An Irish folk tale. (1976). Glenview, IL: Scott, Foresman (Reading Unlimited).

CHAPTER 5 (CURT)

Black, I. S. (1977). *Night cat*. Pleasantville, NY: Readers Digest Services.
Boegehold, B. (1990). *A horse called Starfire*. New York: Bantam.
Bulla, C. R. (1982). *Daniel's duck*. New York: Harper Trophy.

Cameron, A. (1981). *The stories Julian tells*. New York: Random House.

Donnelly, J. (1987). *The Titanic: Lost . . . and found*. New York: Random House.

McGovern, A. (1965). *Wanted dead or alive: The true story of Harriet Tubman*. New York: Scholastic.

Moore, E. (1996). *Buddy: The first seeing eye dog*. New York: Scholastic.

Myers, W. D. (1993). *Young Martin's promise*. Austin, TX: Steck-Vaughn.

Standiford, N. (1989). *The bravest dog ever: The true story of Balto*. New York: Random House.

Udry, J. (1978) "Alfred." In W. Durr et al. (Eds.), *Cloverleaf* (pp. 122–148). Boston: Houghton Mifflin.

Wagner, J. (1969). *J. T.* New York: Dell.

Index

Accuracy, scoring, 30
All Aboard Reading, 205
Alphabet knowledge, 21
  assessment of, 42–43
  in emergent reader, 70–72, 102
  randomized letters for, 66

Beginning consonants, strategies
  for emergent reader, 72–77
Bingo
  for fledgling reader, 149
  vowel pattern, 192–193
Books
  for emergent reader, 108–113
  for fledgling reader, 164–167
  for late-first- to second-grade-
    level reader, 164–167
  new, for emergent reader,
    87–88, 90–91, 93, 100
  rereading, by emergent reader,
    84–85, 89, 91–92, 95–96,
    97–98
Boyd, Betty, 3
*Bravest Dog Ever, The: The True
  Story of Balto*, 215
Buddy, the First Seeing Eye Dog,
  216–217

Cave Boy, 146
Child. *See also* Emergent reader;
    Fledgling reader; Late-first-
    to second-grade-level reader
  readiness of, 4
Chomsky, Carol, 80
Coding, of oral reading, 28–29,
    28f, 29f
Column sorting, 136
  for fledgling reader, 126–128
  for late-first- to second-grade-
    level reader, 189–191
Comprehension
  assessment for late-first- to
    second-grade-level reader,
    221–223
  defined, 22
  in DRTA, 175–176
Concentration game, 71
  for fledgling reader, 127–128,
    135

Consonant blends, 130–132
Consonant digraphs, 128
Consonants, beginning, strategies
  for emergent reader, 72–77
Contextual reading, 22, 68–70, 102
  by emergent reader, 68–70, 102
  by fledgling reader, 137,
    157–158

Daniel's Duck, 211
Decoding ability, 22
Dewey, John, 175
Digraphs, consonant, 128
Directed Reading-Thinking
    Activity, 175–187
  flexibility in, 186–187
  guidance in, 180–181
  lesson planning for, 182–186,
    184f
  model lesson for, 176, 176f, 177f,
    178–180
  predictions in, 180
  tutor–child dialogue in, 182
DRTA. *See* Directed Reading-
    Thinking Activity
Dyslexia, incidence of, 5

Early Steps, 3
  book list of, 108–113
Easy reading
  for building fluency, 205
  for fledgling reader, 137–138,
    147, 153, 156
  for late-first- to second-grade-
    level reader, 210, 213, 215,
    218
Echo reading, 117
  for building fluency, 204–205
Editing, for fledgling reader,
    144–145
Education, group versus
    individualized, 6–7
Emergent reader, 67–113
  books for, 108–113
  initial assessment of, 67–68
  progress assessment of, 101–107
    and advancement through
      graded series, 104–105
    alphabet knowledge, 102

contextual reading, 102
    initial sight vocabulary,
      103–104
    letter-sound knowledge, 104
    phoneme awareness, 102–103
    pre- and posttests, 105–107
  teaching strategies for, 68–84
    alphabet, 70–72
    beginning consonants, 72–77
    contextual reading, 68–70
    lesson plan, 84
    sentence writing, 80–83
    word families, 77–80
    word study, 70–80
  tutoring lessons for, 84–101

Feedback, need for, 4
Flash presentation, 23–24
  technique for, 26
Fledgling reader, 114–169
  book list for, 164–167
  initial assessment of, 114–116,
    115f
  progress assessment of, 157–163
    in contextual reading,
      157–158
    pre- and posttest, 162–163
    in word knowledge, 158–159
    in writing–spelling, 159–162
  short-vowel word families for,
    168
  teaching strategies for, 116–145
    easy reading, 137–138
    guided reading, 116–117
    lesson plan, 116
    monitoring oral reading
      behavior, 121–125
    reading to child, 138, 139t
    short-vowel patterns, 133–137
    short-vowel word families,
      126–133
    support, 117–120
    word study, 125–137
    writing, 139–145
  tutoring lessons for, 146–157
  word family sorts for, 169
Fluency, reading. *See* Reading
    fluency
Fox and His Friends, 210

239

About the Author

Darrell Morris, EdD, is a professor of education and the director of the Reading Clinic at Appalachian State University in Boone, North Carolina. He received his doctorate from the University of Virginia in 1980, after which he began his college teaching career at National-Louis University in Evanston, Illinois. Since moving to Appalachian State in 1989, he has directed the masters program in reading, researched the beginning reading and spelling processes, and helped school districts set up early reading-intervention programs. Dr. Morris lives with his wife and two teenage children in Boone.